Ex Libris

Christine Southwick

SCARLETT,

RHETT,

AND A CAST OF

THOUSANDS

SCARLETT, RHETT, AND A CAST OF THOUSANDS

THE FILMING OF *Gone With the Wind*

Roland Flamini

Macmillan Publishing Co., Inc.

NEW YORK

Collier Macmillan Publishers

LONDON

Macmillan Publishing Co., Inc.

866 Third Avenue, New York, N. Y. 10022

Collier Macmillan Canada, Ltd.

Library of Congress Cataloging in Publication Data

Flamini, Roland.
Scarlett, Rhett, and a cast of thousands.
Includes index.
1. Gone with the wind. [Motion picture] I. Title.
PN 1997.G59F55   791.43'7   75-29463
ISBN 0-02-538670-0

First Printing 1975

Designed by Jack Meserole

Printed in the United States of America

The photographs that appear in this book are from the collections of William Pratt and Roland Flamini, from Culver Pictures (CP), Time-Life Picture Agency (TLPA), Bettmann Archive (BA), and Springer Bettmann Film Archive (SBFA).

In "The Search for Rhett," (pages 10–11), the photographs are from the collection of William Pratt.

In "The Scarlett Girls" (pages 80–83), the photograph of Catherine Campbell is from the December 3, 1936 issue of The Atlanta Journal; the photographs of Mary Anderson, Marcella Martin, and Lucille Ball are from the collection of Roland Flamini; the other photographs are from the collection of William Pratt.

To Janet

CONTENTS

1

An Unwanted
Property

DAVID O. SELZNICK'S
production of
MARGARET MITCHELL'S
Story of The Old South
Directed by VICTOR FLEMING
SCREEN PLAY BY SIDNEY HOWARD
Music by Max Steiner
GONE WITH THE WIND
IN TECHNICOLOR
Starring CLARK GABLE
AS RHETT BUTLER
Leslie HOWARD · Olivia DE HAVILLAND
and presenting
VIVIEN LEIGH
AS SCARLETT O'HARA
A SELZNICK INTERNATIONAL PICTURE
A METRO GOLDWYN MAYER Release

Louis B. Mayer, the most powerful man in Hollywood, isn't completely illiterate, but reading is a struggle for him, and making sense of what he reads a bigger one. So the old art of storytelling flourishes at Metro-Goldwyn-Mayer Studios. He never has to plough through a story, he has it told to him by a woman employed for the purpose. A modern Scheherazade. Except, of course, that at M-G-M it's the fate of the tale, not the teller, that hangs in the balance; if it doesn't meet with Mayer's favor—if, for instance, it offends his complex and sometimes unpredictable sensibilities—it has little chance of reaching the screen.

One May afternoon in 1936 Mayer is sitting on his leather throne, eyes closed, large, soft gray face becalmed, hands comfortably clasped across his stomach, listening to the voice of Kate Corbaly, his storyteller, recounting the plot of a soon-to-be-published outsize novel with a Civil War background. She tells it with skill and feeling, concentrating on the main characters but simultaneously managing to convey its vast canvas.

The heroine is a young Southern beauty, captivating and willful, with a single-minded dedication to a sole objective—her survival. As Kate Corbaly talks, images flash before Mayer's eyes, images in which the heroine assumes the identity of each of his leading women stars: Garbo, Joan Crawford, Norma Shearer . . . but only when the story is over does he stir. Personally, he prefers his heroines softer, less assertive, but it is unquestionably a spectacular woman's part, and good women's parts receive serious consideration at M-G-M, with its preponderance of women stars. So "the little level Jewish voice"—as Graham Greene once described it—says "Let's ask Irving."

Presently, Irving Thalberg enters Mayer's office, a small, pale, fragile-looking man still in his middle thirties and, though he avoids personal publicity, already immovably fixed in a widely acclaimed persona as the man who supplies the creative drive at M-G-M. Mayer is considered the business brain, and the two of them rule with equal power—and an equal measure of hostil-

Poster art for the 1939 premiere, "presenting" Vivien Leigh. It wasn't until after she had won an Academy Award that her status on posters was elevated to "starring." (SBFA)

ity toward one another. Somehow the studio thrives on their differences, for M-G-M is without question both the most successful and the most prestigious of all Hollywood studios.

Kate Corbaly launches once more into the story; once more Mayer closes his eyes and succumbs to the dramatic narrative; but Thalberg immediately begins to fidget and look impatiently at his watch. By the end there is little doubt what his reaction is. "Forget it, Louis," he says, making for the door. "No Civil War picture ever made a nickel." Mayer pronounces the final sentence; "Well, that's it. Irving knows what's right." The following day, the New York agent submitting the novel is told that M-G-M has no interest in buying the movie rights to *Gone With the Wind*.

Recent pictures about the Civil War, including *So Red the Rose* and M-G-M's own *Operator 13*—a vehicle for Marion Davies—had fared no better than they deserved to at the box office. That was enough to give the Civil War a bad name, and such old producers' tales died hard in Hollywood. There was, also, however, a growing popular prejudice against "costume" pictures, especially among less sophisticated audiences. Writing to complain that *Mutiny on the Bounty* had flopped in his theaters, an exhibitor in Uvalde, Texas, told M-G-M that he wanted "no more pictures where they write with feathers." And *Photoplay*, in one of its periodic appeals to the studios to keep the screen's heroes and heroines out of ruffles and breeches, commented, "One bo-bo-bo from Bing Crosby is more exciting than a whole screenful of Crusaders." There seemed, in short, no pressing reason for M-G-M to invest $65,000 in the acquisition of a massive Civil War novel by an unknown Atlanta novelist named Margaret Mitchell.

Turned down by Metro, the agent, Annie Laurie Williams, rushed to Grand Central Station where she knew producer Mervyn LeRoy was on the point of leaving for the West Coast. A few minutes before the Twentieth Century Limited pulled out of the station she came running down the platform and shoved an enormous pile of galley proofs into his hands. "New novel," she puffed. "Very good woman's part."

Intrigued by its bulk, LeRoy's wife, Doris, began to read *Gone With the Wind* and she was still reading when their train arrived in Los Angeles, five days later. She took it directly to her father, urging him to buy it for the screen; she could foresee its enormous appeal to women, and moreover her father had under contract a star who was perfect for the heroine—Bette Davis. Doris LeRoy's father was J. L. (Jack) Warner.

If Metro was the boudoir, Warner Brothers was the men's locker room among Hollywood studios. The accent was on male supremacy as reflected in the cynical, fast-paced Warner Brothers pictures with tough, low-life settings (*G-Men, Petrified Forest, China Clipper*) and biographies of famous men such as Zola, Pasteur, and Reuter. For the most part, Warner's women stars accepted the situation with cheerful resignation, but not Bette Davis, who led an embattled existence at the studio, and in her constant struggle for better parts and greater artistic (and personal) freedom she occasionally came to resemble the neurotic, intractable woman of her best screen portrayals. When Doris LeRoy brought the novel to Warner's attention, Davis was poised on the brink of another act of defiance; against Warner's wishes, she was going to England to appear in a picture.

Warner read a studio-prepared synopsis and sent for her. "Look, don't leave," he said. "I've bought a book which has a marvelous part for you." "What is it?" inquired Bette Davis. "A new novel. It's called *Gone With the Wind*." But the star was unimpressed. "I'll bet that's a pip," she replied. And on that note of bravado, which she would soon regret, she left. Warner had not, of course, bought *Gone With the Wind* and with Bette Davis gone he saw no reason to. But her absence without leave proved short-lived; he sued her in the English High Court for breach of contract and won, forcing her to return to Hollywood.

As the publication date drew near, *Gone With the Wind* found another champion. Lilly Messenger was the story editor at R.K.O., which meant that she mined the publishing world and Broadway for filmable material. She read *Gone With the Wind* on a cruise to Bermuda, her excitement mounting with every page, and then sent the page proofs to Pandro Berman, her studio's leading producer, together with the most ecstatic recommendation she had ever written. In her enthusiasm, she obtained a second set of proofs and gave them to R.K.O.'s big star, Katharine Hepburn.

Overleaf Watched by the Tarleton twins (Fred Crane and George Reeves), Scarlett sprints across the lawn of Tara to meet her father. The cables holding the trees upright are faintly visible at the top of the picture.
(PRATT)

Berman, like Jack Warner's daughter, read the novel traveling by train across the country, but in the opposite direction, from Los Angeles to New York. It impressed him greatly, but what impressed him even more was the sheer scope of the problems awaiting the producer who attempted to film it, chief of which would be the enormous production costs, with casting the main roles—especially the heroine, Scarlett O'Hara—running a challenging second. R.K.O. did have Katharine Hepburn under contract, but Berman doubted whether the gifted, bony New England actress would be believable as the scheming, flirtatious Southern belle of Margaret Mitchell's novel. Her box-office qualifications were also far from faultless; a succession of disastrous pictures such as *Mary of Scotland* (in which, *Time* commented, she acted "like a Bryn Mawr senior in a May Day pageant") had made her unpopular with cinema exhibitors who shortly placed her on their official list of stars considered "Box Office Poison." Unsuitable she might be, but she could also be formidable when in pursuit of a good role, and the most sensible course seemed to Berman to quietly turn down the novel before she picked up its scent. He had reckoned without the zealous Lilly Messenger. (Stars rarely had any say in the acquisition of stories, which was solely the studio's business, and Lilly Messenger was strongly reprimanded for bypassing the system.)

In New York Katharine Hepburn was waiting. Having read *Gone With the Wind,* she saw herself as the inevitable choice to play Scarlett O'Hara, and with characteristic self-assurance assumed that anyone reading the book had to reach the same conclusion. Why then was Berman dragging his feet about acquiring it for the screen—and for her? In vain, he protested that it would cost too much. She kept up a daily pressure of bullying, begging, and wheedling, from which he was at last delivered by the news that the book had been bought by someone else. That someone was David O. Selznick.

Annie Laurie Williams was to be forever known as the agent who sold *Gone With the Wind* to the movies, but the sale overshadowed a long career of finding literary properties for the screen, among them John Steinbeck's novels and the Kathleen Windsor best seller *Forever Amber.* Her appearance and manner gave no hint of the sound business sense and uncanny gift for spotting good motion picture material that made her a legend among studio story editors, for she was small, round, retiring, and rather dowdy. She rarely talked about books other than in terms of their potential as screen properties. But her judgment was hardly ever wrong. *Gone With the Wind* was entrusted to her by Macmillan, the publishers, because Margaret Mitchell had no agent; Annie Laurie Williams instantly saw in it a powerful motion picture. When advance copies did the rounds of the Hollywood studios, however, the response was disappointing. For a while, there was only one firm offer of $35,000 from Darryl Zanuck at Twentieth Century-Fox.

The novel cast a spell on every woman that read it; the only trouble was that studio decisions were not made by spellbound women. Elsa Neuberger, the New York-based story editor for Universal Studios, sent off yet another synopsis of the novel to Hollywood with an enthusiastic recommendation: "I know you told me not to send any costume stories, but I think you ought to consider this one very seriously." Universal replied by repeating its ban on costume pictures.

Annie Laurie Williams submitted *Gone With the Wind* to Katherine (Kay) Brown, head of the New York office of Selznick-International Pictures, the independent production company set up the previous year by David O. Selznick. At first the same pattern repeated itself: Selznick's pretty executive was overwhelmed by it. Soon Selznick himself received the 1037-page novel together with her long synopsis and excited message saying, "I beg, urge, coax, and plead with you to read this at once. I know that after you read the book you will drop everything and buy it." Selznick read the synopsis immediately, but no urgent instructions to snap it up arrived in New York. Like Pandro Berman, he felt that he lacked an important ingredient to do it justice, namely a woman star for the role of Scarlett O'Hara; like Thalberg he regarded Civil War pictures as poor box office prospects. Moreover, the asking price was steep for the resources of a small independent production company with only one completed film to its name (*Little Lord Fauntleroy*) and a second on the way (*The Garden of Allah*). So he cabled Kay Brown: MOST SORRY TO HAVE TO SAY NO IN THE FACE OF YOUR ENTHUSIASM.

The next day, however, he began having second thoughts, and

The Search for Rhett

Ronald Colman

Basil Rathbone

Gary Cooper

Errol Flynn

Clark Gable

a couple of days later he found himself selling the story to Ronald Colman, who was so eager to play the principal male character, Rhett Butler, that he volunteered to spend several months in the South converting his implacably British accent into a Southern one. When it sold an astonishing 176,000 copies (at three dollars a copy) in the first month of publication, Selznick's interest increased considerably; but he still hesitated, torn between his enthusiasm as a producer and his doubts as a businessman. His producer's instincts recognized its potential for drama and spectacle, especially in color. But his business sense continued to signal caution; Hollywood was bestrewn with the wreckage of movies based on best-selling novels. Then Kay Brown shrewdly forced the issue by sending the synopsis of *Gone With the Wind* to the company chairman, John Hay (Jock) Whitney, who unhesitatingly told her that if Selznick decided against buying the rights, he would do so himself.

Selznick didn't relish the prospect of being out-maneuvered by his own chairman of the board and quickly offered $50,000 which was, of course, just as quickly accepted. What was later to seem a fabulous bargain was actually one of the highest prices paid for a first novel up to that time, and Selznick paid it grudgingly, grumbling to Kay Brown in another cable. I FEEL WE ARE EXTENDING OURSELVES CONSIDERABLY EVEN TO PAY SUCH A PRICE FOR IT IN VIEW OF THE FACT THAT THERE IS NO CERTAINTY WE CAN CAST IT PROPERLY. Judging from his truculence, it's conceivable that without Whitney's prodding he might have decided against buying *Gone With the Wind,* leaving the field to Darryl F. Zanuck. As for the deal itself, it was a straight purchase of film rights with no percentage of the box-office profits involved; the amount paid by Selznick was shared equally by the author and Macmillan, with Margaret Mitchell paying the standard ten percent agent's commission to Annie Laurie Williams, who had earned every cent of it.

The biggest news break a producer could hope to get for his picture was "the banner line in Parsons," the lead story in Louella Parsons' column—the Hollywood gospel syndicated in four hundred daily newspapers and countless weeklies. One of Selznick's first acts on buying *Gone With the Wind* was to telephone Louella Parsons with the news, as *The New York Times* said later. The Parsons story was the first pebble in a landslide of news about the making of the picture which, said *The New York Times,* was to fill more newspaper columns than the Neutrality Act debate. And in one important respect it set the tone for what was to follow: it was not entirely true, nor was it completely false. It was Selznick's version of reality, not the perceived reality of the time, nor the truer reality of hindsight, but the reality of what he thought had happened and therefore, in the absence of any contradictory voice, he said had happened. Selznick, Parsons reported, had bought *Gone With the Wind* for $65,000 in the teeth of fierce competitive bidding from the major studios; David had given the studio Goliaths one in the eye.

Next, David Selznick sailed for Hawaii with his wife Irene, Charles Boyer, and, in order to read what he had bought, a copy of *Gone With the Wind.* The novel confirmed his initial feeling that the obvious choice for Rhett Butler was Clark Gable. But for reasons that will become clear later, that was a course he wished, if possible, to avoid. On the other hand, he could think of no female star who fully measured up to Margaret Mitchell's description of Scarlett O'Hara. "The green eyes in the carefully sweet face were turbulent, willful, lusty with life, distinctly at variance with her decorous demeanor."

Returning to Hollywood some three weeks later, he found that sales of the novel had jumped to 300,000 copies ("You had to read it in self defense, if for no other reason," wrote Frank Nugent, the film critic of *The New York Times*) and casting the picture had become a nation-wide topic of conversation—"a dinner sport," as Louella Parsons put it—on a level with King Edward VIII and Wallis Simpson, Roosevelt's re-election, Adolf Hitler, the Spanish Civil War, and the Dionne quintuplets. Into Selznick's capacious lap had dropped the hottest property in the history of the movies.

The filming was to be a Hollywood casebook, unique yet typical: unique in its enormous scope, cost, length, and time spent in the making, for it would be two and a half years before

Overleaf The O'Hara family at evening prayer; Gerald (Thomas Mitchell), Ellen (Barbara O'Neil), Suellen (Evelyn Keyes), Carreen (Ann Rutherford), and Scarlett; Pork (Oscar Polk) and Mammy (Hattie McDaniel). Here is an example of Selznick's insistence on exploring all the angles: for the final edited version, he chose a take which does not show the house servants in the background. (SBFA)

the novel reached the screen; typical in its commitment to Hollywood—its attitudes, resources, conventions, methods and intrigues. As a picture it would straddle two worlds separated, to borrow historian John Wain's phrase, "by one of those seismic cracks in the historical surface"—the closing phases of Hollywood's most successful era, when it was made, of which it can be said to represent a supreme effort, and the first glimmers of the television age in World War Two, when it was released and shown.

It was, for instance, consistent with the canons of Thirties filmmaking that the screen version of a novel drawing so much of its force from its Southern setting would be filmed entirely in Hollywood; during one of his fits of uncertainty David Selznick was to send *Traveltalks* producer James A. FitzPatrick to the South to shoot atmospheric footage, but only some shots of a Mississippi riverboat would find their way into the picture. What was more endemic to the times was that, in contrast to the current tendency of the director to be the dominant creative force in the making of a movie, that role in *Gone With the Wind* was monopolized by David O. Selznick, the producer.

2

The Producer Who
Spelled Sunday

Henry Ginsberg was vice-president in charge of finance at David Selznick's new studio, which meant that he held the purse strings. Holding the purse strings for Selznick was like hanging onto the reins of a runaway horse; the producer was a prodigal spender on his productions, and when Ginsberg read *Gone With the Wind* he was horrified by the scope it offered to Selznick's extravagance. So he marched into Selznick's office and bluntly faced him with the consequences of his intentions. "Good Christ, *we* could never make this picture, it would cost us a fortune," Ginsberg told Selznick. To film the enormous novel was so far out of their financial reach, he argued, that if Selznick attempted it he would probably ruin his studio. The only realistic solution was to try to unload it onto a major studio while it was still selling well, and make a tidy profit.

Perhaps because he was himself having second thoughts about whether the studio's resources were equal to the task, Selznick reluctantly agreed to try for a sale. Ginsberg approached M-G-M first. Irving Thalberg had died in the meantime, but the memory of his opposition to Civil War themes lingered on, and Ginsberg was turned down. Then he approached the head of Paramount, Y. Frank Freeman, himself a transplanted Atlantan whose home in Atlanta was only a few blocks away from Margaret Mitchell's. But he got a derisive refusal—"What, that white elephant?" When other studios also showed no interest, Selznick accepted the inevitable and began to assemble a production team for his picture —as usual, sparing no cost in going after the best. The major studios maintained permanent production staffs (when Cedric Gibbons, head of M-G-M's art department, wasn't designing a movie, he would often be put to work redecorating L. B. Mayer's executive suite or the Metro commissary), but a small outfit like Selznick-International, which did not produce enough films to justify a large payroll, hired additional people for specific productions, either from the pool of freelancers or on a loan-out basis from one of the "majors."

(1 8)

Wearing the green sprig muslin dress, Scarlett waits for her father by the lake at Tara. This opening sequence was reshot later with her wearing a white dress. (PRATT)

Art Director and Designer

Lyle Wheeler, who is credited with art direction of the film, showing David O. Selznick full-color renderings of the tree-lined road leading to Tara and the magnificent double staircase at Twelve Oaks. Wheeler won an Academy Award for interior decoration. (TLPA)

nature had given him one redeeming feature, an electric, boyish, toothy grin. His broad shoulders were set in a permanent stoop which deepened into a hunch when he was tired; he wore good clothes badly.

Without a word of apology for his tardiness, he launched into a discussion of the picture. As he declaimed his views he tramped ferociously up and down the room, bumping into any piece of furniture left out of place because he was nearsighted, and continually borrowing cigarettes. Yet he seemed more readily open to outside arguments and changes of will than other Hollywood producers. He listened intently to what others had to say, bolting ideas down greedily like a hungry hound. He got so absorbed in the discussion that he would strike a match to light a cigarette and then forget about it until it burned his fingers. At least one newcomer noted that Selznick seemed more generous with office titles than he apparently was with wages; virtually everyone on his permanent studio staff was introduced as his "assistant."

His spacious white-paneled office resembled a comfortable study in a large house, with chintz curtains and upholstered chairs and divans. A wide bay window behind Selznick's mahogany period desk flooded the room with daylight; on the desk, along with two telephones, a desk lamp, a cigar box, a white marble clock and pen-and-ink stand, a water pitcher, a filing tray, a push-button for locking the office door from the inside and other paraphernalia, was a jar of cookies that was always kept filled, for Selznick suffered from hypoglycemia, low sugar content in the blood, which tended to make him drowsy until he revived himself by eating something sweet. Hanging prominently on one wall was a large photograph of a grave, heavy-lidded man wearing *pince-nez*. This was Lewis J. Selznick, David's father.

By inheritance, aspiration, application and training, David Selznick was destined to become a movie enterpreneur of the first order. His father was an adventurer who by 1923 had made and lost a fortune in the expanding movie industry. He encouraged —in fact, expected—his young sons to take a hand in the family business. David was eleven when he sat in on the negotiations for the formation of his father's first movie company, World Film Corporation, and twenty-one when he tried vainly to save Lewis

both Douglas Fairbanks (*Thief of Baghdad*) and Rudolph Valentino (*The Eagle, Son of the Sheik*)—and in 1928 received the first Academy Award ever given for best art direction. It was not unusual for him to receive screen credit as co-director on a picture in recognition of his contribution to its overall visual quality, yet the few times that he attempted to direct his own pictures he was unsuccessful, for a sense of screen drama and an ability to handle actors were not among his talents. Without delay, he began compiling a detailed visualization of *Gone With the Wind*, working directly from the novel (since there was no script) on scenes picked out by Selznick, and, as we shall see later, his work was to be a crucial ingredient in the making of the picture.

Selznick also wanted the author to write the screen version of her novel, but Margaret Mitchell turned out to be the exception to publisher Bennett Cerf's complaint that authors had come to regard the publication of their books as "little way stations on the royal road to Beverly Hills—the thing that an author wants most from his publisher these days is a letter of introduction to Darryl Zanuck." She refused to join the writers' gold rush to Hollywood, with its promise of fat weekly pay checks for turning out movie scripts at one of the big studios. A retiring woman, she considered the sale of her book to Selznick the close of a transaction, not the start of a business relationship, and told him she wanted nothing more than to be left alone.

The newcomers to his staff got a taste of what working for Selznick was going to be like when he called his first production conference. They assembled in his empty office to await his arrival; two hours later, he blew in with cyclonic force. In his book *The Movie Moguls,* Philip French writes, "One could have swung a scythe five and a half feet off the ground at a gathering of movie moguls without endangering any lives; several would scarcely have heard the swish." L. B. Mayer, Adolph Zukor, Carl Laemmle, and most of the rest averaged in the region of five foot four or five; at six foot one, Selznick was a tall man by any standards and a positive giant in Hollywood. He had a large, pale, bland face with a bulbous nose, thick lips, eyes that squinted at some distant point from behind thick-lensed glasses, and thick black curly hair (Gene Fowler called him "Chinchilla head");

To direct *Gone With the Wind* Selznick engaged George Cukor, who was both a close personal friend and his favorite director; six of Cukor's twelve pictures to date had been produced by Selznick. Besides being a perceptive observer of the human condition, Cukor had a special gift for breathing fresh life into the popular literary classics much favored by David Selznick and other Hollywood producers, and the pictures he made for Selznick included *David Copperfield* and *Little Women.* In an industry in which labels were easily acquired and stuck fast, Cukor was known as a "woman's director." He handled women stars with unusual skill and insight and it was no accident that eleven of his pictures centered around women's roles—usually played either by Katharine Hepburn or Constance Bennett. Another early recruit was Walter Plunkett, noted for his accurate and imaginative costume designs for historical pictures and period pieces such as *Mary of Scotland;* Plunkett signed a fifteen-week contract with Selznick-International Pictures to create the costumes for *Gone With the Wind* and ended up staying one hundred and sixty-two.

In the fall of 1936, William Cameron Menzies appeared for the first time in Stage Thirteen, a bar across Washington Boulevard from Selznick's studio in Culver City, and spent several hours celebrating his engagement to work on *Gone With the Wind.* He was a stocky, friendly, hard-drinking man in a tweed coat who talked a lot about his Scottish ancestry and his dream of retiring from the movies to open a country pub in England. In a short time there was forged one of those instantaneous associations of person and place; like the pope with the Vatican, the Mona Lisa with the Louvre, Bill Menzies became inextricably linked with Stage Thirteen, where he sought refuge and solace from his exigent and tireless studio boss.

Although he already had a very competent art director in Lyle Wheeler, Selznick had hired Menzies, one of the greatest visual talents to work in the movies, with instructions to make "a complete script in sketch form, showing actual camera set-ups, lighting, etc." The assignment was an indication of how far beyond the business of merely designing sets Menzies had taken his craft. Originally an illustrator of children's books, he had pioneered movie art direction in the Twenties—he worked on pictures with

At the Twelve Oaks barbecue, Ashley (Leslie Howard) woos Melanie (Olivia de Havilland). (PRATT)

William Cameron Menzies, who designed the production. He won an Academy Award "for outstanding achievement in the use of color." (FLAMINI)

J.'s last one from financial collapse. As a teenager, he initialed dozens of film contracts every week on his father's behalf, while his brother, Myron—four years older—was in sole charge of the output of the second largest film company in the world. The Selznick brothers were marinated in movies.

The Selznick legend has it that Lewis J. Selznick never made a major move without consulting his sons. "Show it to David," he would say of a script or a movie; "If he likes it, it will make money." The Selznick legend further has it that David was later able to get his first Hollywood job at M-G-M over L. B. Mayer's objections as a result of having supported Nicholas Schenck, the president of Loew's Inc. (M-G-M's parent company) in a dispute with his father. Somehow, Lewis J. Selznick had managed to get his hands on the rights to fifty percent of the gross receipts of *Ben Hur,* the M-G-M epic famous for its chariot race and its enormous cost, and Schenck had come to try to buy it back. For some time David Selznick listened to the two men haggle themselves into an impasse. Then Lewis J. turned to his son and said, "Let David decide; David, shall we let Mr. Schenck have his fifty percent of the gross back?" David thought for a while and nodded. It's not known how the elder Selznick felt about his son's decision but he abided by it, and a grateful Nicholas Schenck promised David help if he ever needed it.

Lewis J. Selznick felt at home in the rough and tumble of the movie business, which was in the hands of his own kind—Jewish immigrant businessmen who had invested in a goose nobody else wanted, and which was now laying golden eggs. Louis B. Mayer had been in scrap metal, Samuel Goldwyn (nee Goldfish) in gloves, and Selznick's nemesis, Adolph Zukor, in furs; Lewis J. Selznick himself had been in gems. He was born Lewis J. Zeleznick in Kiev, Russia, but David always used to say that his name was Czech for "Man of Iron," and that the family had originally come from Czechoslovakia. It was to Manchester, England, not to Prague or Bratislava, that Lewis made his way at the age of twelve and worked as a factory laborer to earn his passage to the United States. When he was eighteen he emigrated to America, changed his name to Selznick, and settled in Pittsburgh. He found work as a jeweler's apprentice and eventually started his own retail jewelry business, first in Pittsburgh and then on a larger scale in New York. But the movies seemed to offer more scope for his high-powered flamboyance than the conservative jewelry market and in 1911 he sold his business, keeping a handful of stones which he carried around in his pocket.

His rise and fall in the movies is one of the most Byzantine chapters in the industry's turbulent and complex early history. He insinuated himself into films through the back door by undertaking to sell a friend's substantial chunk of stock in Universal Studios (then called Universal Film Manufacturing Co.) to one or the other of the two rivals fighting for control of the company—Patrick A. Powers and "Uncle" Carl Laemmle. With the aid of Selznick's shares, Laemmle emerged on top in the chaotic struggle. When the smoke cleared, the cunning little Bavarian from Wurrtemberg looked around him, discovered that the jeweler from Kiev had installed himself as company general manager, and promptly fired him.

But Lewis J. Selznick had seen enough of the business to be able to form his own World Film Corporation, and he was soon maddening the established companies by raiding them for stars and outbidding them for successful Broadway plays. At the time, the companies made sure of renting out all their movies, regardless of quality, by forcing theaters to accept a quota of less profitable pictures with every film that featured the big box-office stars; Selznick didn't improve relations with his rivals when he broke away from this practice and began offering the films of his top star (and reputed mistress), Clara Kimball Young, separately at considerably higher rates. The others were forced to follow suit and their less saleable movies suffered. He revelled in personal publicity and each coup was exuberantly proclaimed with large advertisements in the trade press personally signed by Lewis J. Selznick. He persuaded Alla Nazimova, the Russian actress, to make a movie by offering to pay her $1000 a day at the end of each working day; the diminutive filmmaker was, of course, photographed handing her the first check.

Another of his inspired stunts was to send a highly publicized telegram to the deposed Czar Nicholas offering him an acting job in movies—WHEN I WAS A POOR BOY IN KIEV SOME OF YOUR POLICE-

Overleaf At the barbecue, the subject is war. (FLAMINI)

MEN WERE NOT KIND TO ME AND MY PEOPLE STOP I CAME TO AMER-
ICA AND PROSPERED STOP NOW HEAR WITH REGRET YOU ARE WITHOUT
A JOB OVER THERE STOP FEEL NO ILL WILL WHATEVER YOUR POLICE-
MEN DID STOP IF YOU WILL COME TO NEW YORK CAN GIVE YOU FINE
POSITION ACTING IN PICTURES. There was no reply from the Czar.
But it's unlikely that Selznick was able to appreciate the full
irony of his own stunt. He probably did not know that Czar
Nicholas despised the cinema, which he regarded as "an empty,
useless and even pernicious diversion."

Even without the help of the former Czar of all the Russias,
by 1920 Selznick was worth somewhere in the neighborhood of
sixty million dollars. The family lived grandly in a seventeen-
room Park Avenue apartment and drove about in two Rolls-
Royces. Twenty-one-year-old Myron Selznick was responsible for
film production at his father's five studios, four on the East Coast
and the fifth in California, making about fifty films a year with
established stars such as John Barrymore, Lillian Russell, and
Olive Thomas (until she was found dead of a drug overdose in
the Crillon Hotel in Paris), and some promising newcomers,
among them Tallulah Bankhead and Norma Shearer. After a
short stay at Columbia University, David also joined his father's
firm on a fulltime basis and was put in charge of distribution.

In the end, the collective cunning of the gnomes of Hollywood
—everyone except Selznick had by now moved to the West Coast
—demolished his empire. Zukor formed a new production company competing for the mass audience of Selznick's Select Pictures,
the successor of World Film Corporation, and Selznick's box-office
earnings took a dive. His rivals began to lure away his big stars
with offers of more money; his creditors began to press him for
payment. Selznick's assets were hopelessly overextended and he
was unable to meet their demands. He and his sons tried desperately to raise more money, but since Selznick had at one time or
another alienated almost everyone, there were no allies to turn to
for help, and the multimillion-dollar enterprise was declared
bankrupt for failing to meet a $3,000 payment.

The Selznick brothers headed for Hollywood vowing vengeance
on all the callous studio heads for ruining their father. They
loved him deeply and saw him as a martyr. Family revenge be-

came an obsession with Myron; it supplied the drive that made him the most powerful agent in Hollywood. As for David, despite his periodic repetition of vows, revenge came a poor second to ambition. He had inherited Lewis J.'s passion for gambling, his extravagance, his tough piratical methods in business, his roving eye, and his flair for personal publicity and self-aggrandisement. Where father and son diverged was in their attitude toward the movies. "Less brains are necessary in the motion picture business than in any other," the elder Selznick told a congressional committee investigating the film industry in 1917. His passions were the theater and the diamonds he carried in his pocket (until he was forced to sell them to raise cash when he went bankrupt), and the movies were merely a quick way to get rich. But from its humble beginnings as a carnival sideshow and vaudeville program filler, the new medium was becoming respectable, and at some point Lewis J. Selznick's rivals had made the subtle transition from successful promoters to leaders of a new industry; in their own limited way they were beginning to take a pride in their movies and to be dimly aware of their enormous potential, and David Selznick, unlike his father, shared this pride and this vision. Yet only Lewis J. Selznick, who was in it for the money, succeeded in establishing a real movie dynasty; the Selznick name is woven three generations deep into the fabric of Hollywood. His sons were leading figures in the industry, and now one of David's sons continues the tradition as a producer.

After a last hopeful fling at wheeling and dealing in a Florida land boom which also came to nothing, L. J. and his wife, Florence, moved to California, where they lived for the remainder of their lives supported by their sons. Lewis J. Selznick never ventured into the movies again, but his sons continued to seek his advice until his death in 1933. David was especially close to his father until the day he was married. Lewis J. came into David's bedroom every night to open the window, talk to him, tuck him in, and turn out the lights; sometimes, he even helped David undress.

David Selznick went to Hollywood in 1926, hampered by a shortage of cash and by his unloved father's name, helped by a thorough knowledge of the business, and propelled by an unquenchable desire to succeed. By 1936, when he bought *Gone*

With the Wind, he had come to full stature as head of his own independent production company, Selznick-International Pictures Inc., with a studio in Culver City close to M-G-M; he earned over $200,000 a year. He was now David O. Selznick, having followed the contemporary trend of adopting a middle initial to make his name sound more imposing, as scores of others, including Louis B. Mayer and George S. Kaufman, had done. Selznick said it stood for Oliver, and encouraged the use of his new initials, DOS.

He had arrived as Hollywood was mastering the revolutionary complexities of sound and welding its fragmented activities into the half-dozen large studios that led its phenomenally successful industrialization. It was the dawn of Hollywood's triumphal age. In the next ten years the movies were to become the fourteenth largest industry in the country after automobiles, steel, the oil companies, and the mail order firms, with a regular weekly audience of eighty million and a business volume of well over seven hundred million dollars a year.* Its rapid growth offered plenty of opportunity to a young man with David Selznick's experience and *chutzpah,* especially in production—the number of producers having jumped from thirty-four the year after his arrival to two hundred and twenty in 1937, an increase of eight hundred percent! (Curiously, the number of directors increased by only twelve over the same period.) Moreover, about sixty producers earned more than $75,000 a year.

Yet when David Selznick first made the rounds of the studios looking for work as an executive, he was told there were no openings. So he lowered his sights and applied for a $50-a-week vacancy in the M-G-M story department. Hollywood was so paranoid about the name of Selznick that if L. B. Mayer had had his way young David would have been denied even that lowly beginning; but Selznick appealed to Nick Schenck and Schenck honored his long-standing debt of gratitude by ordering Metro to hire him. The need for experienced staff worked in Selznick's favor and he was soon supervising (the early term for producing)

---

*U.S. Department of Commerce figures, September 1936. Average daily attendance at movie houses in the U.S. was 11,425,000; the yearly gross from 15,378 theaters was $750,000,000; there was one theater for every 6,724 people. In 1972 there were approximately 15,000 theaters and drive-ins, one for every 13,900 people.

Tim McCoy westerns. But his brashness brought him into inevitable conflict with Irving Thalberg; at Metro that amounted to defying God, and he was dismissed. Next he decided to try to infiltrate Paramount, the studio of his father's arch enemy, Adolph Zukor, and rather to his surprise, he was hired in the same capacity. Again, his boyhood apprenticeship in movie-making, his colossal nerve and determined drive propelled him in a short space of time to the dizzy heights of assistant to the head of production, B. P. Schulberg.

The Selznick brothers also elbowed their way into Hollywood's tightly knit social community, and their tendency to chase girls (usually other men's) and pick fights made them stand out at parties and social functions. Then David met L. B. Mayer's dark, attractive second daughter, Irene, and, to Mayer's consternation, they began to see each other regularly. "Stay away from that *schnook,* he'll be a bum like his old man," Mayer warned her. His opposition only served to draw them closer to each other, and David confided to her his dreams of owning his own studio, and his ambition to become one of "the masters of the industry." David and Irene were married in 1930, with Mayer's reluctant consent.

A year later, David Sarnoff, the head of R.C.A., took over R.K.O. and began casting around for a young executive who could revitalize the lackluster and unprofitable studio. A newcomer to the movies, Sarnoff had no preconceptions about Selznick's name; he was only concerned with the young man's rising reputation. So, at twenty-nine, David Selznick became the head of a Hollywood studio.

At R.K.O., Selznick shaped his philosophy of movie-making and developed his individual working style. At once sentimental and capable of disengaged inhumanity, dynamic and yet lethargic, he was essentially a sublime egocentric. Power and movies were his twin ruling passions and R.K.O. offered enough of both to keep him happy, at least for a while.

At R.K.O., too, Selznick began his association with George Cukor, who directed his first important R.K.O. production, *What Price Hollywood?* Cukor "discovered" Katharine Hepburn on the stage and Selznick—ignoring the derisive comments about her

Overleaf Fighting words on a hot afternoon: Charles Hamilton (Rand Brooks) accuses Rhett Butler (Clark Gable), "a visitor from Charleston," of cowardice; Ashley intervenes and probably saves Charles' life. (PRATT)

lack of conventional screen glamor—launched her film career in *A Bill of Divorcement*. After that the three of them teamed up in *Little Women,* one of Selznick's most successful early productions. Then L. B. Mayer, impressed in spite of himself with Selznick's growing reputation, offered him a two-year Metro producer's contract at four thousand a week which guaranteed him first claim to the studio's great stars and freedom from Irving Thalberg's supervision. Mayer's opinion of his son-in-law had come full circle. Implicit in the offer was the prospect of eventually taking over from Thalberg—who was then convalescing in Europe after a heart attack—for relations between him and Mayer were rapidly deteriorating. Despite the taunts of nepotism ("The son-in-law also rises"), and the thinly veiled opposition of Thalberg's men, the prospect of having the run of the greatest studio in Hollywood was too alluring to turn down and Selznick moved onto the M-G-M lot in February 1933.

His first production was *Night Flight,* a movie about flying mail in the Andes. It was the first M-G-M picture to include the producer's name in the credits, as stipulated in Selznick's contract. All the other producers promptly followed suit and began putting their names on the screen, except Thalberg, who insisted on maintaining his anonymity from the public until his death. Metro gave him posthumous credit for his last film, *The Good Earth.* Next, Selznick produced the Broadway hit *Dinner at Eight.* Taking his father-in-law at his word, he assembled an all-star cast that included John and Lionel Barrymore, Wallace Beery, Jean Harlow, and Marie Dressler. With such a formidible galaxy and George Cukor's deft direction, the picture couldn't help but be both a critical and a box-office success, and Selznick was off to a flying start in Mayer's esteem.

Lewis J. Selznick had imbued David with a reverence for the "classics," meaning by his definition nineteenth-century romantic novels, and had encouraged his young son to compile lists of books that he felt would make good movies. At Metro, Selznick had both the authority and the means at his disposal to indulge his "classic" strain. He engaged novelist Hugh Walpole to adapt *David Copperfield* for the screen. In so doing, he insisted on a degree of respect for the original that was almost unheard-of in Hollywood and which became a hallmark of his other movies based on well-known books. L. B. Mayer wanted Jackie Cooper, an American, as the young David, but Selznick held out for an English boy, Freddie Bartholomew, discovered by George Cukor who was to direct the picture.

Encouraged by the enormous success of *David Copperfield,* Selznick picked two more of his boyhood classics to make into motion pictures—*Anna Karenina* and *A Tale of Two Cities;* later, he would make *Little Lord Fauntleroy, The Garden of Allah,* and *The Prisoner of Zenda* with his own independent production company. Meanwhile, Thalberg had returned to M-G-M, and Selznick, having no desire to become Mayer's pawn in a renewed power struggle between the two rival collaborators, turned down an offer of ten percent of the profits of Loews Inc. and resigned to form his own company. "I am prepared to do with less money if need be, if I fail in the commercial sense," he wrote Schenck in his letter of resignation, "in order to be absolute master from day to day and week to week and year to year of my instincts, my whims and my occasional desire to loaf, my time and my destiny." L. B. Mayer was displeased, and predicted failure. Some of the old antagonism re-surfaced. David Selznick was philosophical: "It's an impertinence to leave Metro's employ," he explained. But those who thought of them as enemies misunderstood their complex relationship. Though he raved against his son-in-law's defection, Mayer allowed him to take Lyle Wheeler as the art director of his new studio (but it was considered folly to try to hire anyone from Metro without Mayer's approval). For David Selznick was still "family"—and the two of them would quickly close ranks against an outsider

Talent, nerve, and extraordinary luck: they were prerequisites of survival in Hollywood and Selznick had them all in generous measure, but he also had two other qualities that set him apart, and he exploited them for all they were worth. Having grown up in wealthy surroundings and received a reasonable education, he had an uncommon social polish and an even less common fluency in speech and writing. In an industry in which business was conducted verbally because its top people were barely literate, David Selznick lived by the written word, and his memo writing will be looked into later. Like his father, he maintained a lavish lifestyle, and the Selznicks' elaborate Beverly Hills house, which had once belonged to John Gilbert, was a focal point of social activity for the movie elite. Selznick's social eminence was enshrined in a *Fortune* magazine article on international café society; only two Hollywood names were mentioned, Countess di Frasso (nee Dorothy Taylor) and the David Selznicks. Their Sunday parties were an institution; to be invited was a mark of arrival. Everybody who was anybody, and visiting notables from the East and abroad, would start drifting in during the afternoon to play tennis, swim in the pool, talk movies, and drink. Then there was dinner and usually a movie.

One typical Sunday, the center of attraction was Orson Welles, a young actor who was making a name for himself on radio. He spent the best part of the evening demonstrating his magical powers; he hypnotized Olivia de Havilland, and "levitated" Selznick by placing his fingers under the producer's armpits.

Selznick was very selective with invitations to his Sunday gatherings. Once Herman Mankiewicz phoned to ask whether he could bring a couple who were close friends. "No, they can't come," David replied, "they just don't spell Sunday." Yet Selznick's parties were an unpredictable mixture of decorum and excess: drunken brawls and arguments were frequent (John Huston's fight with Errol Flynn on the lawn of Selznick's house is famous). One visitor to Hollywood described the Selznick affair he attended as "A beautiful meringue—served in a bedpan."

3

One Foot in
Heaven

David Selznick was ambivalent about his Jewish origins; whenever the subject came up he protested, "I'm an American, not a Jew." He carefully avoided using Yiddish expressions in his conversation, and kept aloof from local Jewish charities and movements such as the Anti-Defamation League. His critics called it snobbery, his friends said it stemmed from a refusal to take advantage of being a Jew in an industry dominated by Jews; it was probably a bit of both. Because of his affluent upbringing, he was socially more mobile than most of his Hollywood contemporaries, and became friendly with a number of rich Gentiles. In fact, possibly the richest Gentile in the country was his business partner. This was John Hay (Jock) Whitney, the dapper young multimillionaire whose father, Payne Whitney, had died while playing tennis in 1927, leaving him the largest gross fortune ever appraised in the United States up to that time.

Hollywood was one of Jock Whitney's favorite playgrounds, and his private railroad car shuttled back and forth regularly between Los Angeles and the more traditional haunts of the Establishment rich. Social life among movie people was a sober shadow of its former self. For one thing, the Depression had put a damper on riotous living; moderation was the keynote now. For another, the advent of sound kept the stars at home learning their lines after working hours. Having spent some time as technical adviser on a picture, Norman Vincent Peale extolled Hollywood's newfound sobriety in glowing terms: "It's a very quiet, sleepy town, and you need a spyglass to see anyone in the streets after midnight. Motion picture people are wholesome, friendly and home-loving folks. These people haven't time to be wild because in Hollywood it's work, work, work all the time. Hollywood has one foot in heaven."

Of course, it was the other foot that attracted the somewhat starstruck Jock Whitney; on arrival he would plunge headlong into a whirl of parties, dates with lovely stars and starlets, and movie premieres. At the time, East Coast money looked askance at movie people, and Whitney's association helped to make them socially more acceptable. In November 1936, he was in Hollywood to discuss Selznick's plans for filming *Gone With the Wind;* he and Selznick were at the Coconut Grove with Joan Bennett and her then husband, Gene Markey, when Dolores Del Rio and Ramon Navarro, who were among the diners, performed an impromptu song and dance act. A few nights later the celebrity photographers patrolling the Strip got pictures of the Selznicks entering the Cafe Trocadero with Whitney and his date, British actress Wendy Barrie.

The Strip, a half-mile stretch of Sunset Boulevard outside the city limits and under the jurisdiction of the more accommodating county deputies, was where most of Hollywood's night life was concentrated. Its focal point was "The Troc," at 8610 Sunset, where the captains and waiters could scent failure as unerringly as buzzards can death; this week's front booth could be next week's pariah by the kitchen door. (But Whitney was immune to the vicissitudes of Hollywood fortune and so was anyone in his company.) The contents of the Troc's superb wine cellar had been personally selected by owner Billy Wilkerson, who was also publisher of the *Hollywood Reporter,* and the food was the best in Hollywood: *broiled pompano maître d', $1.40; brochette of lobster, $1.50; diamond-back terrapin Maryland, $3.50; Chateaubriand for two, $4.50; crêpes Suzette, $1.50; strawberries Romanoff, $1.50.* At 8477 Sunset was The Clover Club, a gambling club where Selznick and other Hollywood notables spent many of their nights and a substantial chunk of their high earnings at baccarat and the roulette tables; it was not how much you won at The Clover Club, but how much you could afford to lose and laugh about it, that rated you. Your limit on IOU's went up and down with Dow Jones accuracy, depending on the current state of your career.

A Broadway angel, Whitney had inevitably become interested in the financial side of picture-making and had begun to invest in it. His first Hollywood venture was to back Pioneer Pictures, formed to make movies in Technicolor, the new color process developed by Herbert T. Kalmus. Technicolor still had a long way to go to win the confidence of the conservative movie indus-

Overleaf Scarlett slips away from the dozing ladies to find Ashley. (FLAMINI)

try; it was offering Pioneer Pictures stock options for every completed film. Whitney's company started with *La Cucaracha,* an $80,000 short film of a Mexican *fiesta* that showed off the process to exciting effect. Then followed *Becky Sharp,* a colorful but commercially unsuccessful screen version of Thackeray's *Vanity Fair;* among the extras in it was Patricia Ryan, who later became Mrs. Richard M. Nixon. When a second feature film, *The Dancing Pirate,* also flopped, Whitney became disenchanted with his collaborator in the enterprise, producer Merian C. Cooper, and David Selznick stepped into the breach. Whitney and Selznick had known each other socially since 1929, and now, brought together by Cooper himself, their friendship crystallized into a business arrangement that salvaged Whitney's investment in Pioneer and provided Selznick with the financing he needed to start his own company.

In September 1935 they announced the formation of Selznick-International Pictures, with Jock Whitney as chairman of the board and David Selznick as president. Whitney recruited his sisters, Joan Whitney Payson, Flora Miller, and Barbara Henry, and his cousin Cornelius Vanderbilt (Sonny) Whitney, and the five of them supplied $2,400,000. The rest came from Wall Street financiers Robert and Arthur Lehman, and John Hertz ($150,000 each), David's brother Myron ($200,000), and Dr. Attilio Henry Giannini, who, as Supervisor of Motion Picture Loans at his elder brother Amadeo Peter Giannini's Bank of America, enjoyed the position of financial godfather to the cinema industry; and as a gesture of support, a silent investment of $200,000 from Irving Thalberg and Norma Shearer bringing the total capitalization to $3,250,000. David Selznick put up no money but had forty percent of the shares, which, combined with Myron's, gave him a controlling interest in the new company. In return for Whitney's backing, Selznick assumed Pioneer Pictures' obligation to make Technicolor movies and Pioneer surrendered its right to stock options at preferred prices to Selznick-International.

Selznick immediately began planning two Technicolor productions. He made *The Garden of Allah,* with Marlene Dietrich, but had to postpone *Tom Sawyer* because he wanted an unknown boy to play the title role and couldn't find one. As an independent producer, Selznick was less likely to give birth to new ideas than he was to give the old ones force and freshness by the genius of their expression. Intellectually and politically, he had his feet firmly planted in the middle of the road. He used to describe himself as a believer in free enterprise and at the same time an admirer of FDR; he planned no searching inquiries into social conditions, no *Grapes of Wrath* or *Oxbow Incident*. His commitment was to quality, and his greatest gift was a genius for inspiring, absorbing, and adapting the ideas of others. Selznick-International, he said, was to concentrate on producing "a few finely made films"; he believed that no matter what it cost in time and money, an intelligently made picture was going to make a profit in the end.

By Christmas 1936, Selznick was talking vaguely of starting to film *Gone With the Wind* in the spring of the following year. A production account was started against which expenditures were to be charged. A team of secretaries was hard at work compiling a master breakdown of the novel, an elaborate maze of cross-referenced lists and charts meticulously classifying its component parts; every incident was catalogued, every appearance of each of the principal characters, their main speeches, their relationships to each other, what they wore, as well as troop movements, battles, political developments . . . Selznick loved lists and charts.

What Scarlett O'Hara seemed to wear most frequently was green, and Walter Plunkett was sent to Atlanta with the dual mission of researching the costumes and obtaining Margaret Mitchell's dispensation to introduce more variety into Scarlett's wardrobe. Her reply was that Selznick was entitled to dress Scarlett in any colors he pleased (green happened to be the author's favorite color and its repeated use was quite unconscious). When word of the designer's visit appeared in the Atlanta papers, he was besieged by Southerners offering to sell him their grandmothers' old dresses. But the second purpose of his trip was not to buy used Confederate clothing; he was to bring back swatches of fabric clipped from the dresses of the period in Southern museums. These swatches were delivered to a textile firm in Pennsylvania which was to supply Selznick-International with all the cotton for the costumes in return for a concession to market the *Gone With the Wind* prints.

Financier and Producer

John Hay (Jock) Whitney, seated far right, who financed and refinanced the filming of *Gone With the Wind*. Seated with him, on the set of *Tom Sawyer*, are Henry C. Potter and Samuel Goldwyn. (CP)

David O. Selznick walking across the Atlanta street set of *Gone With the Wind*. (TLPA)

To make the costumes, Plunkett set up a cottage industry at Selznick's. In addition to seamstresses making dresses and uniforms by the hundreds, there were weavers to reproduce the homespuns of the Blockade period on two old looms, ironmongers to solder the skirt hoops, milliners, shoemakers, and an old woman brought out of retirement who knew how to construct antebellum corsets.

At this point the designer's fifteen-week contract expired. Selznick summoned him to his office and told him that the picture would shortly go into production and that he felt Plunkett ought to agree to work for the remaining weeks without pay. "Every costume designer in Hollywood wants to work on the picture for the prestige," Selznick argued; "some have even offered to pay for the privilege." An emotional, highly artistic man, Plunkett was deeply upset by the suggestion but managed to stammer a refusal. Selznick approached other leading Hollywood designers and secretly invited each one to submit costume designs for *Gone With the Wind* if they wanted to be considered for Plunkett's job. Adrian, Milo Anderson, and Howard Greer all sent him sketches. Selznick then recalled Plunkett and told him what he had done, but announced that he had decided to renew Plunkett's contract— at $400 a week, instead of the $600 a week the designer was originally making. Plunkett was made to feel he had no choice but to accept if he wanted to stay with the project.

Selznick was also preparing to film *A Star is Born*, his second picture about the tensions and uncertainties behind the Hollywood glitter. Director William Wellman and writer Robert Carson had written the original script, based on one of the era's tragedies: the body of John Bowers, a silent screen actor, had been found washed ashore at Malibu two days after he had told a friend he was going to rent a sailboat and commit suicide by "sailing into the sunset" because his career had been ruined by the talkies. (In Selznick's picture the Fredric March character, Norman Main, drowns himself by walking into the Pacific.) Selznick pronounced himself well satisfied with their script but then engaged Dorothy Parker and Alan Campbell to rewrite it; as they wrestled with the Wellman and Carson version, he assigned Carson to rewrite *them;* then he put two young junior writers on his staff, Ring Lardner Jr. and Budd Schulberg, to work revising the Carson revision of the Parker-Campbell rewrite of the original Wellman-Carson script. The fault lay less in the script itself than in Selznick's assumption that the first version of anything, however perfect, was no more than an embryo requiring many additional stages of evolution, and he ordered new versions as a matter of course. Although everyone was sworn to secrecy, each quickly discovered what was happening. No wonder anthropologist Hortense Powdermaker, in her study *The Dream Factory*, observed that "In Hollywood there is far more tension and anxiety than in the society which surrounds it . . . anxiety grips everyone from executive to third assistant."

Still undecided about the casting of the picture, Seznick turned the public's interest to his own advantage by sending out hundreds of cards to PTA groups all over the country inviting nominations for the principal roles; the overwhelming popular choice for Scarlett O'Hara was Bette Davis, followed by Katharine Hepburn, Tallulah Bankhead and a score of other actresses, while Clark Gable and Ronald Colman topped the list for Rhett Butler. Because a star's contract gave the studio total control over his or her professional destiny, Selznick was unable to approach Bette Davis directly. Instead he put out feelers to see if Jack Warner was willing to discuss a loan-out agreement for her to do *Gone With the Wind*. He was.

Warner volunteered to provide part of the financing for the picture, plus Bette Davis and Errol Flynn as the stars, and to distribute it, in return for twenty-five percent of the box-office gross. The deal was a tempting one, but it had one discouraging flaw in the offer of Errol Flynn. The dashing young Tasmanian recently signed by Warner had made an immediate impact as a swashbuckling star in *Captain Blood,* but his good looks and athletic *panache* were not matched by any particularly striking skill as an actor and Selznick felt Flynn would be out of his depth in the role of Rhett Butler. The producer had an unexpected ally in Bette Davis, who was desperate to play Scarlett, but not at that price; the prospect of playing opposite Errol Flynn as Rhett was evidently so repugnant to her professional sensibilities that she flatly refused to co-star with him in the picture, and publicly

Overleaf Posed publicity tableau (not a filmed scene) with Scarlett and Charles, later to be her first husband, on the Twelve Oaks staircase. (PRATT)

voiced her opinion of his acting ability. If she had hoped to influence Selznick and Warner to drop the actor the strategy misfired, for Warner would not break up the "package" to accommodate his wayward star and the negotiations fell through. Bette Davis began to look around for a competitive vehicle and found another Southern story whose heroine could give Scarlett lessons in willful behavior and bitchiness.

Jezebel was rushed into production at Warner's Studios with Bette Davis in the title role, and it was completed in less than eight weeks (when it finally went before the cameras, *Gone With the Wind* was to take twenty-two weeks to shoot). To Selznick's indignation, Warner Bros. milked the similarity of the stories for all it was worth. Jack Warner was quoted as saying that around the studio Bette Davis was known as "Scarlett," and the star herself gave interviews comparing the two roles. When Selznick saw *Jezebel* he was furious; not only did he feel that the general flavor of the picture was strongly reminiscent of *Gone With the Wind*, but there were a number of obvious lifts from it. He fired off an indignant telegram of complaint warning that *Jezebel* would be "damned as an imitation" if such scenes were not deleted, and at least one scene, a dinner conversation on the South's chances in a war against the North, was cut out of the picture before it was released. But damned it was not; Bette Davis was in fine form and gave one of her most memorable performances, and *Jezebel* was an enormous success. The Civil War was no longer box-office poison.

No Bette Davis then, but what about Tallulah Bankhead? Like Scarlett, she came from good Southern stock, having been born in Alabama, the granddaughter of Civil War hero Senator John Hollis Bankhead, and daughter of Democrat Congressman William B. Bankhead, who was Sam Rayburn's predecessor as Speaker of the House. No great shakes as an actress, she had established herself as a stage personality both in London and on Broadway, investing her performances with the force of her colorful, extravagant personality, while the echoes of her rackety life did the rest. Many a mediocre play was prolonged beyond its deserved lifespan by Tallulah's gaudy presence.

A number of her stage successes were made into movies (*Dark*

was a tasseled cord which gave a mild shock when pulled. But the audience laughed in all the wrong places and critic Richard Watts Jr. wrote that *Tarnished Lady* "might have been designed for Tallulah by her worst enemy in a particularly cruel moment."

Selznick was, of course, perfectly aware of all this, just as he was even more aware that Jock Whitney was a relatively recent—and still friendly—old flame. But through Whitney, the producer offered Tallulah a screen test. Tallulah read the novel, was instantly possessed by the conviction that only she could understand and capture its Southern flavor, and felt that her moment had come. On December 20, 1938, she breezed into Hollywood, "with a gusto that must have been felt in Java," as Brooks Atkinson once described her entrances. Selznick met her at Los Angeles' downtown station. In slacks and a mink coat, with her long tawny hair awry, she looked rather like an unmade bed. She talked incessantly in a nervous, husky whisper ("Are you ever taken for a man on the phone?" columnist Earl Wilson asked her one day. "No, are you?" she shot back). An item in Louella Parsons' column delivered a warning to Selznick that her candidacy was not popular in Hollywood: "George Cukor, her friend, is going to direct [the film]. Jock Whitney, another friend, is backing it. So I'm afraid she'll get the part. If she does I personally will go home and weep because she is not Scarlett O'Hara in my language, and if David O. Selznick gives her the part he will have to answer to every man, woman and child in America."

The following morning, a Monday, in a costume that Garbo had worn in *Camille,* Tallulah made a Technicolor test consisting of three scenes taken directly from the book because Selznick was still negotiating with Broadway playwright Sidney Howard to write the script; Cukor cued in her lines. Tallulah Bankhead was the first to test for the role of Scarlett.

On the screen, the sophisticated woman of thirty-four was unconvincing as the sixteen-year-old Southern belle of the early part of the novel, but by the book's end Scarlett O'Hara has married three times, borne three children, and survived the siege of Atlanta, and Tallulah seemed capable of handling the mature drama of the later scenes. Uncertain what to do next, Selznick hedged. He sent her a telegram—with a copy to Jock Whitney—

saying that the tests were promising but voicing his reservations about her ability to portray the younger Scarlett. An immediate answer would have to be "no," he told her, "but if we can leave it open I can say to you very honestly that I think there is a strong possibility."

To bring that possibility to a satisfactory conclusion a Tallulah-for-Scarlett campaign was launched in the South by Marie Bankhead Owen, who was her aunt. The Bankhead political clout was directed toward helping the candidacy of Speaker Will's little girl; letters, telegrams, and copies of pro-Tallulah editorials in the Southern press began pouring in to Selznick. The Alabama Public Service Commission wrote to say that it had passed a unanimous resolution endorsing Tallulah for the role of Scarlett; the Alabama branch of the League of American Pen Women invested $1.26 in a telegram of support "not on the basis of local pride in this daughter of Alabama but solely upon her fitness for the role exemplified by her brilliant acting and colorful personality." From a Mrs. Will C. Oates, Selznick received a huge Tallulah-for-Scarlett scroll bearing the signatures of 1500 top people in the state. The press clippings, sent by Aunt Marie, included an editorial in the *Montgomery Advertiser* and one from a Birmingham paper which, after listing Tallulah's other claims for the role, added, "her speech is still typically Southern—and Hollywood producers in the past have inevitably interpreted the cultured Southern speech in terms of the negro dialect."

Meanwhile, this daughter of Alabama went about her colorful business hopeful that the combined force of her own talent and her friendship with Cukor and Whitney was going to sweep her to victory in the contest for the increasingly coveted role. But Whitney had more business sense than to exert any kind of pressure on Selznick, beyond perhaps making sure that she received serious consideration, and Selznick was a long way from reaching a decision. While she waited, Tallulah impulsively married John Emery, a relatively unknown actor who looked like John Barrymore. The marriage brought sorrow to some of her fans: in Harlem, Gladys Bently, a black chanteuse who wore men's suits and sang dirty songs, composed and performed a lesbian's lament about the fact that Tallulah had married a man!

4

The Search for Scarlett

The sales of *Gone With the Wind* escalated to over a million copies and Mayer began to wonder aloud to his inner circle of subordinates whether Metro had made a big mistake in rejecting the novel. Since the mistake could be blamed on the late Irving Thalberg and not on Mayer himself, they were safely able to agree that it had (Mayer did not exactly dance at Thalberg's funeral, but was seen waltzing energetically at a night club that same evening). But the damage was not irreparable. Press comments and fan mail had already established Metro's Clark Gable as a popular choice for the role of Rhett Butler. With a little help from the studio's publicity department he could well become the indispensable choice, and Mayer, from being out of the game, would find himself holding the last ace in the deck.

Publicity was the fuel that propelled the Hollywood bandwagon; publicity created the stylized theatrical setting in which the star system was able to flourish, and it found its fullest expression at M-G-M. The efficiency and thoroughness of the Metro publicity department was legendary, its power and influence awesomely pervasive. It had a staff of over sixty people, its own three-story building on the lot, and it was run by Howard Strickling. He was a blunt, quick-tempered man whose inner tension frequently erupted in a high-pitched, nervous stutter. His devotion to L. B. Mayer was total. He boasted that he rose at five-thirty each morning because Mayer was usually on his feet by six and might need him. Mayer, for his part, trusted him and took him everywhere he went, including periodic jaunts to Europe. Strickling's detractors used to say that he had no knowledge of himself outside his knowledge of himself as Mayer's man. Mayer's wish was his command. Mayer's idols were his idols, and Mayer's enemies his enemies; thus he admired Herbert Hoover, and hated communists, intellectuals, and homosexuals.

The son of a general store owner in rural Gardena, California, Howard Strickling had dropped out of high school and worked as a sports reporter on a Los Angeles paper before finding his

(59)

Overleaf Mrs. Merriweather (Jane Darwell), Aunt Pittypat Hamilton (Laura Hope Crews), and Mrs. Meade (Leona Roberts) are shocked when the recently widowed Scarlett appears at the Atlanta Charity Bazaar. The shot was dropped from the final version of the film. (FLAMINI)

true metier in the new field of movie publicity. During his tenure as head of Metro publicity, male stars weren't even allowed to appear in fashion layouts, or to accept awards for being well-dressed, because he thought it would make them seem effeminate. His tenure lasted nearly forty years.

Metro concentrated its publicity on the stars—especially the women stars—rather than the movies. Directors, writers, and producers were largely ignored. The aim was to build up a public following that would flock to the movie theaters to see its favorite star, regardless of what the movie was (Metro distributors used to talk of releasing "one Garbo," "two Gables," or "three Crawfords"). It was a seller's market. The demand for "news" from Hollywood was at an all-time peak; the newspapers, with their large rotogravure Sunday sections, had the space for it, and their readers lapped it up. Arthur Schlesinger Jr. talks about the movies in the Thirties being "near the operative center of the nation's consciousness. They played an indispensable role in sustaining and stimulating the national imagination." Wire service agencies considered the Hollywood dateline second only to Washington as a source of personality news, and—with an average daily wordage of 20,000 rattling over the wires—third in volume of copy after Washington and New York.

Strickling was one of the two Metro employees to whom Mayer left money in his will; this was as much in recognition for what the dear public never learned about Mayer's stars—and for that matter about Mayer himself—as for what they had.

When Jean Harlow's husband, Paul Bern, was found shot dead, L. B. Mayer, who was among the first on the scene, found Bern's cryptic suicide note to Harlow and pocketed it, vainly hoping by this action to avert a studio scandal (Harlow, of course, was a Metro star, Bern a Metro executive). But as Mayer was leaving he ran into Howard Strickling, who had heard the news and rushed to the Bern house; the publicity man was aghast when Mayer produced Bern's note, and he persuaded the studio boss to turn it over to the police—to whom Strickling explained that Mayer had taken the note to prevent it from falling into the hands of reporters.

Strickling's next concern was to help Jean Harlow, who was

being besieged by reporters at the home of her mother and step-father, Marino Lo Bello. He found Metro's blond bombshell holed up in a bedroom, paralyzed with shock. She told him that she had been spending the weekend with her mother while her stepfather was away on a fishing trip with Clark Gable. She also told him Paul Bern had been impotent, but this revelation hardly registered in the realization of a new crisis in the tragic chain of events. If Gable was fishing with Lo Bello, then he would probably soon be returning to this house and would run slap-bang into the waiting reporters.

Strickling was anxious to avoid implicating yet another star, especially this star who was widely, and from all accounts not unfairly, assumed to have had an affair with Harlow during the making of *Red Dust,* which had not yet been released. So he stationed secretaries from his department on the two roads lead-ing to the house, to intercept Gable. The plan worked; the star was warned and drove straight to his own home, while Lo Bello slipped in over the back garden fence. Impossible to contain, the scandal flooded the papers in all its sordid detail for weeks; but at least Strickling had saved Mayer from the serious charge of witholding evidence, and Clark Gable from a potentially dis-astrous involvement. (It was not until years later that either of these details came to light.)

A lesser-known instance of Strickling's activities was his role in Gable's marriage to Maria Langham. The couple had been living together for some time, but as Gable's fame grew the studio began to press them to marry. Strickling arranged a secret mar-riage in Anaheim where he was able, through contacts, to have their marriage license backdated by nearly two years.

Strickling operated on a policy of obsessive protection. The world had grown serious and Hollywood, as we have seen, had at least to seem to have grown serious with it; the Hays Office code of conduct had come into being to enforce respectability by statutory regulation. Of course, M-G-M stars would still lapse into the bad old ways, but the paternity suits, adultery cases, and drunk-driving arrests that were once grist for the publicity mills were kept out of the papers by an effective combination of per-suasion, coercion, and advertising pressure. In 1935–36, Holly-

Overleaf Scarlett offers her wedding band to aid "The Cause." "I know how much that meant to you," Rhett tells her. (PRATT)

wood spent over $77,000,000 on press and radio advertising.

The stars' contact with the press and the public was carefully controlled. Each member of Strickling's publicity staff was responsible for one or more Metro stars; the department's deputy head Eddie Lawrence, for example, specialized in handling prima donnas—Norma Shearer, Katharine Hepburn when she moved to M-G-M, and later Greer Garson; Clark Gable was the joint responsibility of Howard Strickling and Otto Winkler; a young U.C.L.A. graduate named Emily Torchia was hired to look after the younger actresses and dreamed up the "Sweater Girl" title for Lana Turner after getting her to pose daringly without a blouse underneath her sweater; Kay Mulbey, another young publicist, became the confidante of Jean Harlow. There was even a publicity man assigned to The Barkies, the team of trained dogs that appeared in a series of Metro short subjects; he would give them dog biscuits while they were being photographed. When the publicity man, Dean Dorn, was promoted to accompanying Irving Thalberg to movie previews, he emptied his pockets of dog biscuits and filled them with mints and gum, which he was expected to hand to Thalberg each time he silently stuck out his hand during the picture.

A member of Strickling's staff was always present when a star was interviewed, and always escorted him or her to public functions and personal appearances. The stars were deluged with invitations of all kinds: the younger ones were asked to college hops and harvest balls, and to be "Sweetheart of Sigma Chi"; the older ones were in demand for conventions, big baseball games, and grand store openings. Although some publicists formed close personal friendships with certain stars that went beyond this role, their principal responsibility was to safeguard the star's and the studio's image of clean, uncontroversial glamor. They were supposed to see to it that the star did not discuss politics, religion, and sex in interviews and conversations, to avoid giving offence. Children were considered unglamorous, rarely mentioned and even more rarely seen. Liquor glasses and cigarettes were removed from sight before pictures were taken.

Every M-G-M publicist also had to fulfill a daily quota of three publishable items of gossip about a Metro star (Clark Gable was going duck shooting with Andy Devine after finishing *Parnell;* Norma Shearer was preparing to play *Juliet* by taking lessons in poetry recitation; Joan Crawford was back from a European vacation, etc.) , and a weekly quota of at least one story suitable for the wire services and one feature story. The department's "planters" would then try to interest someone among the 250 officially accredited reporters from U.S. and foreign publications (including thirty who wrote daily columns) in using the material; one Metro "planter" traveled around the country all year delivering stories and reviews of Metro's own pictures to newspapers which did not have Hollywood correspondents. The obvious effect of this constant flow of studio-generated copy was to discourage too much reporting by the Hollywood press. As the *St. Louis Post-Dispatch*'s Hollywood man used to joke: "Nobody writes too well for me to put my byline on it."

But Hollywood news management—which predated the Washington version by two decades—reached its peak in the studios' censorship of the fan magazines, or "fannies." The fan magazines were expected to submit articles for studio approval before publication, and to use only studio-approved photographs. On one occasion the monthly *Photoplay* decided to test the studios' tolerance by publishing an unauthorized feature story entitled *Unmarried Husbands and Wives,* a thinly disguised catalog of all the stars who were living together—Gable and Carole Lombard, Chaplin and Paulette Goddard, Robert Taylor and Barbara Stanwyck, and so on. "Unwed couples they might be termed," *Photoplay* stated. "But they go everywhere together, do everything in pairs, no hostess would think of inviting them separately, or pairing them with another . . . they build houses near each other . . . take up each other's hobbies, father or mother each other's children, even correct each other's clothes—each other's personalities. Yet to the world their official status is 'just friends.' No more." *Photoplay* soon discovered that the studios' tolerance was very low indeed. Led by Metro, they threatened to cancel their advertising and cut off the magazine's access to their stars if a retraction was not printed. The following month *Photoplay* published a contrite full-page apology to the stars mentioned in the article, ostensibly because newspaper reports about the piece

Overleaf "One hundred fifty dollars in gold for Mrs. Charles Hamilton." The widowed Scarlett causes a scandal by accepting Rhett Butler's bid to lead off the Virginia reel. George Cukor was fired during the filming of this sequence. (PRATT)

had made "these friendships appear in a light far from our original intention." As for the author, his byline didn't appear again in *Photoplay* for months.

At the *Chicago American* the punishment for pulling a boner used to be to stand on a chair in the city room and read aloud Lloyd Pantages' rather precious-sounding Hollywood column. Shortly after Mayer began to covet *Gone With the Wind,* a young reporter at the paper stood on his penitential perch and read that David Selznick was considering Clark Gable for the role of Rhett Butler. Other columnists and wire service stories were drumming home variations of the same Gable-for-Rhett message. Then *Photoplay* came out with a full-page drawing of Gable in an antebellum black coat and polka dot cravat. The fan magazine's caption said it wanted readers to see what Gable would look like as Rhett because he was the popular choice for the part, and it went on to "predict" that he would also be David Selznick's. Considering Metro's tight rein on the "fannies," the drawing could hardly have been published without the studio's knowledge and, presumably, approval. It looked as if Howard Strickling was hard at work on his master's behalf.

The impact was soon felt in Gable's fan mail, which averaged 1200 letters a month, eighty-five percent from women; besides the usual requests for autographed photographs, for advice on how to get into the movies, and for such intimate personal mementos as "a stick of chewing gum you have chewed," and besides the torrid love letters graphically detailing what the writer would like to do with, and have done to her (or him) by Gable, there were hundreds that wanted to see him play Rhett Butler. But more important, mail to Selznick urging him to make up his mind and cast Gable as Rhett, which had been a steady trickle before, now began to arrive by the truckload.

In March of that year, the producer sounded out M-G-M about their conditions for loaning out Gable to Selznick-International, and he was not surprised to learn that L. B. Mayer's price was nothing short of the distribution of the picture. Since it was widely known that Selznick had signed an exclusive distribution contract running through 1938 with United Artists—the releasing organization that handled the movies of independent

filmmakers like Samuel Goldwyn, Mary Pickford, and Chaplin—
and couldn't possibly meet Mayer's terms, distribution was clearly
not what his wily father-in-law had in mind. Evidently Mayer
nursed the hope of seeing *Gone With the Wind* made as a prestigious M-G-M motion picture; to do this he was somehow going
to have to pressure or persuade Selznick to part with the screen
rights of Margaret Mitchell's phenomenally successful novel.
Selznick, of course, had other ideas.

Turning a deaf ear to the growing public clamor for Gable, he
started negotiations with Goldwyn for Gary Cooper to play Rhett
Butler. With Scarlett, the problem was not the pressure of a
popular choice, but the reverse one of a bewildering explosion
of alternatives. Selznick received as great a quantity of mail about
who ought to play Scarlett as he did about Rhett; the difference
was that the Scarlett mail suggested every leading actress of the
moment, from Joan Crawford to Marie Dressler. There was
hardly a Hollywood *diva* who was not convinced that the role
was written for her and couldn't understand why her agent had
failed to convert Selznick to this obvious view. The press had a
field day advancing the cause of this star one day, and that one
the next. When Loretta Young was seen lunching with George
Cukor she was the one; for a while a rumor circulated that Scarlett
would be played by none other than Margaret Mitchell herself
and that she had been secretly training at Selznick's studio
for months!

But after Tallulah Bankhead, Selznick's next serious candidate
was another actress from the South, Miriam Hopkins. She had
recently starred in *Becky Sharp,* and Thackeray's heroine had
many traits in common with Margaret Mitchell's. Miriam Hopkins read for the part but did not make a test (Selznick screened
Becky Sharp instead) ; after a while, however, her name faded
from the headlines and the gossip columns to be replaced by
the recently widowed Norma Shearer, ironically a Selznick-International shareholder.

As Irving Thalberg's wife, Norma Shearer had had first claim
to everything at M-G-M, from movie parts to dressing rooms;
"How can I compete with Norma when she sleeps with the boss?"
Joan Crawford used to complain. No expense was spared on a

Shearer picture. The Capulet garden in *Romeo and Juliet,* one of her most recent films at the time, took up the whole of Stage 15, then the largest sound stage in the world; there was so much vegetation that the moisture from it sometimes formed a cloud that floated like lost mist over the set. The balcony scene took five weeks to shoot, and toward the end the balcony itself had begun to crack under the combined weight of Norma Shearer and Leslie Howard (Romeo) and had to be reinforced. The picture cost over $2,000,000 and failed to recover its cost, but Thalberg immediately went ahead with preparations for *Marie Antoinette,* another costly vehicle for his wife.

On the set, Norma Shearer lived up to her title of queen of the Lot; she was dignified, distant, and demanding. At the mention of her name, George Cukor, who directed *Romeo and Juliet,* would clasp his palms together and raise his eyes towards heaven in silent prayer. On the screen she was bathed in a suffused light that flattered her clear white skin and helped create an illusion of physical glamor, but the rest of the scene was frequently left in dark shadow. When Mrs. Patrick Campbell saw *Romeo and Juliet*—in which she had a small part—she remarked, "Norma Shearer and her cast of Ethiopians."

Now Thalberg was dead and the queen of the lot was fighting a bitter battle with Mayer over her inherited share of the company profits, and refusing to star in any more M-G-M pictures until the dispute was settled to her satisfaction. But *Gone With the Wind* was another matter; Norma Shearer was as anxious to play Scarlett as the next star and, according to Hollywood legend, she secretly made a screen test—something she had not been asked to do for years. Though her career had passed its peak, she was still a name to conjure with at the box office, but Selznick feared that at thirty-seven she was too mature for the younger Scarlett. To test public reaction he leaked the fact that he was considering her for the role to columnist Walter Winchell, who duly passed it on to his eight million radio listeners. The response was not encouraging; the public thought the divine Norma was a bad choice to play a Southern vixen. Her fans complained that the role was undignified, others just felt it was poor casting. One letter said: "She is, of course, enormously popular and everyone prefaces their statements with the remark that they think she is a wonderful actress. However, everyone thinks she is sadly miscast in the part of Scarlett. They think she has too much dignity and not enough fire for the part." The letter was from Margaret Mitchell; it was one of her few comments to Selznick on the casting of the picture.

Norma Shearer announced her withdrawal. Some months later she would tell Bosley Crowther, of *The New York Times*, "We decided against it finally, to some extent on the basis of the fan mail, when we realized it wasn't worth taking the chance. Scarlett is going to be a difficult and thankless role. The one I'd like to play is Rhett Butler."

Though the choice was numerically large, the star contenders were all women rather than girls and the freshness Selznick was seeking just was not there. So he decided to make his own star. He announced that he would tap the vast resources of American womanhood to find an unknown girl to play Scarlett, "a girl whom they [the audience] won't identify with a lot of other roles." Selznick was not convinced that an unknown would be able to cope with the long and complex part, but if nothing else the nationwide talent search was a good device to keep the picture in the public eye until he got around to making it; it was a classic Hollywood gimmick that never failed to get attention. Selznick himself had used it very effectively on more than one occasion. Freddie Bartholomew (*David Copperfield*) was discovered in this way; more recently, the producer had spent months on a widely publicized search for an unknown boy to play *Tom Sawyer*. Day after day he had toured the schools and orphanages of southern California in a school bus that became his office, looking for the right boy to portray Mark Twain's lovable hero. When he drew a blank, his talent scouts fanned out across the country and finally found Tommy Kelly, the son of a parochial school janitor, in upstate New York.

But the search for Scarlett was to become the most famous talent search in history. Already a topic of national discussion, the question of who would play the part quickly reached absurdly widespread proportions—a reflection on both the extraordinary popularity of the novel and the movies' hold on the

Overleaf   Rhett comes calling with a new Paris bonnet. (PRATT)

public's imagination. Selznick bragged with some justification that as a result of numerous arguments over the relative merits of one Scarlett hopeful or another, Margaret Mitchell's opening description of her heroine began to challenge the Bible and Shakespeare in frequency of quotation: "Scarlet O'Hara was not beautiful but men seldom realized it when caught in her charm as the Tarleton twins were. In her face were too sharply blended the delicate features of her mother, a coast aristocrat of French descent, and the heavy ones of her Irish father. But it was an arresting face, pointed in chin, square of jaw. Her eyes were pale green without a touch of hazel, starred with bristly black lashes, and slightly tilted at the ends. Above them, her thick black brows slanted upward, cutting a startling oblique line in her magnolia white skin."

Selznick's announcement had hardly hit the papers when the telephone calls and letters began flooding into Selznick-International Studio. Women wrote to him from all over the country— and also from Europe, where the novel was repeating its American success—enclosing pictures of themselves wearing everything from bustles to bathing suits. Selznick assigned Oscar Serlin, his talent executive in New York, to interview candidates in the East and North; Charles Morison covered the West, and George Cukor himself was dispatched to prospect the South. Morison, a small, sleek, white-haired man, was a former New York agent who had opened the fashionable Mocambo restaurant in Hollywood; he had good social contacts and a discerning eye for screen talent.

In March, Cukor went south, accompanied by two production assistants from Hollywood and Kay Brown, who had befriended Margaret Mitchell, from Selznick's New York office. Movie talent scouts toured the South regularly in search of fresh grist for the Hollywood mills, but of course, this expedition had an almost mystic significance. Wherever they went, they were a front-page story; the *New Orleans Picayune* devoted more space to Kay Brown's arrival in the city than to Edward VIII's abdication, which had occurred the same day. In Atlanta, Margaret Mitchell took Cukor on a personally conducted tour along the red rutted roads of Clayton County where the dogwood was beginning to come out and the flowering crabs were blooming—but she refused to be drawn into any discussion of the picture.

Dozens of debutantes, actresses from little theater groups and stock companies, and students in college drama departments were auditioned for the role of Scarlett. Among the Atlanta socialites who read for the part was Catherine Campbell, who later married newspaper heir Randolph Hearst, and recently made the headlines as the mother of Patty Hearst, the self-styled convert to the Symbionese Liberation Army. The few who showed promise were sent to New York for screen tests. One was Susan Falligant, a striking University of Georgia senior, who was granted a week's leave of absence from school to make the trip; another was Alicia Rhett, whom Cukor had seen and liked in a rehearsal of *Lady Windermere's Fan* in Charleston and who was to play the India Wilkes role in *Gone With the Wind*. But every audition brought him closer to the disappointing conclusion that his Southern trek would not produce a Scarlett.

Every hotel he stayed at immediately came under seige from girls wishing to be discovered, but none was more persistent than a would-be New York actress of Southern descent. Turned down for the role in New York, she followed George Cukor to Atlanta and tried to waylay him at Terminal Station as he left the city. She jumped on the waiting train and for ten minutes tore through it, jerking open stateroom doors, disconcerting honeymoon couples, and arousing sleeping children. The train was in a general uproar and the whole crew was in hot pursuit. Realizing at last that Cukor had not yet arrived, she positioned herself on the platform to wait for him; but Cukor spotted her first and, while one of his assistants diverted her attention, he clambered aboard through the coal car. "I must see Mr. Cukor, if I talk to him he will realize I am the only Scarlett," she pleaded before an audience of interested bystanders. "This is the turning point of my life." The aide took hold of her hand and told her that Cukor had decided to leave Atlanta by car. "I would advise you not to chase him," he told her as she tried to start for the train. "Men don't like being chased. The more you pursue him the less chance you have. Go home and forget about it, and perhaps when we come back to New York we'll see you." He continued to hold her hand until the whistle sounded and then leaped on board the moving train, leaving her weeping on the platform.

Meanwhile, a sign had gone up beside the driveway leading to David Selznick's office; it said "Scarlett Way." Girls arrived at the studio gates in droves demanding screen tests. They came in buses, in taxicabs—and in boxes. One morning, a packing case was delivered bearing the sign OPEN AT ONCE. The case contained an attractive girl who, on being released, ran straight to Selznick's office and began to recite one of Scarlett's speeches while simultaneously peeling off her clothes. But the most bizarre moment of the search came on Christmas Day 1937, when a gift-wrapped package was delivered to Selznick's Beverly Hills house by two liveried footmen. In it was an enormous book-shaped object wrapped in a facsimile of the *Gone With the Wind* dust jacket. The front cover swung open and out popped a young girl in antebellum costume: "Merry Christmas, Mr. Selznick. I am your Scarlett O'Hara."

At one point Selznick invited all the other Hollywood studios to send their stock players to audition for Scarlett, promising them second use of the girl who landed the part. Among the R.K.O. starlets was a young newcomer named Lucille Ball who was already making a name for herself as a comedienne. Privately, she considered her chances negligible, but as a stock player hers was not to reason why; she dutifully studied the three short scenes she was given and went to be auditioned by Selznick himself.

A cloudburst drenched Los Angeles that afternoon, and she lost her way to Culver City. Arriving at Selznick Studios very late and somewhat wilted, she was determined to tell the producer that she was not interested in reading for the role, but he had not yet arrived. A brandy was thrust into her hand and she was led into Selznick's office where she began drying herself kneeling in front of a blazing fire. When Selznick entered, he seemed huge from her low vantage point. She read the scenes, with the producer supplying the cues. "Thank you very much, Miss Ball, that was very nice," Selznick said afterward. It was then that she realized that she had auditioned on her knees. Years later, Lucille Ball (with husband Desi Arnaz) bought Selznick's old studio which became the home of her successful television show, and occupied Selznick's old office herself. On occasion, she would still lose her way getting there.

The flow of eager young women may not have produced a Scarlett, but from all accounts it occasionally helped gratify Selznick's overwrought compulsion to assert an aggressive masculinity. His life was an unsolvable tension between his passionate appetites, his obsessive drive to establish himself as a force in Hollywood movies, his genuine fondness for Irene, and his weakness for physical bravado. His wife was genuinely fond of him in return, but without illusions, no doubt realizing that she had to take him on his own terms.

The "Scarlett" Girls

Joan Fontaine

Alicia Rhett   Norma Shearer

Loretta Young

Miriam Hopkins

Catherine Campbell

Paulette Goddard

Susan Hayward

Joan Crawford

Tallulah Bankhead

Mary Anderson

Joan Bennett

Marcella Martin

Jean Arthur

Katharine Hepburn

Bette Davis

Lana Turner

Lucille Ball

5

The Search for Scarlett (Continued)

Mayer never completely accepted the fact that his second daughter, Irene, was not a son, so her upbringing had been a combination of lessons in traditionally feminine occupations such as cooking and what her father regarded as more manly pursuits—golf, tennis, riding. He would rout her out of bed early in the morning for a pre-breakfast horseback ride across the sand in front of their house in Santa Monica, which preceded Malibu as the beach movie colony. Yet when she asked to go away to college, Mayer's ambiguity vanished in a storm of opposition to his daughter leaving home except as a married woman. Where his daughters were concerned his exigent propriety was a throwback to the Victorian era.

Irene stood out in Hollywood; she was an intelligent girl, with her father's drive and a mind of her own. But her strong urge to express herself never had a chance, for the principal role of a producer's wife was to bask decoratively in her husband's reflected glory. Selznick sought her advice and listened to it, but he never permitted her any active involvement in the making of his movies. She tried to take a hand in designing the costumes for *Gone With the Wind;* David wouldn't allow it. At the time, it was even rumored that Irene had persuaded Selznick to let her test for Scarlett. Then she tried her hand at scouting talent, and a lovely hat model named Edythe Marrener, whom she spotted in a New York fashion show, was also tested for Scarlett. Edythe Marrener certainly looked the part, but her performance was stiff and amateurish and she did not get the role. However, as we shall see later, the screen test set her on the road to stardom.

Kept on the periphery of Selznick's working life, Irene threw her considerable energies into running the household to best suit his chaotic hours; his occasional philandering she accepted with apparent forbearance. There was a kind of innocence in the way Selznick went about doing his own thing—whether it was philandering, gambling until dawn, or running his studio—with little regard to its effect on other people and complete indifference to

Overleaf Melanie and Scarlett anxiously scan the casualty list of the battle of Gettysburg; Ashley's name is not on the list, but the names of many of their friends are. With them is Uncle Peter (Eddie Anderson).

the harm it caused them. And since he was talented, clearly very charming, and a producer in an era when producers enjoyed absolute power, he got away with it.

The job of converting all that Scarlett activity into endless column inches of publicity was carried out with shameless abandon by Selznick's publicity director, Russell Birdwell, universally known as "Bird." The aptness of his nickname extended to his physical appearance; small gimlet eyes, longbill nose, and a small body perched on spindly legs. The Texas-born son of an itinerant revivalist preacher, he was steeped in the idiom of yellow journalism, having spent twenty years working for a succession of Hearst papers—mostly as a police reporter—from the old *Dallas Dispatch* to the *New York Daily Mirror*. While on the *Mirror* he scooped the world with the only eyewitness report of Lindbergh's take-off on his historic solo flight across the Atlantic. Birdwell was the *Los Angeles Examiner*'s star crime reporter when he was recommended to Selznick to fill the job of publicity director at the new studio; the producer hired him at $250 a week and was delighted when he learned Birdwell claimed to be getting $1000.

Birdwell provided the creative response to Selznick's strong urge to see his name in print, a legacy from his father. He had a flair for dreaming up newsworthy stunts that wound up on the front page rather than in the movie section with all the other news from Hollywood. One of his favorite tricks was to hitch his publicity to a breaking news story. When *The Garden of Allah* was released, he persuaded Robert Hichens, author of the novel, to issue an invitation to the recently abdicated, and therefore homeless, King Edward VIII and Wallis Simpson to stay at his house on the Nile, conveniently called Garden of Allah; the story was widely played as a sidebar to the main abdication development.

About the same time that Selznick bought Nancy Bruff's bestselling novel *The Manatee,* a series of murders by the notorious Collier brothers was filling the newspapers. Shortly afterward, the Colliers were arrested; reporters noticed a stack of copies of *The Manatee* in their hideout and had a field day speculating on the significance of the find. Somehow, Birdwell had managed to smuggle in the books following the arrest, before the reporters gained admission. On another occasion, he flew thirteen of the inhabitants of a Canadian township called Zenda to New York for the premiere of *The Prisoner of Zenda*. Its fourteenth inhabitant was an old woman who, with a little help from Birdwell, decided she was unfit to travel; naturally the wire services wrote stories about her, calling her the Prisoner of Zenda. There were some failures, too: the town of Fairbanks, Alaska, refused to change its name to Douglas Fairbanks Jr. in honor of Douglas Sr.'s son, a Selznick-International star. Thirty-five years later Birdwell would still be up to his old tricks, trying to sweet-talk the home town of his client, singer Bobbie Gentry, to change its name to Gentry.

But the high point of the Selznick-Birdwell association was the search for Scarlett, conceived during one of their brain-storming sessions in David Selznick's office. The producer genuinely hoped that it would lead to the discovery of an unknown girl; Birdwell saw it more as a sure-fire way of sustaining public interest in the picture. But if they differed somewhat on its objectives, they were in perfect accord about its scale. Selznick and Birdwell hardly ever disagreed on the question of scale; the biggest was never big enough for either of them.

Not content with merely publicizing the search, Birdwell tried his hand at discovering a potential Scarlett himself. She was a pretty, twenty-one-year-old redhead who had come to Hollywood from her home town of Austin, Texas, nursing the same ambition that brought thousands of other girls to Hollywood every year—to become a movie star. What she did become was a secretary in the publicity department at Paramount Studios while taking acting and singing lessons, and regularly doing the rounds of the studio casting offices. A chance meeting with Carole Lombard was the turning point, for the zany Selznick star was taken with her fresh, *gamine* looks and enlisted Russell Birdwell's help to advance her career. Birdwell's inventiveness appealed to Carole Lombard's sense of fun and she had been his willing accomplice in a number of stunts: he had once talked the Culver City authorities into declaring a "Carole Lombard Day" and appointing her honorary mayor. Her first official act was to declare a studio

Overleaf Reunion among the wounded at the Atlanta railroad station. Ashley comes home on Christmas furlough. (PRATT)

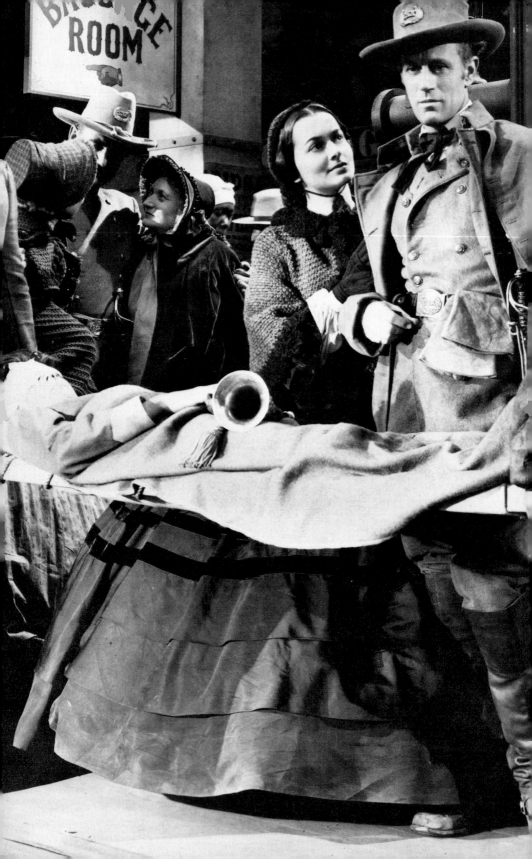

holiday and all the studio employees went home for the rest of the day. Selznick was not amused.

Between December 1936 and mid-March 1937 Margaret Tallichet, the unknown girl from Texas, was mentioned five times by Louella Parsons. She was reported dining out with King Vidor, with Jerry Wald, and with two successive "fiancés"—Selznick contract player Alan Marshall and a German baron—and she was listed among the guests at a big Chaplin party. Birdwell had been at work masterminding her social life and planting items about her in the gossip columns. Her first screen appearance was a fleeting shot of her sitting on a settee in *A Star Is Born;* Birdwell engineered that too. Then she had her picture taken in a Birdwell-designed cellophane swimsuit, edged with blue and red— the edging was necessary to show where the swimsuit ended—and the Sunday "rotos" ran the picture.

The accumulated effect of this exposure was to bring Margaret Tallichet to the attention of David Selznick, who put her under contract as a Scarlett candidate, gave her a small part in *The Prisoner of Zenda,* and then sent her to New York for drama training. Before she left, Birdwell announced that he had insured her Southern accent with Lloyds of London for a million dollars. When a skeptical reporter challenged this story, Birdwell smugly produced a Lloyds policy . . . for one day at $26.

Birdwell tried to publicize the picture by its initials, but with the exception of the trade papers, the press generally failed to respond to the notion of calling it *GWTW*. His efforts to embroil Margaret Mitchell publicly in the production of *Gone With the Wind* were equally unsuccessful.

"Life has been awful since I sold the movie rights," Margaret Mitchell complained in a letter to Selznick. In different ways the press, the public, and the Selznick organization combined to push her into an involvement she did not want, and a notoriety she was determined not to accept. In desperation she asked Louella Parsons to publish her disavowal of any connection with the Selznick production, and any influence with the producer: "Several ladies have advised me that their little daughters tap dance beautifully and do the splits elegantly and can't I get them into *Gone With the Wind* (no, they have not read the book, they admit) .

People also turn up with their colored cooks and butlers and demand that I send them to Hollywood to play Mammy and Uncle Peter." But it did no good. People continued to ambush her in the street to insist that Katharine Hepburn would never do as Scarlett and the only girl for the part was their daughter, or simply to tell her that Clark Gable *must* play Rhett Butler. One morning, the door burst open and in came a woman carrying a pot of lamp black, which she proceeded to smear on her face while at the same time explaining her concept of Mammy's role in the book.

When they didn't appear in person they wrote. "I am convinced that no one could do Scarlett the justice she deserved except someone who really understood her," said one young lady. "I feel that you and I are the only ones who really understand her . . ." And the French publisher of *Gone With the Wind,* Gaston Gallimard, cabled to ask, CAN YOU MANAGE THAT [the picture] IS CALLED AUTANT EN EMPORTE LE VENT? (the French title of her novel).

Margaret Mitchell's stock reply to this avalanche of requests and entreaties was "I'm sure David O. Selznick, the producer of the picture, would like to hear from you." Privately, she would say that any competent actor or actress could portray Rhett and Scarlett and that the more complex characters of Ashley and Melanie would be harder to cast well; privately she would confide that she was not enthusiastic about Gable as Rhett and would prefer Basil Rathbone. But she resisted the temptation to state her preferences openly. Her one recommendation to Selznick was to hire her friend Susan Myrick, a columnist on the *Macon Telegraph* in Georgia, as technical adviser on Southern speech, manners, and customs. "Sue is the youngest child of a Confederate soldier and God knows she's heard enough about the old days," Margaret Mitchell wrote to Selznick, "and good grief, what she doesn't know about negroes! She was raised up with them. And she loves and understands them. But the main thing that recommends her to me is her common sense and utter lack of sentimentality about 'The Old South.' " She also suggested that Selznick hire Wilbur Kurtz, an artist and noted expert on Atlanta before and during the Civil War. Selznick hired both of them.

Though resentful of its pressures, Margaret Mitchell had a

Overleaf Aunt Pittypat prepares to pour wine from the last bottle in her cellar. (FLAMINI)

movie fan's fascination for the production and when "the Selz-nickers," as she called the producer's representatives, began combing the South for Scarlett, she proved quite helpful and cooperative in providing an *entrée* to colleges and local theater groups. That was all the encouragement Russell Birdwell needed to release a story that the author of *Gone With the Wind* was assisting its director with the auditions and conferring with him on the making of the picture. Margaret Mitchell took fright and fled with her husband to Kentucky where, to avoid recognition, they registered in a hotel under an assumed name. After that, Birdwell's requests to her to make statements or give interviews fell on unproductive ground.

It seems incredible that anything as monumental as *Gone With the Wind* could have come about as the result of an accident, but in a sense it did. When she was a child, Margaret Mitchell permanently damaged her left ankle in a bad riding fall. And in 1926 she was confined to her apartment in Atlanta hobbling about on crutches, having severely sprained her damaged ankle in another fall from a horse. Her second husband, John Marsh, an advertising executive with the Georgia Power Company, suggested she try writing to keep herself occupied. Writing had been her favorite diversion since she was six; the sprain had forced her to give up a $25-a-week reporting job on the Hearst *Atlanta Journal* which she had held for four years.

So Margaret Mitchell—or Peggy Marsh, as she was known in Atlanta—rather tentatively started work on a novel about the Civil War. She had no clear plot in mind except for the beginning and the end, and started with the last chapter, in which Rhett Butler walks out on Pansy O'Hara, as she first named Scarlett; Melanie was originally Permalia, and Tara, Fontenoy Hall, but Rhett Butler was Rhett Butler from the start. She continued to write out of sequence, stuffing each completed chapter in a large manila envelope.

Peggy Marsh was tiny—less than five feet tall—pretty, and quiet-spoken. People sometimes mistook her mildness for timidity but wrapped inside the soft cheerful exterior was a will of iron, as David Selznick was shortly to discover. She was reserved without being unsociable: on the contrary, she loved being with friends,

On the steps of the hospital, Scarlett and Melanie are accosted by Belle Watling (Ona Munson), who wants to give gold to the Confederate cause. Sam Wood directed this sequence. (PRATT)

and dancing; she was an entertaining raconteur, and an excellent conversationalist on many topics, but extremely reticent about herself. For example, she never mentioned her first marriage, which had lasted only a few months before she was divorced and married to John Marsh, the best man at her wedding. Because she lacked assurance she kept quiet about her novel. Only the instigator of her endeavors, her husband, was permitted to read the contents of the growing pile of envelopes. One or two close friends knew of its existence, among them Lois Cole, who worked for The Macmillan Company in Atlanta. The rest of her circle only suspected what she was up to, but they accepted the mysterious project as a fact of her intensely private nature. Over the next four years the mysterious project grew and with it their curiosity, for Peggy Marsh continued to work in secret.

It doesn't take much literary detective work to trace the influences in *Gone With the Wind,* and see how the ideas developed. In her youth—she was born in 1900—the Civil War was still fresh in the memory of many relatives and friends and, to some degree, in the physical appearance of her native Atlanta. The stories she heard of war and defeat haunted her and became the genesis of her novel. When she began writing she went back and spoke to many people who had fought in, or lived through the war, and delved into Confederate medical records and Civil War documents.

By 1932 Lois Cole had been transferred to Macmillan in New York and the two of them corresponded regularly; however, repeated inquiries about the progress of the book went unanswered. In fact, it was more than two-thirds completed; it still lacked several chapters, including an opening chapter, and not all of what had been written was by any means in final, polished form. For a title she had gone from *Bugles Sang True,* to *Tote the Weary Load,* to *Tomorrow is Another Day,* but none seemed right. But once she had recovered and was able to go about her business and resume her social life, Peggy Marsh appeared to lose all interest in the massive project, and the mass of envelopes had been piled in a cupboard and had not been touched in two years.

Then, in April 1935, a trade books editor and vice president of Macmillan named Harold S. Latham was touring the South in

Scarlett tending the wounded. (FLAMINI)

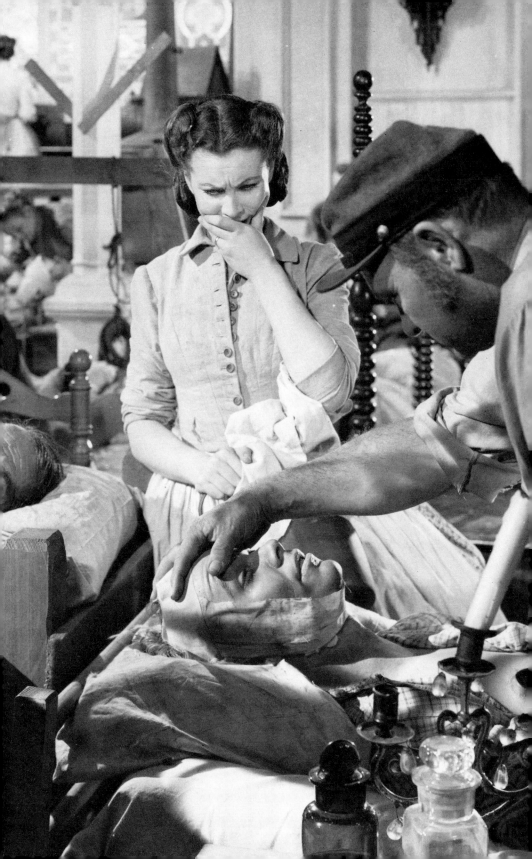

search of new authors and manuscripts. He had been tipped off about Peggy Marsh's novel by Lois Cole; in Atlanta, several people suggested vaguely that if he was looking for new Southern writers he ought to meet Peggy Marsh. The two met at a literary luncheon given by Rich's, the Atlanta book store, at the Atlanta Athletic Club, but when Latham dropped in a casual question about her novel, she replied, "I have no novel." Later, Harold Latham brought the subject up again. Peggy Marsh snapped: "Please stop talking about this. I have nothing to show you." "Very well," Latham replied, "I will drop it—provided you promise me that if you ever do have a manuscript for the consideration of a book publisher, you will let me see it first." "Oh, yes, if I ever do have a book manuscript you shall see it first," she replied in a tone implying that it was an unlikely possibility.

That evening the phone rang in Latham's hotel room; it was Peggy Marsh: "I'm downstairs. Could I see you for a minute?" When Latham went down to the lobby he saw a mammoth manuscript piled on a divan next to her. Her husband, who was a strong believer in her talent, had persuaded her to let Latham see it. "Here, take the thing before I change my mind," she said, and disappeared.

Latham bought a suitcase in which to carry the manuscript and left for New Orleans. Its messy state made it difficult to read, but despite the yellowing, dog-eared pages and the heavily corrected typescript, Latham quickly sensed a potential best seller. In New Orleans, he found a telegram waiting for him. It said: SEND THE MANUSCRIPT BACK HAVE CHANGED MY MIND. Instead, Latham astonished her by offering to publish the novel. Peggy Marsh's first reaction was to refuse, partly because she lacked confidence and partly because she was worried about its reception in the South. "It wouldn't do me any good to be trafficking with you Northerners if my own people don't like what I have done," she told Latham. But once again her husband prevailed, and she signed a contract, receiving a $250 advance on royalties.

She spent the next six months rewriting some portions of the novel, completing others, checking the historical details for accuracy, and producing more than seventy versions of Chapter One before she was finally persuaded to part with it. And she settled on a title. It was a line she had read one afternoon in a poem by Ernest Dowson: "I have forgot much, Cynara! Gone with the wind."*

When the novel was published it was clear that Latham's instincts had been right. The reviews ranged from glowing to patronizing; J. Donald Adams, on the front page of the Sunday *New York Times* book section wrote. "It is, in narrative power, in sheer readability, surpassed by nothing in American fiction," and called Scarlett "selfish, unprincipled, ruthless, greedy and dominating, but with a backbone of supple, springing steel. . . . She is a memorable figure in American fiction." The *New York Sun* called it "profoundly stirring and what looks now like a great novel," and the *Herald Tribune Book Review* said: "The story, told with such sincerity and passion, illuminated by such understanding, woven of the stuff of history and of disciplined imagination, is endlessly interesting."

Robert Nathan remarked: "The three best novels I read this year were *Gone With the Wind;* to *Time* magazine it was "remarkable in other ways than its extreme length." And Stephen Vincent Benét, writing in the *Saturday Review of Literature,* described it as "a good novel rather than a great one . . . the book moves swiftly and smoothly. . . . It is a solid and vividly interesting story of war and reconstruction, realistic in detail and told from an original point of view." Some complained at its lack of "social consciousness," and the *Sunday Worker* called it "an insidious glorification of the slave market." But even its severest critics conceded its power and romantic appeal. Sales climbed by leaps and bounds, and Peggy Marsh almost vanished in the general explosion of interest in Margaret Mitchell.

---

*Dowson's poem is entitled *Non Sum Qualis Eram Bonae Sub Regno Cynarae.*

6

One Smart Young Fellow

By the end of 1937, Selznick-International had released six movies. Five made modest gains at the box office (*Prisoner of Zenda, Little Lord Fauntleroy, Tom Sawyer, A Star is Born, Nothing Sacred*); the sixth—*Garden of Allah*—had barely broken even. Selznick's grand design of producing only a small number of high-quality pictures was costly at the best of times, requiring lengthy periods of preparation and filming as well as high salaries for top talent, but in his own dilatory hands it was even worse. His lack of discipline and his inability to stay out of anything— the costumes, the music, the set design, the hairdressing, the publicity—resulted in inevitable delays, and the soaring overheads wiped out the profits from his previous pictures.

The studio books told their own story: fresh transfusions of capital were needed before *Gone With the Wind* could be made. So just when his backers could reasonably have expected to begin seeing a return on their investment, David Selznick was back asking for more money. The Whitneys can hardly be said to have eagerly embraced his request. One evening, Joan Payson was at a Hollywood dinner party where Selznick's praises were being sung. "Everyone assures me that Mr. Selznick's pictures are the best and that they make money," she commented dryly. "But I've never received a dollar of return."

Fully aware of his son-in-law's predicament, L. B. Mayer telephoned him and made an offer which Selznick immediately transmitted to Jock Whitney in these terms: "They would be interested in buying *Gone With the Wind* together with my services as producer on an outright purchase, including, of course, repayment of our complete investment plus a substantial profit." Selznick sounded very tempted by the offer, glossing over the obvious loss of prestige to his own studio, and stressing the advantages—no financial problems, use of Metro's facilities, and the assurance of getting Clark Gable as Rhett Butler. If his enthusiasm was a deliberate ploy to loosen the Whitney purse strings by playing on Jock's pride, it worked. Whitney told Selznick that another $1,250,000—half the estimated cost of the production at the time—would be made available to him, but he would have to find the other half himself.

The obvious place to look for it seemed to be Metro; talks with Sam Goldwyn for Gary Cooper to play Rhett never really got off the ground, partly because Selznick was never fully convinced that anyone but Gable could fill the part, so some form of negotiations with Mayer were now inevitable. Neither Selznick nor Mayer took part in the lengthy loan-out negotiations that began between their two studios shortly after that, for both were anxious to avoid giving any hint of nepotism to their respective superiors in New York (Mayer was not actually a corporate officer of M-G-M, but an executive whose salary and bonuses of $1,296,503 in 1937 made him the highest-paid employee in the country). Mayer now actually took credit for the marriage he had so vehemently opposed. "Irene thought she'd like to marry a poet or a painter but I held on until I landed Selznick," he boasted. " 'No, Irene,' I would say, 'I'm watching and waiting.' So David Selznick, he's performing independent now."

The Metro side consisted of E. J. (Eddie) Mannix, Mayer's burly right-hand man, a former fairground barker who brought a strong touch of Irish bluster to the negotiations; Bennie Thau, the diminutive executive in charge of "talent" who was so soft-spoken you had to lean forward to hear what he was saying; and Metro's head of distribution, Al Lichtman, a tough, wily bargainer who had once worked for Selznick's father. Selznick sent Henry Ginsberg and occasionally Daniel O'Shea, a dewlapped Boston-born lawyer who had drifted into the arcane field of show business law straight from Harvard because other legal jobs were scarce, and had remained to temper Selznick's wilder flights of fancy first as general counsel at R.K.O., and then as Secretary of Selznick-International. After every meeting, Ginsberg would give Selznick a full report and receive fresh instructions for the next one. But the instructions were usually followed by a bewildering barrage of often contradictory memos.

The memo was Selznick's chief method of communication. Thousands of words issued forth from his office every day. Lunging back and forth across the room, sometimes shoeless, sometimes

As Sherman nears Atlanta, panic and disorder sweep through the streets; Rhett rescues Scarlett as she seems about to be run over by the fleeing crowds. (PRATT)

munching his sugar cookies, he kept three secretaries busy with his dictation: an often unintelligible *obbligato* of exhortations, protests, reprimands, flat lies, open insults, blandishments, and grunts of approval to his employees and stars. At the top of each yellow memo page was printed, "Dictated but not read by DOS," as if Selznick never felt he needed to revise a line that he had written, and the tone was one of ringing self-assurance.

This wasteland of repetitions, divagations, and tergiversations ranged in length from one line to dozens of pages, and in scope from a minor filming detail to everything Selznick knew about movies—which in his case were synonymous with life. During the negotiations for Clark Gable there was an epidemic of "the runs" in Hollywood; Selznick circulated a memo to his staff advising them that a few drops of vinegar in the water when washing vegetables acted as a disinfectant to kill germs. Every evening in the bars around the studio, Selznick's staff would compare the memos they had received that day like football players comparing scars after a game. To Susan Myrick, who with dialogue director Will Price was teaching the cast Southern speech: "It is probably superfluous for me to remind you that the Yankee officer in the jail scene [with Clark Gable] is not to be coached in the Southern accent." To Percy Westmore, the irreverent, gossipy make-up man on *Gone With the Wind,* pointing out that Melanie's child is one year old in one scene and two years old when he next appears, "kindly see that the child is properly aged."

The memos were partly a pretentious display of literacy—a child performing cartwheels in front of another who doesn't know how—and partly a way of getting the last word in an argument, since it is impossible to talk back to a piece of yellow paper. But they were also the result of his obsessive sense of history, the same obsession that caused Richard Nixon to bug his own office in the White House. Selznick was writing for posterity. The recipients of his memos sometimes received only a copy, while the original remained in his files.

By June, the historic loan-out deal had been worked out. M-G-M agreed to lend Gable to Selznick for the role of Rhett Butler, and contributed $1,250,000 toward the production costs, in exchange for the distribution rights of *Gone With the Wind* and a sliding-scale percentage of the gross profits starting at fifty percent and going down to twenty-five percent over a number of years, so that Selznick-International would eventually receive seventy-five percent of the profits from the picture. A distribution fee was also added to Metro's income from the picture. A couple of days later, on June 23, Louella Parsons reported that Gable had at long last been signed to play Rhett Butler, having been tipped off by the Metro publicity department; but the official announcement was delayed for two months, because Selznick's distribution agreement with United Artists did not run out until the end of the year and he didn't want to give the impression that he was ready to start production. Both Mayer and Selznick were on hand for the ceremonial signing of the contracts. "My son-in-law is one smart young fellow," chirped Mayer. "He'll go far in this business now that we're uniting our interests and will work hands in glove together. We have just finished a very pleasant visit. We agreed that the past is past and next year is another year." Selznick smiled wanly, for once at a loss for words. And no wonder; he had been forced to give away half his picture to get the star he felt was indispensable for its success. The object of the negotiations was never consulted, nor would he share in the gleeful distribution of the spoils. M-G-M was well aware that Clark Gable didn't want to play Rhett Butler. He felt the part was beyond the range of his essential screen personality, and he was scared of it. "Too big an order," he told Selznick. "I don't want any part of him." But the system was not one that consulted the players, and his $7,000-a-week star's contract did not include the right to turn down parts. To have done so could have led to suspension, which he could ill afford because of his financial obligations to his estranged wife, Ria Langham. Mayer knew this; he was a close friend of Ria's lawyer and was urging him to keep up the pressure on Gable. So Gable was forced to agree, amid assurances of paternal concern from Mayer. The studio that had dubbed him "The King" also demanded total obedience; no wonder that stardom had done nothing to calm his naturally suspicious nature.

As a consolation prize, Mayer undertook to pay a $400,000

Overleaf Scarlett searches the railroad yard strewn with wounded and dying Confederate soldiers for Dr. Meade, to ask him to come deliver Melanie's baby. (PRATT)

divorce settlement to Ria Langham so that Gable and Carole Lombard could get married. Since the *Photoplay* article, Mayer had become increasingly concerned over the publicity surrounding their romance. On the screen, Gable's image was one of aggressive sexuality—a man for the stormy season of the post-Depression, who coped with women and adversity with the same confident, cocky assurance of knowing what he is and where he is bound for; his furrowed forehead, challenging tilt of the eyebrows, half-closed eyes, and sardonic, arrogant grin were all visible proof that he had seen life. As the ever-graphic Sam Goldwyn once told Hedda Hopper: "When a person like Robert Montgomery comes on the screen you know he's got balls. When Clark Gable comes on you can hear them clacking together. That's the difference." But in his off-screen relations with women Gable seemed to have been more often dominated than dominant.

An orphan shortly after his birth—in Cadiz, Ohio—he was brought up by a doting stepmother. As a raw, stage-struck young farm boy with protruding ears and bad teeth, his acting career progressed by amorous stages from one aging theater star to another, including Alice Brady, Jane Cowl, and Pauline Frederick, who gave him parts in their plays and sometimes paid his dentist's bills. But all the time he was married to drama coach Josephine Dillon, who was fourteen years his senior, and somewhere in that relationship the essential Clark Gable emerged. At twenty-six, he was taken up by, and eventually married Maria (Ria) Langham, who was forty-three, the widow of a wealthy Texas oil man and backer of a Houston stock company. She first took him to New York to help him get established on the Broadway stage, and then backed the Los Angeles production of the Broadway stage hit *The Last Mile* on condition that Gable play the lead—Killer Mears, the condemned man who leads a prison break—hoping that it would lead to a studio contract, which it ultimately did.

As an obscure contract player at M-G-M he embarked on an affair with Joan Crawford, who insisted on having him as her leading man in one of her pictures. Mayer put a stop to the affair because he felt that the gossip might damage the career of one of his top female stars. But as his fame grew, Gable took to philandering in a big way, as if to prove that the screen lover had his equally successful counterpart in real life. The gossip magazines would hint at his escapades with starlets, Broadway showgirls, and debutantes; but his friends knew he was most comfortable with the fifty-dollar girls from the house of Lee Francis because "I don't have to pretend that I'm Clark Gable."

By 1938, his affair with Carole Lombard had been going on for two idyllic years. Her zany humor complimented his gloomy nature, and moreover, she didn't mind his false teeth. Metro had tried to keep the unromantic truth about Gable's teeth a secret for years. To Gable himself, they had evidently come to represent the restrictions of studio life, for he once told Andy Devine that he would consider that he had reached the pinnacle of his career "When I walk down Washington Boulevard, take out my upper rack and throw it through L. B. Mayer's window."

Off the screen, Howard Strickling (who took a personal interest in Gable's publicity) depicted him as a rugged, sporting lover of the outdoors. The studio publicity talked about his guns, horses, and sports cars; stories were released about him going on long hunting and fishing trips, camping around the Kaibab Plateau on the northern rim of the Grand Canyon; he was photographed on horseback or astride a Harley-Davidson motorbike with his cronies Victor Fleming, the director, and actor Ward Bond. Yet when he got his first film role—in a William Boyd western, *The Painted Desert*—he had had to lie about being able to ride a horse; then his agent, Minna Wallis, rushed him off to Will Rogers Park for a crash course in horseback riding. As for hunting, he hadn't known the difference between a Purdy and a pea shooter. But he came to like the outdoors; he learned to fish well and was a good shot. People assumed he had been at it all his life. Sometimes, it seemed, so did he.

Now that the problem of Rhett Butler had been settled, and a deadline of February 1939 had been established by M-G-M for Gable to start work on the picture, the matter of finding a Scarlett became more acute. Governor Bibb Graves of Alabama cabled Selznick: WHY DON'T YOU GIVE TALLULAH BANKHEAD THE PART AND BE DONE WITH IT? But Selznick still clung to the hope of finding an unknown girl. He consulted his brother, Myron, with

Overleaf Inside the makeshift hospital; Dr. Meade refuses to abandon the wounded. (CP)

whom he had a very close relationship. Myron advised him to find someone as soon as possible. Ten years earlier Myron had hit upon the idea of representing actors and directors in contract negotiations with their studios and securing high salaries for them as a means of revenging the wrongs done to his father. Mayer and Zukor—Lewis J.'s archenemy—were his most hated targets, but his avowed purpose was to bring all the studios to their knees by transferring the money and power to the stars and filmmakers. In a short space of time, he succeeded in raising the earning power of the stars to astronomical levels and, almost incidentally, started the modern talent agency business. Both developments were to have far-reaching consequences for the studio system. His clients included Carole Lombard, Merle Oberon, Fredric March, and Fred Astaire and Ginger Rogers; the search for Scarlett had been profitable for him, since his brother would send promising unknown actresses to be represented by his agency. In due course, Myron would reciprocate by producing an actress to play Scarlett.

7

A Very Important
Gentleman from
Hollywood

A mutual dislike characterized Myron Selznick's relations with most of the movie-star clients who were making him rich. He resented their strutting pretentiousness and, above all, their endless demands for attention; they complained that he was contemptuous, brusque, and unconcerned about their careers except as a means of gaining his own objectives. But the stars were Selznick's most powerful weapon in his fight against the studios (otherwise, he would happily have limited his clients to directors and writers); Selznick was their best guarantee of ever higher salaries and it was thus worth putting up with his ill-concealed animosity.

To keep friction down to a minimum the stars were handled by other agents in Myron's employ. For many years they were the responsibility of Frank Joyce, Myron's affable partner; but since Joyce's death in 1936, Leland Hayward had inherited the task. However, Myron continued to be personally responsible for a number of favored clients, including William Powell, Fredric March, and Paulette Goddard. Powell and March were old friends, and Paulette Goddard was—well, Paulette Goddard.

She would perch on the edge of his desk, cross her legs, and ask: "What have you got for me today?" What was it she wanted? Myron would reply. The banter would frequently end with an expedition to the stores on Wilshire Boulevard where Paulette Goddard would pick out an expensive trinket, and Myron would pay for it. One day, she asked for the role of Scarlett O'hara. It wasn't for sale on Wilshire Boulevard but she had come to the right man, for, on his brother's recommendation, David Selznick willingly agreed to test her. The result proved to be one of the high points in the quest for Scarlett. In appearance, Paulette Goddard came closer to Selznick's conception of the character than anyone had before. She was more classically beautiful than Scarlett's description, but her bold, dark looks and spirited personality held the promise of a fiery performance. Though she looked right, she obviously lacked acting experience, so Selznick put her under contract and engaged English stage actress Constance Collier as her coach, determined to see her fulfill that promise.

Paulette Goddard wasn't yet a movie star, but because of the publicity surrounding her association with Charles Chaplin both on and off the screen, she was already a celebrity. Chaplin had plucked her out of the chorus line (*The Kid from Spain*) and launched her in movies as his co-star in *Modern Times,* and in the top echelons of Hollywood society as his wife. However, their affirmations of marriage were widely disbelieved; as the famous *Photoplay* article put it: "No one has ever been able to say definitely whether the gray-haired Charlie and his young, vivacious Paulette were ever married." Whatever the exact nature of their relationship, it had evidently seen better days. She still presided over Chaplin's rare, lavish dinner parties, fascinating George Bernard Shaw with her combination of physical beauty and hard-nosed business talk at one, and causing John Steinbeck to become openly infatuated with her at another; but otherwise they went their separate ways.

While "the gray-haired Charlie," who was fifty, brooded at home over the embers of his colorful past, his twenty-four-year-old Paulette was cutting a notorious swathe through the present as a glamorous girl-about-town, with vigilant gossip columnists keeping track of her progress like scientists following the course of a space ship. One night she was sighted at the Mocambo, another night it was the Troc, and the next the Victor Hugo; and each time with a different escort, for her taste in men was eclectic enough to include Jock Whitney's aristocratic English cousin Lord Wakefield, who was trying to get into pictures, and a *jai alai* player encountered in Tijuana, the squalid Mexican frontier town where the newly respectable Hollywood of 1938 went to indulge its old penchant for high jinks.

Chaplin learned that Paulette Goddard had signed a five-year contract with David Selznick from Louella Parsons' column, hardly the most intimate channel of communication between a husband and wife; this meant, Louella Parsons added, that Paulette was now virtually certain to play Scarlett O'Hara in *Gone With the Wind.* Star and producer soon felt the hot blast of Chap-

Overleaf Prissy (Butterfly McQueen) prepares hot towels, and Scarlett offers moral support. The scene was reshot in silhouette, and the silhouette version is used in the picture. (FLAMINI)

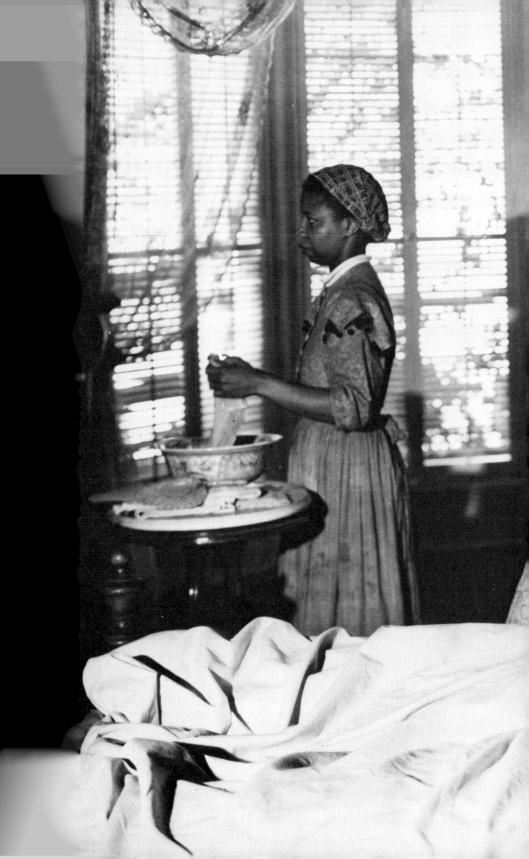

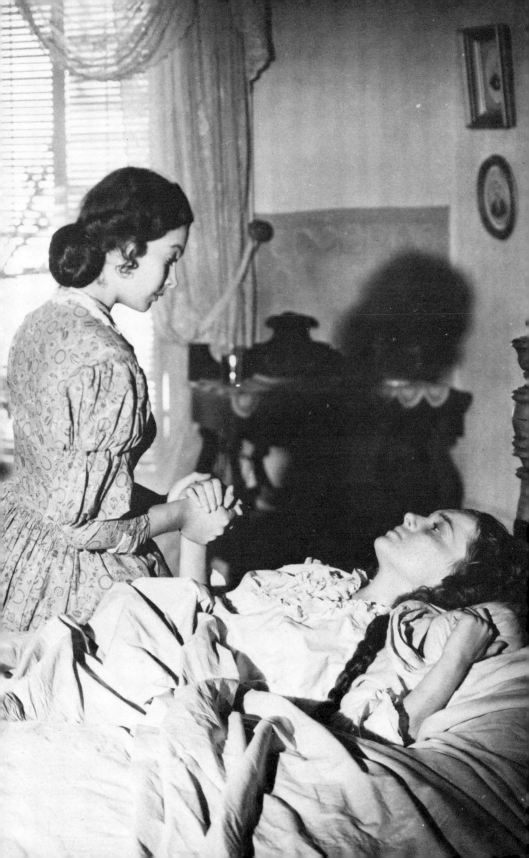

lin's anger. In a prepared statement he said Paulette Goddard
was his star, and he had not given his consent to a contract with
Selznick, or anybody else. Moreover, he had no intention of per-
mitting her to appear in any picture but his own. Paulette's rejoinder was that she was a free agent, since no contract existed
between them. "He said my first talking picture had to be with
him as co-star, in a story he was writing for us both," she explained to friends, "but I have no faith that the story will ever
be completed. He's told me dozens of times that he had a story
ready—only later he tears it up and says it wasn't right. He gets
so enthusiastic over an idea and then, before it's completed, he
starts another entirely different."

In fact, no contract did exist but the couple had evidently
reached an understanding that Paulette's next appearance on the
screen would be in Chaplin's long-awaited first talking picture,
and Chaplin was trying to hold her to it. Paulette Goddard preferred to play Scarlett O'Hara and was prepared to go to considerable lengths to get the role—as indeed what Hollywood
actress was not?—but if possible not to the extreme of sacrificing
her relationship with Chaplin, toward whom she felt a great loyalty, in her own fashion. So she persuaded Selznick to seek his post-
dated approval of her contract. (It has to be said that Paulette
Goddard was no golddigging starlet; she had a tidy income from
a number of rented houses in Los Angeles, which she and her
mother had bought for a song during the real estate slump of
the Depression.)

Obtaining Chaplin's approval was a tricky undertaking, for
besides his possessiveness toward Paulette Goddard there was the
additional obstacle of his dislike for David Selznick, whose entry
into United Artists as a partner he still regarded as a personal
intrusion. When Daniel O'Shea approached him, he at first played
hard to get. But at last, O'Shea succeeded in reaching him by
telephone and Chaplin began to equivocate. He questioned
Selznick's motives in putting Paulette under contract. O'Shea
protested that Selznick's motives were perfectly genuine. Then
he switched tactics, saying he felt a long-term studio contract was
not in her best interests.

Suddenly, his manner changed: "It's all right, Miss Goddard

After the birth of Melanie's baby, Scarlett comes downstairs to find
Rhett Butler in the doorway; he chides her for never at any important
time in her life having a handkerchief, and offers her his. (PRATT)

Clark Gable

Clark Gable with his Irish setter Queen on the set of *Red Dust,* in which he costarred with Jean Harlow under Victor Fleming's direction. (BA)

Clark Gable about to kiss Carole Lombard but thinking of a "big, tender, rare steak" in a scene from *No Man of Her Own*. (BA)

Clark Gable, Ward Bond, and Victor Fleming astride their *macho* machines.

Poised in a sulky, ready to take the trotter for a turn around the track at his valley ranch . . . or so said a press release issued during the filming of *Gone With the Wind*. (BA)

has left now, and I'm alone," he said, immediately becoming more businesslike, and O'Shea was able to establish his conditions for endorsing the contract, namely the insertion of a "Chaplin clause" which gave him a claim to Paulette Goddard's services for the occasional movie. Next, O'Shea received a call from Paulette herself, who seemed to know exactly what had transpired. Had Chaplin briefed her, asked O'Shea? "No, I was hiding in a closet and heard it all," Paulette answered.

In quick succession, she was given a small role in the Selznick-International picture *The Young in Heart,* shipped to New Orleans to work on her Southern accent, and tested a second time. A rising Warner Brothers newcomer, Jeffrey Lynn, played Ashley in the test. He was younger and more robust than Leslie Howard, but cast in the same sensitive mold, and he had come to Los Angeles in the road company of the Broadway play *Brother Rat.* As far north as Seattle, he had begun to prepare for his arrival in Hollywood. If it seemed more like preparation for a physical fitness test than for a screen test—early nights, running on the beach, swimming, a rigid diet—it was because, like every young actor of his day, he knew the premium that the studios placed on a well-toned muscle. All that strenuous effort paid off, for he was the only member of the play's cast to be tested and put under studio contract. He made an impact in his first movie, *Four Daughters,* and a local leather goods manufacturer named a three-quarter-length coat after him. Now, less than six months after his arrival in both senses of the term, he was trying out for a leading role in the most talked-about picture in Hollywood, opposite one of the town's most talked-about women.

For three weeks Paulette Goddard and Jeffrey Lynn were trained in the accent by Will Price. "Try to bring an English-Southern tone to this, not a Southern drawl," he instructed them. "In the nineteenth century, Southern speech was closer to English." The test itself took all day, with a full camera crew under George Cukor's direction, and consisted of two scenes; one in which Scarlett first declares her love to Ashley in the library at Twelve Oaks, the other with Ashley in the woodshed at Tara after the war, when Scarlett makes another, more passionate declaration of love. (Accustomed to the less lavish conditions at Warners, Lynn mused, if this is a test, what must the real thing be like?) Outwardly as cool as always, Paulette Goddard felt stiffly tense in his arms, but she gave a forceful performance, and her kisses were full of unforgettable abandon. She's a real gypsy, Lynn thought, she's going to get the part, and after viewing the test several times Selznick began to feel the same way.

Nothing came of Lynn's brief flirtation with the coveted role. He was too raw to bring any depth to the character and Selznick told his associates he was "completely unimpressed" with him. Lynn went back to a short-lived career at Warners which would fail to revive after a long war absence, so that he would find himself relegated to "B" movies, and eventually to selling insurance in Los Angeles, which he still does.

Just when it seemed that nothing could stand between Paulette Goddard and the role of Scarlett—Louella Parsons had taken to calling her Scarlett O'Goddard—the uncertainty about her marriage to Chaplin came home to roost. Letters began pouring into Selznick's studio from women's clubs all over the country protesting against the role being given to an actress suspected of being the mistress of a leading Hollywood star; the protest was picked up by the press, and the threat of a large-scale boycott of the picture hung in the air. The target was as much Chaplin as it was Paulette Goddard herself; his movie *Modern Times* had come under criticism for its left-wing views. At first, Paulette flashed defiance. When Russell Birdwell, instructed by a nervous Selznick to obtain proof—a marriage license, witnesses, anything—told her: "If you're announced in the part and there's a press conference they will certainly ask you when and where you were married," she snapped back: "It's none of their goddam business."

Selznick was genuinely alarmed, however, and made it clear that bravado just wouldn't wash. What he wanted was ammunition with which to silence his critics. Already, at the company's annual general meeting, he had been harangued by women's club lobbyists and had been unable to defend himself. Paulette Goddard's explanation, when it came, was anything but iron-clad: she and Chaplin were married on a yacht anchored off Singapore; later, the vessel had come under guerrilla attack, and its records were destroyed. In 1940, Paulette Goddard would go to Mexico

Overleaf Atlanta in flames. Rhett's buckboard dashes through the burning railroad yard with Scarlett beside him and Melanie, her new baby, and Prissy hidden in the back. Doubles were used in this sequence, which was the first one to be filmed. (PRATT)

and obtain a divorce from Chaplin, but the question of whether they were ever married, and more significantly when, would never be satisfactorily cleared up. In his autobiography, published thirty-four years after this episode, Chaplin dismisses the subject in one line ("During this trip," he writes, referring to the Orient cruise, "Paulette and I were married."). But the prevalent belief at the time of their divorce was that, having finally decided to go their separate ways, they had in fact married only a few months earlier in order to be able to carry their fiction to its logical conclusion.

With no marriage license forthcoming, Selznick next considered having Paulette Goddard take a public oath that she was married, but further reflection brought home the possible hazards of such a course. Discouraged, and uncertain what to do next, he adopted the most effective way he knew of marking time: he resurrected the search for Scarlett.

In these sexually permissive times, when no press interview with a movie actress is considered complete unless she has named who she is living with and enumerated the offspring born out of wedlock, it may be difficult to appreciate why David Selznick felt so imperiled. The simple answer is that, considering the size of his investment, he was not prepared to risk reaping the whirlwind of adverse public opinion by making *Gone With the Wind* with an unpopular girl. But there was a more fundamental reason: Selznick shared in the general devotion to the box office and, in consequence, was conditioned to avoid giving offense at all costs. Like every other major Hollywood producer, he accepted as one of the guiding precepts of the industry the total avoidance of the problems and complications of contemporary life. (The fact that *Gone With the Wind* owes some of its success to the tensions of the times, being released at the start of World War II, is no credit to Selznick, who embarked on the project in 1936, when the threat of a major war did not yet exist.)

Under this precept, the public was indulged as a capricious and unreasoning infant. At the first whimper of protest, however hesitant, productions came crashing to the ground like houses of cards, regardless of the investment or the worthiness of the project; a completed picture was sent back for further editorial surgery

to eliminate the offending section, often with little consideration
for its coherence in the expurgated form. Obviously, this timidity
only encouraged further pressure: the American Newspaper Guild
campaigning for a better screen image, the Billiard Association
threatening to boycott all movies that depicted pool halls as dis-
reputable places, the glass bottle industry complaining that the
movies were furthering the interests of the canning industry, and
the canning industry accusing Hollywood of showing favoritism
toward glass bottles, all produced spasms of anxiety, as did coal
industry requests to Warner Brothers to soften the story of *Black
Fury,* with which the studio complied, and Standard Oil Company pressures on the same studio to tone down the tragedy of
the hero's death in *Oil for the Lamps of China*—another victory
for the lobbyists.

As a result, if the whole span of movies made in 1938 (Selznick's included) survived as the sole record of the year's events,
who would guess that it had been an era of confrontation between
democracy and dictatorship, of civil war and international conflict, of hunger, unemployment and industrial unrest, of social
changes and upheaval? Since forty percent of Hollywood's
revenue came from foreign markets, the studios were as sensitive
to foreign pressures as they were to domestic ones. With Poland
overrun, L. B. Mayer still refused to produce movies that might
give offense to Germany for fear of jeopardizing the market in
central Europe, which was rapidly coming under German control. Metro stars were discouraged from making anti-Nazi statements. Melvyn Douglas, whose political activism was a constant
source of friction with Mayer, was once instructed to retract a de-
nunciation of Nazi Jewish persecution delivered before the Anti-
Nazi League, which he had helped to found, because the Berlin
government was threatening to retaliate by holding up distribution of two Metro productions.

But Germany wasn't Hollywood's only foreign bogy. As a result of Italian government protests, the script of *A Farewell to
Arms* was altered to avoid showing the Italian army in retreat;
France compelled Columbia to change the villain in *Beau Geste*
from a Frenchman to a Russian; Paramount films were banned
in Spain because *The Devil Is a Woman* showed the Civil Guard

drinking and taking bribes. And in *Blockade,* Walter Wanger managed the extraordinary feat of producing a picture with a Spanish Civil War theme without ever establishing whether Henry Fonda, the hero, was a loyalist or a fascist.

Meanwhile, the Californian summer dissolved into fall which, if anything, was even more scorching than the previous months had been, and still there was no sign of Scarlett. As usual, there was no shortage of aspirants, among them some old faces, and some new ones. In October, Mrs. Ogden Reid, vice-president of the *Herald Tribune,* introduced guest speaker Katharine Hepburn at the Eighth Annual Women's Forum on Current Problems at the Waldorf-Astoria as "my candidate for Scarlett O'Hara in *Gone With the Wind."* When she went on to announce that Katharine Hepburn had Margaret Mitchell's endorsement as well, the 3000 women present gave her a standing ovation. From Atlanta the next morning, Margaret Mitchell sharply squelched Mrs. Reid's sensational revelation; what she had told Mrs. Reid, she explained, was that she had seen *Little Women* and thought Miss Hepburn looked very good in hooped skirts. "I don't know anyone in the movies who looks like Scarlett," she insisted once again. "I have never expressed a preference, and I never will."

Even so, Hepburn's cause had more influential backing than that of Mrs. Reid. George Cukor had just completed *Holiday,* in which she starred, and had come to Selznick full of enthusiasm for her ability. It was a tempting way out of the impasse. She was a mature and stylish actress, as Selznick knew better than anyone; yet he was bothered by her lack of obvious sexuality. Would Rhett Butler's years of pursuit be believable with her as the object? He wanted her to demonstrate—as he told Cukor in the inevitable memo—"that she possesses the sex qualities which are probably the most important of all the many requisites of Scarlett." But Katharine Hepburn stubbornly held out against a screen test, arguing that Selznick—of all people—ought by now to know her professional worth. Besides, Selznick was also concerned about her continuing unpopularity. She was still formally labeled "Box Office Poison" by distributors and one recent fan magazine popularity poll had ranked her fifty-eighth.

Even someone as totally professional and outwardly self-possessed as Katharine Hepburn herself could betray an occasional longing for Hollywood glamor. Once at a studio screening of one of her M-G-M movies, she overheard the producer complain that in one scene her neckline was too revealing. As soon as the movie was over, she sped to the costume department. Flushed and out of breath, she said excitedly, "You darlings, I love you all. You've given me cleavage! *Me,* with cleavage!" By contrast, cleavage was the principal asset of Lana Turner, the new Metro sex symbol, who tested for Scarlett under her real name, Jean Turner. Her low-cut green dress showed off her physical endowments to good advantage; unfortunately for her chances, her lack of experience was also very evident. Margaret Tallichet, fresh from a successful season of summer stock, also went before George Cukor's cameras in the ritualistic test scenes. But she too failed to make the grade; shortly afterward William Wyler, the director, secured her freedom by buying the remainder of her contract from Selznick for $65,000 and married her.

From the start, the obvious choice for Ashley Wilkes was Leslie Howard, who had for years occupied a unique position as Hollywood's gentle, brooding hero (*Petrified Forest, Of Human Bondage,* etc.) . The problem with casting Howard as Ashley was that the choice lacked both originality and youth. Once again, Selznick yearned for a new face, alive with the energy of recent discovery, but he had left it too late to launch a search for Ashley. In a half-hearted attempt to find an alternative, he tested Melvyn Douglas with Lana Turner, but decided he looked "too beefy physically"; Irene reasserted herself briefly with the suggestion that Ray Milland be tested, but he never was.

When Selznick finally faced up to the inevitable and offered Howard the role, he was alarmed to discover that the British actor wasn't interested: he was forty-five and beginning to feel uncomfortable about his romantic screen image, and he shared Selznick's reservations about his age. The steady blue eyes were too often glazed and tired; the high, arched forehead was lined, and the neat brown hair was thin and graying. Three years earlier he had tried unsuccessfully to avoid playing Romeo to Norma Shear-

Overleaf "Take a good look, my dear. You can tell your grandchildren how the South disappeared in one night." (PRATT)

er's Juliet because he thought he was too old, and he now felt the same reluctance toward the idealistic young Southerner Ashley.

But Selznick knew of Howard's hopes of escaping behind the camera as a producer, and possibly even as a director. He had already formed his own production company and bought a few properties, including *They Shoot Horses, Don't They?*, which for over thirty years was to be considered unfilmable because of censorship problems. So Selznick offered him a tempting package: *Gone With the Wind* first, with a job as associate producer of *Intermezzo* to follow. For in the midst of his other activities, Selznick had signed a young actress from Sweden, Ingrid Bergman, and was planning to star her in his re-make of the Swedish production in which he had discovered her. Howard agreed in a spirit of complete indifference—"Money is the mission here, and who am I to refuse it?" he wrote to his daughter; and his attitude would not alter throughout the making of the picture.

Having Howard thrust upon him served to increase Selznick's resistance toward Katharine Hepburn, because, he complained, with a cast of Howards and Hepburns, "we can have a lovely picture for release eight years ago." So the search for a new Scarlett was resumed with renewed vigor, reinforced by the arrival of Maxwell Arnow, who had been a noted casting director at Warner Brothers until his contentious nature brought him into conflict once too often with Hal Wallis, the young head of production at the studio. Arnow was an ambitious, hard-working former law clerk from the Bronx with a flair for spotting potential screen talent; Errol Flynn was among the star finds of his Warner days, but he would later give starts to dozens of well-known actors and actresses, among them Jack Lemmon and Ernest Borgnine. Unfortunately Arnow himself possessed as much tact and finesse as a runaway bull. His final showdown with Wallis, who by temperament and position was his frequent adversary, centered around the casting of a small female role in *Angels With Dirty Faces:* Wallis wanted his current girl friend, Lola Lane, one of the four Lane sisters, while Arnow was anxious to try out a newcomer named Ann Sheridan. When they appealed to Jack Warner, Arnow won the battle—Ann Sheridan got the part and it began her career—but lost his job. Irritated by the internal squabbling, Warner replaced him with a less capable but more accommodating man whose main credential seemed to be that he was Warner's regular tennis partner.

David Selznick knew there were no openings for an unemployed studio casting executive at the time, and he stepped in with an offer for Arnow to take over the search for Scarlett—at half his former salary, plus a bonus of $10,000 if he were successful. Arnow had no choice but to accept, but with characteristic brashness he was convinced that he would win the bonus. By coincidence, his last undertaking at Warners had been to catch a rejected Scarlett on the rebound; Edythe Marrener, the stunning redheaded New York hat model discovered by Irene Selznick, but dropped at the end of her six-month contract. Arnow had hired her, changing her name to Susan Hayward—a tribute to two men he admired, agent Leland and actor Louis Hayward. Now he was to be at the hub of a new, and as it turned out final, surge of Scarlett activity. He was sent south for a more systematic search of the ground covered a year earlier by George Cukor. He was to visit colleges and little theater groups, and also interview the best prospects from among the hundreds of applicants who continued to write to Selznick every week.

In the studio system, casting directors had an important selective function: they were the coarse-grain sieve through which hundreds of hopeful men and women who annually besieged the studios were sifted; only those who got through were given screen tests. There were, of course, other roads to stardom besides through the casting office, but the overall influence of the half-dozen top casting directors on the physical appearance of not only the stars, but every level of screen characterization, was pervasive. Collectively, their taste tended to be conventional and safe; in 1937, for example, thirty-five girls and seventeen men were put under contract by the seven major studios. They included Betty Jane Schultz, whose name was changed to Betty Jaynes; Rebecca Wassem, who became Sheila Davey; Harry Ueberroth, who became Alan Curtis; Bud Flanagan, whose name was changed to Dennis O'Keefe; and Jean (later Lana) Turner. All had regular features. Twenty-six of the girls were blondes; the tallest was five feet eight, the average was five feet six, and the heaviest weighed 124 pounds. Typically, Arnow's preferences ran to tasteful sexiness: good features, attractive eyes, a full rounded figure (but nothing exaggerated), plus an ability to wear clothes. He attached little importance to brains or intelligence, but a great deal to sexual impact. Arnow set out from Hollywood in the late fall of 1938.

In New York, his first stop, he got off to a promising start by finding, through a Manhattan agency, a striking, well-built blond model named Doris Jordan who seemed a strongly possible candidate. At first, Selznick shared Arnow's enthusiasm for her; renamed Doris Davenport, she was signed to a six-month contract, and brought to Hollywood for training and a screen test. But he rapidly lost interest and—as with Edythe Marrener—her option was not picked up. She would, however, remain in Hollywood and have a brief screen career, the high point of which was playing opposite Gary Cooper in *The Westerner*.

In October, Selznick left by train for New York, en route to Bermuda, and Henry Ginsberg made another attempt to scuttle *Gone With the Wind,* in the higher interests of saving the company from financial ruin. One of the executives he tried to recruit for his palace revolution was Maxwell Arnow. In a secret telephone call, Ginsberg told him that *his* cost projections were far in excess of the $2.5 million budgeted for the picture by Selznick and a profit was virtually out of the question. "Max, we are going to lose a fortune on this picture, and when you talk to David I want you to tell him so. See if you can't convince him to take his first loss" (that is, stop production and write off his losses to date). But Arnow was the wrong man to approach. He was convinced that the $10,000 bonus was as good as in his pocket; secondly, like many people working on *Gone With the Wind,* he had come under the spell of the project; thirdly, he didn't care much for Henry Ginsberg. Far from being a losing picture, *Gone With the Wind* was going to be a blockbuster, was his rejoinder. "Max, it's going to cost so much money we'll lose our shirts on this thing," Ginsberg wailed. But Arnow wouldn't be swayed, and Ginsberg's plot fizzled out soon afterward for lack of support. The production continued to gather momentum, as did David

Selznick. Before sailing for Bermuda he cast Milton Vaughn, elevator boy at the Savoy Plaza, as one of the Tarleton twins, and packed him off to Hollywood.

For six weeks, Maxwell Arnow zig-zagged across the Southern winter by train, taxicab, and—on the rare occasions when there was one—commercial aircraft, holding auditions for college drama students in the daytime, and attending local theater performances in the evening. From St. Petersberg, Florida, to Birmingham, Alabama, daughters of Dixie who saw themselves as the incarnation of Margaret Mitchell's heroine paraded before him like racehorses in the auctioner's ring, and at night serenaded him by telephone calls, offering intimate forms of Southern hospitality in return for the coveted prize.

As the emissary of a Hollywood prince, he enjoyed special privileges. One morning, he was making a dash across New Orleans in a taxi to catch the Texas & Pacific noon express to Shreveport. With three minutes to go before the train's departure, and several miles of city traffic to cross, the situation seemed hopeless, but Arnow instructed the cab driver to stop at the first gas station; lowering the window, he threw the young pump attendant a half dollar and shouted, "Call the T & P railroad station and say there's a very important gentleman from Hollywood who has to make the noon train. He's on his way and will be a few minutes late." It was a full ten minutes before Arnow arrived at the station, to find the train waiting for him. He celebrated in the dining car by ordering a "shovel steak," so called because it was put on a shovel and cooked on the coals of the locomotive; it was the first charbroiled steak he had ever eaten.

Not everyone, admittedly, was imbued with the same sense of awe. At Agnes Scott College, Atlanta's noted institution for the daughters of old Southern families, he got a curt reception. As an elocution expert (she was one of the founders of the Georgia Speech Association), Frances K. Gooch, the head of the drama department, despised Hollywood; as a Southern snob, she despised it doubly. In her view, none of her girls were sufficiently advanced in speech technique to appear in a Hollywood picture, and they certainly weren't going to get any better once they got there. However, she reluctantly allowed them to audition, telling

Overleaf The last Confederate soldiers desert Atlanta, leaving it
to rioters and looters and Sherman's army. (PRATT)

them they were trying out for a part in *Gone With the Wind,* but omitting any mention of Scarlett O'Hara. Each girl was pushed into a room to give an unrehearsed one-minute reading, and pushed right out again.

It soon became apparent to Arnow that Frances K. Gooch attached more importance to who should play Rhett Butler than Scarlett O'Hara. "Is it true that Clark Gable is going to play Rhett?" she asked him suddenly, halfway through the parade of girls. Something in the way she said it told him that he was not talking to the guiding spirit behind the Gable for Rhett Butler movement, so he hedged: Gable had been mentioned as a strong possibility, yes. "Well, he's all wrong," she snapped. "There's only one actor in Hollywood that can play it and that's Basil Rathbone." Then she embarked on a lengthy explanation to support her choice. Anyone with any knowledge of the history of the South (which in her mind clearly did not include anyone in Hollywood) knew that the Charleston area where Rhett Butler came from had been settled by the English only a couple of generations earlier, and Rhett Butler ought therefore to have a marked English accent. Moreover, apart from linguistic considerations, she implied strongly that Gable was incapable of bringing to the character the qualities of a Southern gentleman.

Arnow promised to pass on this valuable information to David Selznick and, as soon as he was able, beat a hasty retreat, at the back of his mind thinking inconsequentially how much she reminded him of Beulah Bondi. Shortly afterward, Frances Gooch learned that Clark Gable was to play Rhett Butler and for a year proceeded to make her students' life miserable with her daily lectures on Hollywood's perfidy generally, and that of David Selznick in particular.

Despite endless auditions (one girl drove 750 miles with a week-old baby to try for the part), and hours of often indigestible local theater productions, Arnow's expedition was a failure. On a couple of occasions he felt close to the moment of discovery, only to sense it fading away upon closer scrutiny. At the Shreveport, Lousiana, Little Theater he spotted a lively looking brunette in the audience who seemed just right; she turned out to be a new member of the theater, Marcella Martin. When she read the inevitable test scenes, with Arnow feeding Ashley and Mammy lines, as he did several times a day throughout the trip, he knew that she was both too young and too sweet for Scarlett, but she was packed off to Selznick studios to fill one of the minor roles.

His hopes of earning the $10,000 rapidly fading, Arnow returned to Hollywood expecting to confront a disappointed Selznick. Instead, he found that the burning of Atlanta had been filmed, and a new name was bringing excitement and anticipation to Selznick-International. It was Vivien Leigh.

8

Vivien Leigh:
The Fame-in-a-Night
Girl

Selznick-International's studio was a mile east of the mighty Metro on Washington Boulevard, but in appearance they were lightyears apart. M-G-M was a vast, impregnable fortress, surrounded by high, orange-colored walls; Selznick's fantasy factory was hidden from view behind the colonnaded elegance of a white antebellum-style mansion standing incongruously in a neighborhood of rundown bars and seedy apartment hotels, like a rose bush in the middle of the California desert. It had a sweep of red brick steps leading up to the front door from a semi-circular driveway with a wooden gate at each end, and a spacious lawn planted with a row of young oaks and edged with low oleander bushes. Selznick felt that it lent tone to his enterprise, and he used the facade as the screen trademark of his productions together with the slogan: IN THE TRADITION OF QUALITY.

His office was on the first floor with his executives scattered all over the building and in outlying bungalows; Ginsberg fretted and plotted in a room directly above him, with O'Shea poised watchfully next door; George Cukor confronted the endless procession of role-seeking talent in a small gatehouse beside one of the two wooden gates. In the rear of the house, hardly visible from the busy boulevard, were the eight sound stages; huge, windowless hangar-like buildings running north-south, with heavy sliding doors, the most massive—Stage Sixteen—bringing up the rear. A water tower on three long steel stilts loomed over it like a giant sentinel, painted silver with the words *Selznick-International* emblazoned in black script. And behind that was the back lot, a forty-acre spread of trees and vegetation sufficiently nondescript in botanical terms to be disguised as the African jungle, the English countryside, or the cotton plantations of the South. It was criss-crossed by dirt roads and culminated in a sizeable hill covered in thick, brown brush. The impression that Selznick's domain extended from Washington Boulevard all the way to the hill was, however, illusory. A road and several rows of small houses ran behind the studio, bisecting the area and isolating the back lot, which was reached from a separate entrance at the end of a cul-de-sac named Ince Boulevard running down one side of the studio.

Thomas Ince, the film pioneer, had been the original owner, followed by Sam Goldwyn and Pathé. Then the studio was the scene of Joseph Kennedy's fling at the movies to indulge Gloria Swanson (Russell Birdwell had installed himself in Gloria Swanson's old bungalow, and claimed to have found bullet holes in the wall and a primitive bugging device hidden in the ceiling of her dressing room). Eventually it passed into the hands of R.K.O., which began leasing space to Selznick when he formed his independent production company in 1935. R.K.O. would regain possession when Selznick-International was dissolved in 1940.

Selznick, of course, subscribed to the prevalent Hollywood belief that any setting could be reproduced better than the original at the studio; he never entertained any serious notion of shooting *Gone With the Wind* on location in the South. Instead, he gradually increased the area he leased from R.K.O. in order to film the picture in his studio, with a minimum amount of nearby location work. After all, if Catalina Island could pass muster as the South Seas in *Mutiny on the Bounty,* and the Arizona desert as the Sahara in *Garden of Allah,* the San Fernando Valley, its earth tinted the right shade of red, ought to do for Tara; by the time shooting was due to begin, he controlled all the studio's facilities.

By a combination of cajolery and Scottish canniness, Bill Menzies had succeeded in overcoming Selznick's tendency to procrastinate and had obtained his approval of designs for several key sets so that they could be constructed. Some had proved more difficult than others; the Art Department submitted numerous sketches of the exterior of Tara, but Selznick rejected them all. Trying to discover from Selznick what he wanted was often like having him pour water into your cupped hands: by the time you ran back to the office the water had trickled away and there was nothing there. Selznick knew he wasn't getting the vast, romantic evocation of Tara that he envisioned, but as usual, he was unable to communicate his vision to the staff. When Selznick threw out the twenty-fifth design, Menzies bided his time for a couple of days. Then he dug out the very first design he had submitted,

On the road to Tara, Rhett gives Scarlett his pistol, kisses her goodbye, and departs to join the routed Confederate army. (FLAMINI)

called it "Number 26," and took it to Selznick, saying, "David, I think I've got it." "That's it, Bill, you finally got it," Selznick exclaimed. "That's Tara."

But before it, and the other exteriors, could be put up (work on the principle *interiors*—Tara, Twelve Oaks, the Atlanta Bazaar —was already underway on Stage Sixteen), a space had to be cleared on the back lot, which was crammed with old sets, some of them dating back to the silent days. To dismantle them was going to prove costly and time-consuming. Then Menzies had a brainwave: put false fronts on the old sets and use them for the burning of Atlanta. That way the back lot would be cleared and Selznick would have some welcome footage in the can. Selznick had logically thought of Sherman's sacking of Atlanta as one of the closing sequences of the production, when the sets constructed for the picture could safely be burned down, but he was quick to see the value of starting the shooting literally in a blaze of publicity. The peeling remains of *The Last of the Mohicans, King Kong, Garden of Allah, Little Lord Fauntleroy,* and half a dozen productions of earlier vintage were hurriedly repaired and repainted. Because it was to be a night scene, and the detail would be obscured by the flames and smoke, a few false fronts, cupolas, signs and other embellishments were sufficient to convert the motley cluster of wooden structures into a convincing silhouette of pre-war Atlanta.

The idea was particularly appealing because, with *Made for Each Other* completed, Selznick-International had fulfilled its commitment to United Artists and David Selznick had lost his main delaying tactic. Pressure for an early starting date was intensifying from all sides. There was pressure from the Whitneys and the other financial backers anxious to see some return on their investment.

There was pressure from Metro; the redoubtable Mannix kept up a barrage of telephone calls pressing Selznick to make a start, reminding him that Clark Gable had to begin work by the second week in February, and there was no guarantee that he would be available for more than the specified twenty weeks. And there was indirect pressure from the industry, which looked upon the long-delayed production as a costly indulgence of an overweening conceit. Shop talk dominated Hollywood social life and David Selznick dominated the shop talk. When not predicting his imminent financial ruin, they were telling jokes about him; no one in the motion picture business missed the point when Cecil B. De Mille announced he was launching a nationwide search for a ferocious-looking cigar store Indian to use in a scene in *Union Pacific,* and then reported that having failed to find one that looked fierce enough he was going to have it made at the studio after all. And Sid Grauman, owner of the Chinese Movie Theater and a social figure in Hollywood, gave a large dinner party at which was exhibited a life-size wax statue of David Selznick as a very old man, leaning on a cane; at the foot of the statue was a placard reading: "Selznick after the final shot of *Gone With the Wind.*"

Finally, Whitney, who to preserve their relationship avoided personal confrontations with Selznick, sent an emissary with an ultimatum; shooting must begin no later than the middle of January. The emissary complained that with the increase in costly staff such as Menzies, Plunkett, and Platt engaged in pre-production work, higher leasing costs as a result of having taken over the entire studio, and the actual pre-production costs, overheads at Selznick-International had skyrocketed to an all-time high. Realizing that Whitney meant business, Selznick somewhat truculently agreed. "How much money are we in the hole?" he asked Whitney's emissary. "About a million," was the reply. "Is that all? I can make that back on one picture," Selznick said airly. "Well, all we're asking you to do is make the picture, David."

On the evening of December 10, Los Angeles city desks, the wire service news desks, and a handful of leading Hollywood correspondents began receiving anonymous telephone tips that the Selznick back lot was in flames. The anonymous tipster was Russell Birdwell. A simple announcement that the long-awaited filming of *Gone With the Wind* had finally begun would have sufficed to bring them flocking to the studio, but a simple announcement was not Birdwell's style. Everything he did was calculated to propagate the notion of the filming of *Gone With the Wind* as a continuing news event. Reporters who tried to check back with Birdwell could not find him, but the red glow lighting the sky over Culver City told them that Selznick-International was the place to be.

They arrive to find the fire—the biggest ever staged in a motion picture production, as they were to report later—at its fiercest. Flames and smoke leap from some thirty or more acres of tinder-dry old sets with a great crashing and roaring, and as bits of debris soar into the air, firemen shoot them down with their hoses. Three pairs of doubles as Scarlett and a white-suited Rhett Butler are filmed escaping from the burning, collapsing city on three identical buckboards, with Melanie, her newborn baby, and Prissy the servant hidden in the back. All of Technicolor's seven existing cameras are deployed around the periphery to film the blaze from different angles and perspectives. One camera photographs a high brick wall, originally used in *King Kong*, at almost point-blank range as it burns and distintegrates in an avalanche of flame (the resulting footage was used in *Gone With the Wind*, and also found its way into the burning of Manderly sequence in *Rebecca*).

In an early wide-screen experiment, two synchronized cameras are positioned to film the same scene, with the aid of two angled mirrors. Selznick's plan is to open the screen to panoramic proportions for the fire sequence. When the resulting footage was shown on two projectors side by side in the Hollywood premiere of the picture at Grauman's Chinese Theatre, it proved very effective. But it was considered too impractical for general distribution and was never shown again. Thirty-two years later, the entire picture would be reprocessed for showing on a wide screen.

As with everything else connected with the picture, the start was delayed. Myron Selznick, as usual, was late; he was entertaining some clients at dinner and while David refused to give the order to go ahead without his brother present, those involved brooded over their private anxieties. For example, Ernest Grey, the Culver City Fire Chief, had had nightmares since he had first learned of the fire in which it ran amok, wiping out the studio and most of Culver City with it. The studio's own fire department had been strengthened by the addition of some 200 voluntary helpers from the Selznick staff, but anticipating the worst, Grey had marshalled every available fire company in the area as well. The normally cheerful Lee Zavitz, the man who had planned the fire the Fire Chief was afraid couldn't be contained, looked grave. Zavitz was the movies' number-one "powder man," or demolition expert. The burning of Atlanta was the most complex assignment he had ever undertaken. He had laid two contiguous networks of pipes among the old sets at three levels (one on the ground, one on the second floor, and one hidden from view among the roofs) and fitted them at regular intervals with sprinklers. A composite of 20 percent rock gas and 80 percent distillate would be pumped through one network of pipes and ignited. To control the flames, the flow of liquid was turned off and doused with a mixture of water and extinguishing solution from the other network. To boost the flames the process was reversed. The flow was regulated from a console like a small piano keyboard which Selznick insisted on operating himself. It consisted of three rows of pushbuttons—one for each level of pipes—which turned on and off specific parts of the sprinkler system.

Bill Menzies and *Gone With the Wind* production manager Ray Klune were also worried; the originators of the idea, they had stuck their necks out even further by standing up to Eddie Mannix when he tried to persuade an undecided David Selznick that models would be cheaper and more effective.

And finally, David Selznick himself, perched high on an observation platform surrounded by a group of henchmen and friends including Daniel O'Shea, and his mother, trying to conceal his tenseness under a barrage of final and largely futile instructions. What if Mannix was right? What if the Culver City Fire Chief's fears were justified? For an hour he barged nervously about on his perch, an elephant confined in a treehouse, peering into the darkness for signs of the missing Myron, until, at last, he was persuaded he could delay no longer.

Since this was technically second unit work, there being no actors involved, it fell to Menzies to call the first "Action" on *Gone With the Wind*. Selznick turned on the oil sprinklers, which were set alight, and the area quickly became an inferno.

Selznick gazed on the acres of flaming buildings with mixed feelings. The sight gave him a visceral thrill of triumph and power; Mannix had been wrong, the Fire Chief had been wrong,

Overleaf The tragedy of famine and defeat at Tara: Gerald O'Hara, mentally unmoored since his wife's death; Suellen, Carreen, Prissy, and Mammy; Scarlett in the background. (PRATT)

the whole of Hollywood had been wrong. *Gone With the Wind* was going to be a resoundingly successful motion picture, and the fire sequence one of its most dramatic sequences. Yet at the same time there was the sobering thought that it signaled the start of the filming. These were the flames of reality, and there was no turning back. There was no leading lady either, but luck was coming to Selznick's rescue, for out of the ashes of the old sets would emerge not only Margaret Mitchell's Atlanta, but also her Scarlett O'Hara.

The fire was started and stopped eight times during the night for retakes. The last burning structure had come crashing down and the flames were fighting a losing battle with the water now pouring out of the sprinklers; a light wind from the sea carried the black clouds east toward Beverly Hills, where they dissolved over the mansions of Hollywood's aristocracy as they sat playing gin rummy and probably discussing David's folly. Then Myron Selznick appeared on the observation platform, together with his dinner guests. David charged angrily forward, but Myron brushed aside his complaints, saying loudly, "Here, genius, I want you to meet Scarlett O'Hara." Myron often called his brother "genius," especially when, as now, he was drunk. In the fading glow, David Selznick was conscious of a pair of large, arresting gray-green eyes, a cascade of auburn hair under a black halo hat, and a slight, trim figure wrapped against the cold evening air in a mink coat. Her voice had that limber pitch, every consonant hammered firmly into place with precise emphasis, until she laughed, when it became full-throated, a trick she shared with many trained actresses.

Years later, Selznick was to romanticize his first meeting with Vivien Leigh as the epiphanic moment when Scarlett was chosen —a scene from his own *A Star Is Born*. "I took one look and knew that she was right," he wrote in a magazine article about her "discovery." "At least, right as far as appearance went. At least right as far as my conception of how Scarlett O'Hara looked. . . . I'll never recover from that first look." Doubtless, Selznick was impressed with his first sight of Vivien Leigh—in the circumstances that was hardly surprising. But the truth about how she landed the part is more complex, and more protracted, than his version of it.

All of Hollywood knew two things about Vivien Leigh. The first was that she was having an affair with Laurence Olivier. The second was that she had been indirectly connected with a recent story about L. B. Mayer's legendary temper. In 1937, M-G-M decided to produce movies in England. The studio's first foreign venture was to be *A Yank at Oxford,* with Robert Taylor and Maureen O'Sullivan, and to show his new English subsidiary that he meant business, L. B. Mayer had decided to lead the Metro contingent himself.

Arriving in London, Mayer perceived that his London production chief, Michael Balcon, had cast an unknown (at least to Mayer) girl just out of drama school in the second female lead —the college vamp who tries to lure Taylor away from O'Sullivan—and was paying her too much. Mayer at once ordered him to find a replacement with a bigger name. A highly civilized and intelligent man, Balcon assumed that as the executive responsible for the operation he was at least entitled to try to justify his choice. He argued with Mayer that the girl was a promising young starlet worth developing and furthermore was perfect for the character. But Balcon had never dealt personally with Mayer before. At the first sign of resistance Mayer launched into a screaming attack on Balcon's handling of the production, ostensibly in the privacy of the Englishman's office, but positioning himself so as to be seen and heard outside. The affronted Balcon resigned but the girl in question, who happened to be Vivien Leigh, remained in the picture, which turned out to be a dismal introduction to American audiences. *A Yank at Oxford* was too self-conscious to be any good—"made by Metro in England and in awe," as Alistair Cooke's review put it. Selznick had screened the picture, briefly considered this girl he now found so right for Scarlett, and decided against her; George Cukor had agreed with him, telling London reporters that he thought she was beautiful, but lacked sufficient temperament for the part!

Throughout Vivien Leigh's life, people would note her exquisite manners. Years later, when they were making *Streetcar*

Named Desire, Marlon Brando would grumble, "Why are you always so damned polite? Why do you always have to say good morning to everyone?" The answer was India. Vivien Leigh was born Vivien Mary Hartley in 1912 in Darjeeling, at the foot of the Himalayas, into a society not unlike the one in which Scarlett O'Hara grew up—a fact that may have later helped in her understanding of the character. It was not just that the cornerstone of Vivien's world, like Scarlett's world, was white domination of a larger, non-white population. In the India of the British Raj a child was still brought up with the rigid formality of Victorian times, or the antebellum South, even in 1912. When she was six she began making the annual trek "home" to an English convent boarding school, returning to India for the long summer vacation, and the experience endowed her with an independence and rock-like resilience that was to prove useful in Hollywood.

At eighteen, after attending several European schools, she entered the Royal Academy of Dramatic Art, but her marriage to London barrister Leigh Holman (hence her professional name) and then the birth of their daughter caused her to break off her training. When she was twenty-two, after a year of miniscule parts in British movies and one previous stage appearance, she won acclaim in an indifferent sentimental drama, *The Mask of Virtue.* James Agate, the leading London critic, wrote her a poised eulogy. The next morning her billing was changed to "Vivien Leigh—the fame-in-a-night girl." Alexander Korda, the head of London Films, saw the second performance, and by the end of the week had signed her to a five-year contract. The Fleet Street popular press, thirsting as always for an overnight sensation, did the rest.

She and Laurence Olivier first appeared together as Elizabethan lovers in *Fire Over England,* her debut as a Korda contract player. Then Korda put them in *The First and the Last,* the screen version of Galsworthy's novel about a youth who accidentally kills the evil husband of the girl he loves and spends three weeks with the girl before deciding to give himself up. It was inevitable that they would become a romantic team—the ravishing, talented newcomer and the country's dashing leading actor. It was probably equally inevitable that life would eventually follow art, and the romance would spill over into their private lives. In the fall of 1937, Olivier played Hamlet and Vivien Leigh Ophelia in the Old Vic presentation of *Hamlet* in Elsinore; on the battlements of Kronberg Castle, where the play was performed, they made their decision. Returning to London, they broke the news to their respective spouses that they were in love. The following winter found Vivien Leigh petitioning for divorce from her husband of five years, Leigh Holman, and Olivier seeking an annulment of his twelve-month marriage to actress Jill Esmond.

Olivier was asked to play the lead in Sam Goldwyn's production of *Wuthering Heights*. At first he refused, expressing the suspicion and disdain for Hollywood deemed proper for a serious English actor. Then he had second thoughts and tried to get Vivien the part of Cathy as a condition for accepting, but Merle Oberon had already been cast. Vivien was offered Isabella Linton, but refused—it was Cathy or nothing. "You'll get nothing better than this for your first part in Hollywood," William Wyler, who was to direct the picture, told her. Olivier then cabled his Los Angeles agent Myron Selznick about Vivien's prospects of finding work in the Hollywood studios. The reply was even less encouraging: Myron advised her to stay at home. But Vivien still refused the offer of Isabella. In the end Heathcliff, plus Hollywood's high rates of pay, proved irresistible to Olivier and he reluctantly left for the U.S.

For Vivien Leigh, unemployment in Hollywood seemed preferable to a long separation from Olivier, and ten days after his departure she impetuously followed. During the Atlantic crossing she kept to herself, reading *Gone With the Wind*. Arriving in Hollywood three days before the shooting of the burning of Atlanta sequence, she confided to Olivier her desire to play Scarlett. The trade papers had that day carried one of Selznick's periodic denials that Paulette Goddard had definitely been cast, so it was not too late for Vivien Leigh to enter the Scarlett stakes. Olivier took her to Myron, who in turn put her in the hands of associate Nat Deverich. Deverich was a former jockey, and his knowledge of horses and the racetrack was his entree to the Hollywood studios. He had introduced several executives to the sport of

The star is reluctant. Clark Gable manages to muster a sheepish grin as Louis B. Mayer holds the loan-out agreement committing him to play a role he doesn't want; David O. Selznick hovers over them. (SBFA)

The Signing of Rhett
and Scarlett

The "Scarlett hour" arrives. Vivien Leigh is signed and then photographed in Selznick's office with the producer, George Cukor, Olivia de Havilland, and Leslie Howard. (CP)

kings, including Myron himself, whose horse Can't Wait had finished third in the 1937 Kentucky Derby.

Deverich approached O'Shea, a racetrack friend, and O'Shea talked to Selznick: was it all right to hand this girlfriend of Larry Olivier's, Vivien Leigh, to George (Cukor) for a test? She was a wonderful actress. . . . Selznick appeared not to recognize her as the girl he had turned down, and Vivien Leigh's name was included on the Scarlett short list that was to be tested the week after the burning of Atlanta. Selznick met Vivien Leigh at the shooting of the scene, and, over a drink in his office later, he asked her whether she was seriously interested in testing for the role of Scarlett. Vivien thought it best not to remind him that a test had already been scheduled.

The Monday after the burning of Atlanta, having first savored the wide coverage it had received by reading through the pile of newspaper clippings on his desk, Selznick fired off a memo to Henry Ginsberg requesting him to "lay out the schedule of the remaining tests of our principals for *Wind*. . . . Scarlett will definitely be decided upon as a result of this next group of tests." There were now four actresses in the list. Paulette Goddard, in spite of the complications, was still, in Selznick's view, the most promising candidate; then there was Joan Bennett, who seemed to owe her last-minute inclusion to a dark wig. She was well known to Selznick both socially—as one of the Selznicks' circle of friends—and as the blonde ingenue in dozens of movies, but he had never shown any interest in her as a potential Scarlett until he saw her as a sultry brunette in *Trade Winds,* a South Seas saga. Then he asked her to read for the role, but Joan Bennett replied that she would prefer to take a screen test.

At thirty-three, Jean Arthur was the oldest of the four. Over the years she had had several cracks at Hollywood from Broadway, but one of her drawbacks was a "difficult" face. Virtually every star had a "good" side and a "bad" side before the camera, but Jean Arthur's was an extreme case. "Half of it's angel, the other half horse," was how Harry Cohn put it. And when, after failing to get the role of Scarlett, she was cast by Frank Capra in *Mr. Smith Goes to Washington,* the sets of the picture had to be constructed in such a way that her entrances showed only her "good" side. Selznick had been in love with her before he married Irene Mayer, but if the test began as a sentimental gesture, this original and interesting actress had showed such promise in the early readings that she was now under serious consideration.

There was the usual preliminary work with Will Price and Susan Myrick; then, each actress had her day before the camera under George Cukor's direction in a full-dress black-and-white test, in the three test scenes.

The first to test was Jean Arthur. She was an agonized performer; when the cameras stopped she would dash into her dressing room, lock the door, and collapse in tears. Called for another scene, she virtually had to be dragged on to the set, looking wilted and protesting about not being ready. But forced in front of the camera the limp, apparent nervous wreck blossomed into a poised and confident actress. Joan Bennett followed some days later, and then Paulette Goddard, tanned and confident after a trip to Bermuda with the Whitneys and their English cousin, and sporting a new, two-inch cabochon diamond-and-ruby bracelet on her slim brown wrist.

Six days before Christmas it was Vivien Leigh's turn, and for George Cukor, who had maintained a wary neutrality ever since Katharine Hepburn had been dropped from the running, the search for Scarlett was over. He was struck by the passion of her performance, by her immediate understanding of the character. Where other actresses had been coy, or seductive, or tentative, Vivien Leigh attacked the scenes with an urgent drive.

Selznick viewed the tests intercut in order to see each of the four actresses consecutively playing each of the three scenes. Like Cukor, he was impressed with Vivien Leigh's intensity; here, indeed, was a find. The fact that her English accent frequently overwhelmed her attempts at Southern speech he regarded as only a minor problem. But Selznick faced the obvious dilemma: how would the public react to the announcement that an *English* girl was to play Scarlett? Would it create irreparable adverse publicity? At a time of widespread isolationist sentiment, it seemed inconceivable that it would not. There was also certain

to be resentment in Hollywood to contend with; people were getting tired of foreign actors getting all the good parts.

His other worry was Vivien Leigh's love affair with Olivier. Its implications were driven home one morning following the tests when Vivien Leigh told him her first task, if she were cast as Scarlett, would be to go out and find a house for herself and Larry to live in while they were filming. "Oh no, not again," groaned Selznick, remembering his problems with Paulette Goddard, whereupon Vivien quickly assured him that both had divorces pending and planned to get married. In the next five days he screened Vivien's Scarlett test over thirty times on its own, and in conjunction with the other three; he had blow-ups made of each of the four actresses from close-ups in the tests and would gaze at them for hours; he held lengthy staff conferences to discuss the relative merits of each performance; the tests were shipped to Whitney in New York and his opinion sought. But Whitney replied that the choice was up to Selznick. The producer was to say later that, realizing that further searching was out of the question because of the pressure of time, he was waiting for someone to challenge his preference for Vivien Leigh by strongly supporting one of the other women. When no challenge came, he finally decided on Christmas Eve to take his chances with public hostility and the industry's pique and cast her in the role. He believed that the fact that Vivien Leigh was English was potentially more dangerous than her affair with Olivier. Both of them were comparatively unknown in the U.S. and, with a little judicious supervision, their romance could be kept in the background.

Ironically, the search for Scarlett ended with a whimper of legal jargon, as Selznick and Korda—who had Vivien Leigh under contract—haggled over the terms of their agreement. Vivien Leigh learned the news from George Cukor at a lunch party at his house on Christmas Day 1938. When she arrived with Olivier, Cukor told her the part had been cast. She assumed it had gone to one of the other actresses, but then Cukor said: "I guess we're stuck with you." Enjoined to secrecy, Vivien Leigh and Olivier continued their social round; at Merle Oberon's party for Myron Selznick they met Alexander Korda, who again took Vivien aside.

Scarlett discovers a Union deserter looting the house and shoots him with Rhett's pistol. The deserter was played by Paul Hurst, a character actor who played hundreds of gangsters, outlaws, and cops. (PRATT)

He told her he thought she was making a big mistake because she was completely wrong for the part, but that negotiations for the transfer of her contract to Selznick had begun.

Knowing that Selznick had no time for protracted bargaining, Korda squeezed tough terms out of him. Besides the proceeds from the contract sale, he was to have the use of Vivien Leigh in her third picture after *Gone With the Wind*; if he were proved wrong about her in the role and she became an international star, he wasn't going to live to regret it. In addition, he insisted on being prominently mentioned in the casting announcement. There was nothing Selznick could do except grumble helplessly to Jock Whitney: "The lucky Hungarian had fallen into something, and we're going to make a fortune for him."

What *The New York Times* once called "the most exciting and intensive publicity campaign Hollywood has ever seen" was to remain the most successful non-event in the annals of movie publicity. No one has succeeded in equaling its scope, its scale, or its durability. For two years, isolationist America found more relevance in the latest story about who was going to play Scarlett O'Hara than it did in Neville Chamberlain's missions to Munich, the Austrian *Anschluss*, or the latest offensive in the Spanish Civil War. Selznick was handling an enormously successful best-seller at a time when Hollywood's mystique was at its highest, and the stars were national idols. The search represented a new kind of American fantasy, a new promise of instant fame and wealth, supplanting the Protestant ethic in which hard work and virtuous living were supposed to guarantee success, but since the Depression hadn't.

In all, 1400 candidates were interviewed and 90 tested in the search for Scarlett. At $92,000—including the cost of 142,000 feet of black-and-white film and 13,000 feet of Technicolor film shot in the tests—it was a bargain. It had achieved its main purpose of keeping Selznick's project before the public until he was ready to tackle it—and in the process made David O. Selznick a household name; it had also been a genuine attempt to find an unknown actress for the part, and in this it was partially sucessful, since Vivien Leigh was virtually unknown to American audiences; it had even been the subject of a satirical Broadway comedy by

Clare Booth Luce, *Kiss the Boys Goodbye,* in which an egomani-acal Hollywood producer launches a nationwide search for a girl to play the heroine of his Southern epic, Velvet O'Toole. Before the filming had even begun, enough had been published about *Gone With the Wind* to fill a book several times as thick as Mar-great Mitchell's massive novel. When Lee Garmes, the camera-man, received Selznick's cable in London asking him to take on the cimematography of *Gone With the Wind,* he was surprised, since he was sure, from all the publicity he had seen, that the picture must be over. But it was only just beginning.

9

The Biggest Bust in Town

The Selznick brothers had opposite attitudes toward entertaining. Myron was too much of a maverick to play the Hollywood nabob, but his brother did it with relish. David and Irene lived grandly, maintaining a full domestic staff that at one time included two shifts of cooks so that David would find food ready at whatever hour he came home. Life at Myron's on Santa Monica beach had a barrack-room austerity; since his divorce, he had lived alone with one or two servants, and social occasions at home were limited to poker sessions or drinking bouts with cronies. On the rare occasions when he did entertain on a large scale, he generally left the planning to one of his agents, Collier Young, a polished Southerner whom David used to call "a fugitive from F. Scott Fitzgerald."

Shortly after Christmas, Young was summoned by Myron and found both brothers sitting in the yard of the Santa Monica house, behind a screen that served as protection from the ocean wind. He was handed a guest list and told to organize a New Year's weekend at Hillhaven, Myron's Lake Arrowhead Lodge.

On the afternoon of New Year's Eve, a chartered bus wafted the guests through the orange groves of San Bernardino toward the mountains beyond; drinks were served, a small combo in the back played such current hits as *Alexander's Ragtime Band*. But as the nature of its composition dawned on the members of the party, a deadening awkwardness settled like lead upon the bus. The male guests included David Niven, Arthur Hornblow Jr., Errol Flynn . . . all regular members of the Selznick social set, nothing unusual there. But among the women were Vivien Leigh, Paulette Goddard, Joan Bennett, Miriam Hopkins, plus one or two lesser contenders for the role of Scarlett; they became edgy and their anxiety did not diminish when the Selznick brothers were observed apparently enjoying a huge private joke. Was David hatching some diabolical way of announcing the winner of the crown, which persistent Hollywood rumor already placed on Vivien Leigh's head? At the lodge that night the New

Year's Eve party was somewhat strained, but the Selznicks remained inscrutable. Throughout the weekend the edginess persisted whenever the party came together; when everyone went their separate ways, however, things loosened up, and some of the men returned to Los Angeles limping, scarred by the bramble bushes around the bedroom windows.

Thanks largely to Alexander Korda's persistence, twenty days elapsed between the decision on Vivien Leigh and its official announcement. By then it was no longer a secret, since she had begun to report to the studio for make-up tests, costume fittings, dialogue training and sessions on Southern deportment with Will Price and Susan Myrick. Vivien made no secret of disliking Hollywood—"their standards are purely financial," she complained in a letter to her estranged husband—or of her grave misgivings about signing a seven-year contract. But in the end, as in the case of Laurence Olivier and Heathcliff, the lure of the part overcame all her other reservations. She was reassured by the presence of George Cukor; with his theatrical background, he was closer to her world than the majority of movie people and there was a note of reliance in her description of him to Holman as "a very intelligent and imaginative man, and seems to understand the subject perfectly."

Selznick had meanwhile also succeeded in borrowing Olivia de Havilland from Warner Brothers to play Melanie—on which more later—and was thus able to name a full cast of principals. Never one to boil things down, he released the news in a 750-word statement mainly notable for its clever evasions. It referred to Vivien Leigh's "recent screen work in England," without actually stating that she was English. In fact, having read of her birth in India, schooling in England, France, Germany and Switzerland, her French father and Irish mother (in both cases, a tenuous matter of distant descent), the reader was hard put to guess *what* nationality Vivien Leigh really was. Blithely ignoring the pending divorce and the presence of Laurence Olivier under the same roof, Selznick described her as being in private life "Mrs. Leigh Holman, the wife of a London barrister." Hollywood proprieties had to be observed. As usual, no ages were given and no reference made to Vivien Leigh being eight years

Carreen and Suellen watch in horror as their father is thrown from his horse and killed. (PRATT)

older than Scarlett at the start of the book, and Leslie Howard twenty-two years older than Ashley Wilkes.

On the night of the Scarlett announcement, Margaret Mitchell was on hand in the city room of her old paper, the *Atlanta Constitution,* to help with the story. It was already close to the paper's deadline when Selznick's press release began arriving by telegram at the Western Union office on Peachtree Street where John Marsh was waiting. It came in sections because it was too long to send in a single transmission; Marsh delivered it to the *Constitution* a few pages at a time, and they were quickly set in type. By the end of the evening Marsh had made the trip six times. One oldtimer at the newspaper told Margaret Mitchell that he could recall only one other instance when the story kept coming in chunks right up to deadline time; that was the sinking of either the *Titanic* or the *Lusitania,* but he didn't remember which. The paper could only unearth one photograph of Olivia de Havilland, a publicity cheesecake shot of her in a bathing suit. When Margaret Mitchell said she thought it didn't seem to go with the announcement that the actress was to play Melanie, the editor replied: "We can explain that Sherman's men had gotten away with the rest of her clothes."

Later that night, when reporters began calling her from all over the country for her reaction to Selznick's choice for Scarlett, Margaret Mitchell's only comment was that Vivien Leigh "looks like she has plenty of spirit and fire, not at all like a languid Hollywood girl." Selznick, who was torn between relief that the author had not denounced his Scarlett and chagrin at her refusal to impart her blessing, officially interpreted the remark as an endorsement. He was quickly corrected.

Playing down Vivien Leigh's nationality probably yielded dividends in public support: A Gallup Poll taken after the announcement showed that thirty-five percent approved the choice and sixteen percent disapproved, while twenty percent were undecided, and though the news was carried by virtually every newspaper in the country and broadcast by every radio station coast-to-coast, twenty-nine percent said they hadn't heard it. The shrillest protests came from Hedda Hopper, who accused Selznick in her column of insulting every American actress with his choice. But the Daughters of the Confederacy, another expected source of opposition, were so relieved the part hadn't gone to a Yankee actress that they passed a resolution accepting Vivien Leigh.

On the day of the announcement, Joan Bennett received a large bowl of orchids and a note from Selznick that began: "The Scarlett hour has arrived, and the decision unfortunately is against our Joanie. I am more grateful than I can say for your effort which was magnificent . . ."; Paulette Goddard—flashing a new diamond necklace—was taken aside by Selznick for a consoling chat at the Douglas Fairbanks Jr.s' dinner party for Elsa Maxwell, but she was too full of her role in Chaplin's new production, *The Great Dictator,* to care much about the loss of Scarlett; coming face-to-face with Jeffrey Lynn at a screening, Selznick told him, "I'm sorry, Jeffrey, but I couldn't resist the name of Leslie Howard." But with Scarlett enthroned at last, Selznick wasted no time mending fences. Turning his back on the debris of wrecked hopes and sinking careers, he directed his energy to completing the cast of the picture.

At the time, Selznick was ardently pursuing Joan Fontaine, twenty years old and under contract to R.K.O. Though she had the will of a woman twice her age and was successfully keeping him at bay, or perhaps even because of it, he offered to test her for Melanie. But Joan Fontaine thought she was the stuff that Scarletts were made of, not Melanies. "If it's Melanie you're interested in, why don't you try my sister?" was her disdainful reply.

Her sister, Olivia de Havilland, had been signed by Warner Brothers to play Hermia in Max Reinhardt's film version of *A Midsummer Night's Dream,* but she was now better known as the damsel in permanent distress in Errol Flynn's swashbuckling capers, having appeared in virtually every one of them from *Captain Blood,* his first, to *Robin Hood,* the latest and most successful. Why not Olivia de Havilland, Selznick thought. There was a limpid loveliness about her that seemed just right for Melanie. Because Jack Warner was notoriously opposed to loaning out his stars to other studios, she had to be contacted in secret; without notifying Warner, she stole over the hill from Burbank to Culver

Costumes, Makeup, and Hairstyling

Walter Plunkett, who designed the costumes for *Gone With the Wind,* adjusts the collar of Ashley's Confederate army uniform. (FLAMINI)

Trying on their costumes for the barbecue: Evelyn Keyes (Suellen O'Hara), Mary Anderson (Maybelle Merriweather), Leslie Howard (Ashley Wilkes), Ann Rutherford (Carreen O'Hara), and Alicia Rhett (India Wilkes). (FLAMINI)

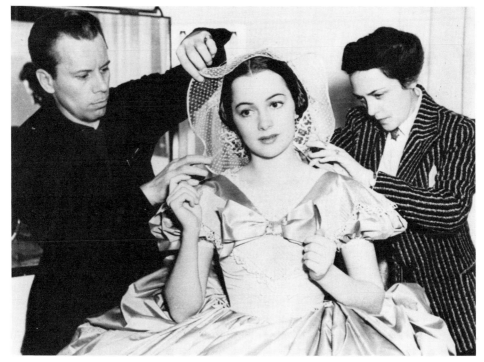

Monty Westmore, who is credited with makeup and hairstyling, and his assistant Hazel Rogers adjust the snood that Melanie wears to the O'Hara-Hamilton marriage. (FLAMINI)

Vivien Leigh waits in position while extras receive last-minute costume and makeup changes. (FLAMINI)

City to read for Cukor, and then to Selznick's house for a second reading a few days later. While Selznick stood listening with his arms folded, Cukor read Scarlett's lines with great emotion. At the sight of the pudgy, bespectacled director clinging passionately to the drapes in Selznick's paneled study, Olivia—dressed for the part in black velvet with a demure lace collar—felt herself losing control of what she was doing in a fit of suppressed laughter. But whatever it was that she was doing, it was right, for when she had finished Selznick said, "Well, you're Melanie. You're what we want. The problem now is to convince Jack Warner." Then Selznick took her into the playroom, which also served as projection room, and showed her the screen tests of six other Melanies. Olivia recognized Elizabeth Allen, Andrea Leeds, Frances Dee, and Ann Shirley (whose real name was Dawn O'Day, the child extra who became a child star). Privately, she thought them all wonderful, but she felt that this was the moment to keep her own counsel.

For Olivia de Havilland, the role of Melanie held the promise of deliverance. Firstly, deliverance from the stultifying rut of being rescued by Errol Flynn. She had enjoyed the costume roles at first, particularly since she had developed a crush on the dashing hero. But as she bounced backwards and forwards in history, her career remained at a standstill—and as Flynn's fame grew, so did his ego. In her one big scene, usually an appeal to him for help against the Sheriff of Nottingham, Indian mutineers, or some other cinematic embodiment of evil, he had taken to such distracting tactics as fiddling with the hilt of his sword, or swatting the air with his long leather gloves. As if this were not bad enough, in their love scenes he would gaze upwards at her hairline instead of into her face, because his wife, Lili Damita, had told him he had small eyes. Deliverance, secondly, from Warner Brothers itself, where male stars like Cagney, Robinson, and especially Paul Muni, who was surrounded by a mystical foreign prestige, dominated the lot; where there was room for only one woman star and Bette Davis seemed as immovable from that perch as the Statue of Liberty.

But there was still Jack Warner to be converted. When she went to his office Warner was playing with an electric train, ostensibly a Christmas gift for his son. The tracks were laid out all over the floor, and rail cars were clattering busily in and out from under the chairs, the desk, and the couch. Actors made Warner nervous; they were a mysterious, alien breed beyond his understanding. Producers and writers he respected, and in his own fashion even trusted; from actors he demanded obedience. To refuse a film part was to incur the highest form of royal displeasure, suspension. At Warner Brothers this went beyond mere loss of salary to banishment from the lot for an indefinite period. (The lot was the heart of the actor's universe. While filming, he was there twelve hours a day, six days a week. It was where he met his friends, ate his meals, placed his racing bets, made his assignations, received the press and his adoring fans, and found a dozen other ways to indulge his ego. To be barred from the lot was considered by many actors as great a deprivation as the loss of income.) Equally, an actor played a role outside the studio at Warner's pleasure, and Warner was obviously in no mood to be agreeable. While he continued to dart about in pursuit of the little trains criss-crossing the room, he asked her: "Why do you want to play Melanie? Scarlett's the part, and they've cast it." But Olivia stood her ground; it was Melanie that interested her, she pleaded, not Scarlett. "Oh, you don't want to be in that, it's going to be the biggest bust in town," Warner remarked, terminating the audience. "Besides," he added, getting to the nub of his opposition to loaning out his actors, "you'll come back, and you'll be difficult. . . ."

By rights, that ought to have been the last word on the subject, but beneath the docile facade, Olivia was canny and resourceful. The most delicate bloom in Jack Warner's garden she may have been, but the bloom was cast in tempered steel. Discovering, for example, that the wardrobe and make-up departments received scripts well in advance of forthcoming productions in order to get a head start on any major problems, she had gone to work on the department staffs, who were soon slipping her their scripts so that she, too, had a head start on preparing for auditions. The wardrobe and make-up departments weren't likely to be of much use in this situation but Olivia had her sights set on someone who would—Warner's wife. Knowing her influence with her husband,

Olivia played a very effective tea-and-sympathy scene with her at the Beverly Hills Brown Derby, appealing for her help as a former actress.

Mrs. Warner and David Selznick then joined forces to lay siege on Warner's opposition, while Selznick tried to effect a breach by offering him the use of other actors in exchange—for Warner coveted the stars of other studios as much as he refused to part with his own—Mrs. Warner applied wifely persuasion. Realistic as always, Selznick also began looking for an alternative; a year earlier, a young actress named Marsha Hunt under contract to Paramount had impressed him with her reading for Melanie, and he impulsively decided to audition her a second time. When she had finished, Cukor applauded, and Selznick enfolded her in a bear hug and exclaimed, "I have found my Melanie." Thrilled by Selznick's convincing display of enthusiasm, Marsha Hunt mentally bid goodbye to her position as undisputed queen of Paramount's string of vapid boy-meets-girl movies aimed at the juvenile market, the precursors of the beach pictures of the early Sixties. But Selznick swore her to secrecy, ostensibly because he wanted to go through the formality of seeing her alongside Vivien Leigh to compare appearances before making his choice public, but obviously because he still had not abandoned hope of shaking Olivia de Havilland loose from Warner Brothers. In fact, less than twenty-four hours later, J. L. Warner reluctantly capitulated. The role of his wife in Warner's change of mind is not known, but what in the end tipped the balance was Selznick's irresistible proposal to transfer an option he had on the use of James Stewart, Metro's rising new star. Stewart was immediately signed to appear in Warner Brothers production of *No Time for Comedy,* and Olivia to play Melanie in *Gone With the Wind.* Marsha Hunt read the news in the *Hollywood Reporter* the following morning while waiting for a call from Selznick which never came.

Warner's fears were to prove well justified: having drunk the heady wine of big-time stardom, Olivia de Havilland would have no stomach for studio discipline and begin to take suspensions in preference to some of the film roles assigned her, roles that attempted to return her to the mold of Errol Flynn's demure heroine. Improbably, she was to become the focus of actor unrest on the Warner lot, challenging the authority of the second largest Hollywood studio in the courts and winning a landmark case in the downward slide of the studios from control over their stars, and eventually over their own destinies.

By the end of her contract in 1943, Olivia de Havilland had piled up seven suspensions amounting to a total of nine months, which Warner ordered tacked on to the end of her seven years. Olivia brought suit, and after sticking to her case through three courts in eighteen months, the Superior Court of California ruled in her favor: a seven-year contract was binding for no more than seven years. Warner took the case to the appellate court (at the same time shutting off any hope of other employment by warning every Hollywood producer by telegram that she was still under contract to him) ; his argument was that suspension time did not constitute time worked. But again the decision was a victory for Olivia: to add accumulated suspension time to the seven calendar years of her contract, the judge ruled, "would amount to virtual peonage." Stars returning from war service, such as James Stewart and Melvyn Douglas, had occasion to be thankful for her dogged determination, for they found their old contracts close to expiry and were able to negotiate new ones at postwar prices, often on a profit-sharing basis.

That was all in the future. There were no signs of rebellion in the docile young actress who reported for work at Selznick-International one drizzly morning in January 1939, though it could perhaps have been foreseen in her extraordinary determination to land the role. She set to work at once on her accent and her appearance. When Cukor suggested two alternative hairstyles—one with ringlets and the other, more authentic but more severe, with flat wings covering the ears—she had no hesitation in choosing authenticity over glamor. Pleased with her own artistic scrupulousness, she showed the costume shots to her current beau, but he was furious over the way she had allowed herself to be deglamorized. "What have they done to you?" he cried. "*And they've made you flat-chested.*"

Olivia de Havilland's beau was Howard Hughes. For another one of the incongruities of her personality was her hectic love life; from her arrival at Warners in 1935, she seemed to have

Overleaf Desperate for $300 to pay the new taxes on Tara, Scarlett goes to Ashley; he talks about the fall of civilization; she asks him to run away with her to Mexico. (PRATT)

been linked romantically with a number of Hollywood men, including James Stewart, Fredric March, and director Anatole Litvak, to mention but three. Her relationship with Hughes had begun shortly after she accepted a ride back to Los Angeles in his plane from a desert location. Hughes himself wasn't on the plane, and in fact Olivia had never laid eyes on him, but Louella Parsons got wind of the story and ran an item in her column jumping to two conclusions: one, that Hughes had been piloting the plane, and two, that Olivia must then be the latest in the long string of Hughes' "fiancées."

The day the item appeared Olivia de Havilland received a telephone call. "This is Howard Hughes," the caller announced. "Now that we're engaged, don't you think we ought to meet?" She accepted his dinner invitation, splurged on a fur wrap, and borrowed a gown from her friends at the studio wardrobe department. She did not know that Hughes' conception of a date differed from current Hollywood practice. He hated wearing formal clothes, he hated crowded fashionable restaurants and nightclubs, and above all he hated the limelight. So when Olivia de Havilland began to see him regularly in the winter of 1938, she stepped into a social backwater of out-of-the-way chop houses and quiet, unknown bars. Their first evening set the tone; they watched two movies in the screening room of his green stucco Hollywood office on Romaine Street, followed by a meal in an Olympic Boulevard steak joint. Still, there was the thrill of being out with Hollywood's young mystery man (he was thirty-three) and the excitement of listening to him talk about his grand design for living in which a specific number of years were to be devoted to science, to the movies, to aviation, and to other worthwhile pursuits.

With the shooting date of *Gone With the Wind* now firmly set for January 26, a procession of actors and actresses of all ages, shapes, and reputations, from every level of achievement in the theater as well as the movies, from Broadway and the provinces, from Metro and the studios of "Poverty Row," trekked in and out of Selznick's studio trying out for supporting roles. Lionel Barrymore was considered for Dr. Meade, but he was now con-

fined to a wheelchair and the part went to Harry Davenport.
Billie Burke set her heart on playing Aunt Pittypat, and though
Selznick felt that she was too youthful and shapely to play Scarlett's bustling, dumpy aunt, he gave in to her entreaties for a test.
Encased in a heavily padded costume, her delicate features fat-
tened by a rubber double chin and cotton stuffing in her cheeks,
she lumbered resolutely to the set looking like a kingsize Thanks-
giving turkey. In her excess baggage she was overwhelmed by the
heat of the studio lights, and almost fainted. She managed to reel
through the scene, stumbling over her lines and her clothes, and
totally oblivious to Cukor's directions; a few days later the part
was entrusted to the doughty presence of Laura Hope Crews.

At times the choice was so clear that Selznick was forced into
an untypically quick decision. Thomas Mitchell was virtually the
only serious contender for Gerald O'Hara, Scarlett's father, and
Selznick had to agree to a special clause in his contract that he
wouldn't have to ride, because he was terrified of horses. But the
producer's uncertainties were very much in evidence during the
casting of Belle Watling, the Atlanta madam. When Selznick
complained, during a dinner party given in honor of the Grand
Duchess Marie, that the part was proving difficult to fill, his old
ally Mrs. Jack Warner slipped into a Southern drawl and Selznick
jokingly offered to test her; whereupon practically every woman
around the table followed suit, with different degrees of success.
The Grand Duchess looked puzzled.

Selznick never did test Mrs. Warner, but the list of actresses
considered included Joan Blondell, Loretta Young, and Gladys
George; many of them could have filled the bill, but Selznick
continued to hold out for a quality which, as usual, he was not
able to define, but knew he would recognize if he ever saw it.
Then he had one of his inspirational flashes and cabled Kay
Brown to approach Tallulah Bankhead about playing Belle as a
"stunt," or cameo role. Selznick was well aware that there was
no saying how the fiery Tallulah, as a rejected Scarlett, would
react to the suggestion, and he prudently warned Kay Brown:
"For God's sake, don't mention my name in connection with it,
simply saying that it is an idea of your own that you haven't yet

Overleaf Frank Kennedy (Carroll Nye), one of Scarlett's beaus
and soon to be her next husband, returns from the war. (FLAMINI)

taken up with me." She chose to ignore this assignment, and it was never mentioned again. But once again, David Selznick's extraordinary intuition was coming to his rescue.

A young woman appeared in the wardrobe department to be fitted for a test as Belle Watling. She was New York actress Ona Munson, and at first sight she had about as much in common with a Southern madam as Hitler did with Santa Claus. She was tall, freckled, and flat-chested; her hair was worn in a short bob. But if Selznick wanted to test her, it was not theirs to reason why, and the wardrobe and make-up staff went to work. On the screen, the result was electric. There was a lush, Rubensesque figure with a creamy Ingres skin, glossy red hair, flashing jewels on a breathlessly plunging, ruffled neckline. The scene was Belle's meeting with Melanie outside the church that had been converted into a hospital, and Melanie's lines were thrown to her by Will Price, off camera. Belle's voice was low and throaty and full of sex. At the end of a fluent and touching performance, the lights came on in the small studio projection room and there was silence for a while, and then Selznick's voice broke it: "Well, there's Belle."

In his attitude toward blacks on the screen Selznick was, as usual, in the mainstream of Hollywood pragmatism. Mae West used to insist on having a black servant in every one of her films; when Henry Hathaway, the director, once asked her the reason, she told him: "Lissen, don't forget that one out of every four people in the galleries is colored. They're my public and I gotta show 'em I'm democratic." Blacks had their place in the scheme of things, and that place was in the kitchen, or on the plantation. Selznick eliminated the Ku Klux Klan from *Gone With the Wind,* fearing that it "might come out as an unintentional advertisement for intolerant societies in these fascist-ridden times," as he wrote to Sidney Howard, but he seemed to have no quarrel with the more insidious racism of Margaret Mitchell's novel, its suggestion that somehow the South had won an ideological victory since the war had changed neither the social nor the economic reality of black dependence on the white race.

Yet the symptoms of black urban congestion were already well advanced in cities like Detroit and Chicago, and if it is too harsh a judgment to say that by their indifference, producers like Selznick actually inhibited the cause of race relations in America, they cannot be said to have acted as the spur and model for greater racial understanding. This is perhaps one of the great missed opportunities of the movies, but at the time Hollywood believed that messages were best left to Western Union. Thirty-five years later, the place of blacks in films was to shift to the police precinct house and the whorehouse, as another generation of producers discovered the black audience and exploited it with traditional rapacity in a series of violent, sex-filled cops-and-pushers potboilers, and the aggressive sexual stud and his ravishing but flint-hard soul mate were to become even more improbable black screen stereotypes of the Seventies than the comic butlers and fat mammys that Selznick was busily casting in *Gone With the Wind* had represented the black race in the Thirties.

Always on the lookout for a good publicity story, Selznick tested Elizabeth McDuffie, the White House cook, for the role of Scarlett's Mammy—"with the blessing of Mrs. Franklin D. Roosevelt"—after reading that she was the star of the White House servants' amateur dramatics. But inevitably, he turned to Hattie McDaniel to play the part. This black actress of immense and cheerful presence had started her career as a singer, touring the country with Prof. George Morrison's Colored Orchestra, and had been the first black woman to sing on network radio. Then she had come to Hollywood and quickly established herself as the quintessential screen mammy, a role she was content to play for the rest of her working life.

Butterfly McQueen came from the stage. When she was signed to play Prissy she was appearing in the Benny Goodman—Louis Armstrong musical inspired by *A Midsummer Night's Dream,* entitled *Swingin' On a Dream.* After *Gone With the Wind,* the world of black squeaky-voiced comic maids could have been her oyster; she played the same character in four successive movies, and then issued a statement saying she would no longer accept such parts. Her refusal to be typecast damaged her film career, but Butterfly McQueen would stick to her decision, even walking out of a Jack Benny show rather than resurrect Prissy. In his autobiography, Malcolm X recalled his racial embarrassment upon seeing Butterfly McQueen as Prissy when he was a young man. Moody and unpredictible, Butterfly McQueen could well have felt that way about it herself.

What of the highly publicized Southern belles discovered by George Cukor and Arnow and brought back to Hollywood like rare birds from a distant land? Marcella Martin ended up as Cathleen Calvert, Mary Anderson as Maybelle Merriwether, and Alicia Rhett, as we have said, as India Wilkes; Southern starlet Evelyn Keyes was borrowed from Cecil B. De Mille, to whom she was under contract, to play Scarlett's sister Suellen. Ann Rutherford, best known as Andy Hardy's girlfriend, was signed to play the other sister, Careen.

One starlet under consideration for a speaking part ran, weeping and disheveled, into the arms of a surprised production assistant, saying that she had been attacked by David Selznick in his office. Evelyn Keyes, a pert, shapely blonde from a tough working-class district of Atlanta, was better able to look after herself. When Selznick lunged, she ran around his big mahogany desk with the smouldering producer in hot pursuit until he was out of breath, and then she made her getaway. Some years later, she was to be drawn into his social circle by her marriage to John Huston (Jennifer Jones, then Selznick's mistress, was maid-of-honor at her wedding), and though Selznick never gave the slightest hint that he remembered their skirmish in his office, she was to see that they never found themselves alone together.

Sexually, Selznick was more attracted to women than women were to him. He was intelligent enough to be aware that he was physically not cut out for the role of successful philanderer, particularly in a community that set such store by good looks. So he resorted to the studio head's *droit de seigneur*, accepting a high ratio of rebuffs for the occasional surrender. But for a young actress, the lecherous studio executive was a fact of Hollywood life, and more than one career owed its origins to the hurly-burly of the casting couch.

To Selznick's eternal credit, he bore no grudge when repulsed, unlike some of his nastier counterparts. Evelyn Keyes was cast in the picture. Joan Fontaine, who had already turned down the role of Melanie, was under consideration for the lead in *Rebecca,* a film version of the Daphne Du Maurier novel. When she continued to reject his advances, Selznick at first contemplated retaliating by turning her down for the part, but eventually he faced up to the fact that the tests had shown her to be ideal for it ("I can't do it, we've got to have the Fontaine girl, go get her," he instructed a close aide). And shortly after releasing *Gone With the Wind,* Selznick was to put under contract a stunning redheaded high school senior, Rhonda Fleming. She had, however, failed to tell Selznick that she was a rather unusual schoolgirl, in that she had a husband and a newborn baby. Around one o'clock one morning there came a call from David Selznick. Obviously surprised when her husband answered, he demanded to speak to Rhonda. "Who was that man?" asked Selznick. "My husband," replied Rhonda. "You never told me you were married." "You never asked me," Rhonda replied. At the studio the following morning Selznick reproached her for keeping her marriage a secret, but the episode had no effect on her career at Selznick-International. He never did tell her—and Rhonda Fleming never asked—the purpose of his one o'clock call.

Later on, his infatuation with Phyllis Isely, a young actress whom he renamed Jennifer Jones, was to have a deep and often crippling influence on his decisions as a producer. But until that fateful encounter, and certainly in the early days of 1939 with *Gone With the Wind* about to go into production, movie priorities always took precedence over sexual priorities; film was Selznick's real mistress (as Irene Selznick knew well) , not the seductive young things he chased around his office, and to film he gave total fidelity. From noon, when he generally arrived at the studio, until the small hours of the following morning when he often collapsed from exhaustion at his desk and had to be carted home, Selznick presented a picture of total, unchallenged control over his enterprise. His statement that, as producer, "my function is to be responsible for everything," incarnates the justification and aims of his entire film career. His insistence on personally approving every detail of the intricate weave and lattice of film produc-

Overleaf Rhett, now a prisoner of the Yankees, plays a profitable card game with his captors. (FLAMINI)

tion meant that, from its inception, the whole movie existed in his head, and in no one else's.

In the last frantic days before filming started, a swarm of associates orbited around David Selznick like satellites around some planet, seeking his endorsement or advice. On a typical afternoon, while the sun blazed on the white facade of the Selznick-International studio, the casting department needed him to pass on two featured extras (a featured extra appears in a shot either on his own or alone with one of the stars of the picture); Walter Plunkett pushed through the last of some 400 costume designs that made up the wardrobe of the fifty-nine principal characters; from Bill Menzies came the daily ration of sketches of set-ups from the picture (which finally totaled 2500 or so, and left Menzies with calloused fingers from holding his brush), and from the writers their daily submission of revised pages of Sidney Howard's script. The acountants came to deliver a warning of mounting costs. As night fell he joined Hal Kern, his chief cutter, in the cutting room to work on the editing of *Made for Each Other.*

As if *Gone With the Wind* were not a formidable enough project, Selznick was also preparing three other movies to go into production concurrently with it. One was *Intermezzo,* another was *Rebecca,* which was to launch the British director Alfred Hitchcock in Hollywood pictures; *Prom Girl* was the third, a college musical in Technicolor to star Ginger Rogers, with music by Rogers and Hart, and of course a nationwide search for the six most beautiful coeds to appear as chorus girls—but the picture was finally abandoned.

As an employer, Selznick was bullying, exacting, and inconsiderate, but he was also stimulating, loyal, and prestigious. Olivia de Havilland was impressed with the "community of purpose" that existed on *Gone With the Wind,* despite the tensions, and Menzies once told Selznick that he had the ability to make people transcend themselves; more than one associate of mediocre ability made headway in the industry on the strength of some distinguished piece of work that had been bludgeoned out of him by Selznick, and never came close to reaching such a peak again.

Selznick often pushed his staff to their physical, as well as mental, limits. While he slept the morning through, others who had toiled with him through the night were expected to be at work, facing the exhausting prospect of yet another wakeful night with him. New secretaries were at first attracted by the prospect of unlimited overtime money and such perquisites as catered dinners from the Hillcrest Country Club in Beverly Hills, and the chance of being part of Selznick's caravans to New York, with first-class rail travel and accommodations. But exhaustion soon took the thrill out of their increased earnings, and the dinners frequently had to be swallowed on the run because Selznick wanted to dictate another marathon memo. Even the New York trips were often a disappointment, since Selznick expected his secretaries to be on continuous call in their rooms. One pair of girls (so legend has it) spent two and a half weeks in the Sherry Netherland Hotel waiting for a summons which never came, and then were told to pack their bags and return to California without having put their noses outside of the building.

Selznick was, of course, too much of an egotist to be aware of the punishing pace he was setting for his staff, and the staff was too conscious of the despotic nature of studio managements to risk protesting too loudly. The top echelon of his executives accepted his excesses as another privilege of office, with only a few mild complaints. One night, after they had worked late on *Gone With the Wind* casting problems, he dragged Dan O'Shea to a nightclub where they drank and talked shop until nearly 5 A.M. Finally, O'Shea got up to leave, pleading that he had to be back at work in less than five hours. Having experienced a number of these all-night sessions he knew that they did not carry dispensation from work the following morning. "Oh, you don't have to be there early," said Selznick, urging him to stay on. "I don't expect to be down until noon." "Yeah, but you don't work for the same son-of-a-bitch as I do," O'Shea replied.

At the end of another day shortly afterward, Menzies and several other members of the production staff were summoned to a conference. Arriving in Selznick's office about 7 P.M., they found it empty, but there were instructions to wait. They sat in a circle smoking, making small talk, listening to Menzies' anecdotes, and pining for food and drink—especially drink. Two hours later

Selznick breezed in and, without a word of apology as usual, launched into the conference. Presently, a waiter from Chasen's restaurant arrived with a tray, which he set down on Selznick's desk. The producer continued the discussion as he ate his dinner. Menzies was quietly furious, and thereafter always had a meal before Selznick's evening conferences.

10

Fade in:
Front of Tara:
Long Shot

"Don't get panicky at the seemingly small amount of final revised script," David Selznick wrote Jock Whitney on the night before the shooting began. "It is so clearly in my mind that I can tell you the picture from beginning to end, almost shot by shot." The less reassuring truth was that after two and a half years of preparation, the script was still a shambles. This was nothing new for Selznick. When *Garden of Allah* was being filmed on location in the Arizona desert, the writing barely kept pace with the camera; script pages had to be telexed to Yuma railroad station from Washington Boulevard every night so there would be something to shoot the following morning. On *Gone With the Wind* the situation was rather different. It was not that he had no script, but that he had too many.

One of his first acts on buying the novel had been to engage as scenarist Sidney Howard, the Pulitzer Prize-winning dramatist and movie writer (*Dodsworth, They Knew What They Wanted, The Silver Cord*). Howard was both an outstanding writer and also an outstandingly fast one who could lock himself in his study and turn out twenty-five pages of polished dialogue a day. All this discipline didn't appeal to Selznick's chaotic nature, but he acknowledged Howard as one of the two best screenwriters not under contract to a major studio. The other was Ben Hecht, and when the inevitable break came with Howard, the producer was to turn to Hecht for help. Selznick suffered his first misgivings when he learned that Howard disliked California and refused to work there; he had recently written *Dodsworth* for Sam Goldwyn at his Eighty-eighth Street apartment in Manhattan and proposed to do the same with *Gone With the Wind*. Selznick tried in vain to induce him to change his mind, grumbling to Kay Brown, who was conducting the negotiations: "I never had much success with leaving a writer alone to do a script, without almost daily collaboration with myself and usually the director." But Howard agreed to come to Hollywood for conferences with Selznick and Cukor, but then withdrew to the East to work. A friend of Mar-

Wearing a dress cut from the green drapes of Tara, Scarlett visits Rhett in the hope of borrowing the $300. (PRATT)

garet Mitchell's met him in Hollywood and sent her this description: "He's tall, Scotch looking—a little mustache—an incisive speech—a tendency to preoccupation—and very pleasant." The playwright also relayed a message: he was glad she had not come to Hollywood. After the conferences, Howard called on Selznick to say goodbye, promising to deliver the first draft of the script within two months. "He will, too. He's a businessman writer," Selznick remarked to an executive later.

One may wonder why Selznick felt the necessity for daily collaboration with a writer of such standing. Though he may not have admitted it, Selznick subscribed to the prevailing Hollywood view of the scenarist as the medium of the producer's message: a craftsman whose main task was to articulate the producer's ideas and transfer them to paper. It was a view that had been swallowed by the writers themselves, many of whom lacked sufficient courage or creative confidence or talent, or a combination of all three, to resist it. So they learned, in the words of Sancho Panza, to itch where they could scratch, demanding and receiving huge salaries in return for suppressing their creative independence. "Half the sum paid to me for writing a movie script was in payment for listening to the producer and obeying him," Ben Hecht once admitted in an interview. "The movies pay as much for obedience as for creative work."

Out of sight did not mean out of range of Selznick's memos, and Howard was the target of an intensive bombardment of instructions and suggestions on how to get the best out of Margaret Mitchell's novel for the screen. Structurally, *Gone with the Wind* owed a lot to the movies and Howard's principal task was to boil down its monumental length to screen proportions. Selznick's studio once worked out that to film the entire book would have resulted in a picture 168 hours, or one week, long, but the producer was thinking in terms of between two-and-a-half and three hours. And though Howard observed to Selznick that Margaret Mitchell "did everything at least twice," it remained a colossal undertaking. Selznick issued repeated warnings against tampering with what he called "the chemicals" of the novel. Most producers showed little respect for the properties that they bought and often ended up transmuting literary gold into base metal

The calluses on Vivien Leigh's hands were made from a rubber
solution and applied by Monty Westmore, the makeup man. (SBFA)

on the screen, but Selznick observed certain rudimentary precepts of fidelity, on the theory that the same elements that drew people to a classic or a Broadway hit or a best-selling novel would attract them to the movie. Discussing screen adaptations—one of his favorite topics—with Bosley Crowther, he said: "If there are faults in construction it is better to keep them than to try to change them around because no one can certainly pick out the chemicals which contribute to the making of a classic. And there is always the danger that by tampering, you may destroy the essential chemical."

Howard was encouraged to cut out large chunks of the novel, but to leave individual scenes intact. Audiences, Selznick felt, understood the conventions of the movies and were prepared to forgive omissions, but were less tolerant of interpolations of new scenes and distortions of familiar scenes; subordinate characters could be reduced to one or two lines, as long as their identity survived. As an example, he was fond of pointing out that Barkis in *David Copperfield* was left with only two lines of dialogue— "Barkis is willing" and one other that had actually been a chapter heading—but the audience hadn't objected.

Punctually, Howard produced a first draft quarried from the 1037-page novel. Despite massive cutting, it was a tome of 400 pages which would have run on the screen for over six hours. Selznick briefly contemplated making two pictures out of it, the first one ending with the marriage of Scarlett and Rhett, and a second shorter picture starting with the honeymooning couple in New Orleans, but he abandoned the idea when several movie distributors advised him that it would be unpopular with audiences. So Howard grudgingly returned to Hollywood where, in long sessions that dragged on into the night, he and Selznick began the task of paring down his script to at least half its length. The going was slow. When Selznick wasn't thumbing through the studio-prepared master breakdown of the novel in search of a more telling line of dialogue or a more filmable incident to replace what Howard had written, the two of them were arguing over what should stay in and what had to go. In Howard, Selznick's irresistible force met its immovable object. To make his point the producer would charge around his office, a Juggernaut

"You can drop the moonlight and magnolia, Scarlett." (SBFA)

on the loose, gesticulating wildly and bumping into furniture, but Howard, planted firmly on the office couch, held his ground.

The going was very slow. To reduce the crowded canvas to more manageable numbers, several characters had to be eliminated altogether, but which? The ax fell upon, among others, all members of the O'Hara family not living under the same roof at Tara, and Scarlett's children from her first two marriages. Her child by Frank Kennedy was dropped as a compromise after Howard talked Selznick out of cutting Kennedy altogether. But Bonnie Blue, who was not in Howard's script, was restored to the picture. Selznick was unwilling to lose the tear-jerking potential of her scenes in the movie. Complaining about "the lack of variety and of invention in what Rhett does," Howard proposed writing some new sequences showing Rhett doing his stuff as a blockade runner. But Selznick kept him to the rule that no new scenes or new characters were to be added—"I urge that we abide by Miss Mitchell's failures as well as her successes."

Selznick asked Howard to write what he called "a night of love" for Scarlett and Rhett even though he knew it was unlikely that the Hays office would allow it to be shown on the screen. No such scene was ever filmed; Selznick settled for a shot of Rhett carrying Scarlett upstairs followed by a morning after shot of Scarlett in bed positively purring with satisfaction. Of course, if *Gone With the Wind* were to be filmed today, the camera would follow them into the bedroom and remain for the duration, but Selznick could only suggest the sex in the story, leaving the rest to the audience's imagination.

It was inevitable that their opposite and mutually incompatible natures would make prolonged collaboration difficult. Howard's insistence on punctuality was even harder for Selznick to take than his apparent immunity from browbeating. For once in his life Selznick was being forced to be on time; when he was not in his office at the appointed hour, the writer had a tendency to walk out and disappear until the following day.

After several nights the script sessions petered out, ostensibly because other productions claimed Selznick's attention, and to their mutual relief, Howard took the train back to New York. The script of *Gone With the Wind* was shelved, along with piles of notes and revisions, and for several months it was largely ignored, except for occasional moments when Selznick would pick at it in a desultory fashion, the way a man with no appetite picks at his food.

In October 1938, with the shooting date three months away, the need for a completed script began to press upon Selznick and he made fresh overtures to Sidney Howard, inviting him on a trip to Bermuda he was planning so that they could resume where they left off. Howard declined. "I have a cow with calf," he explained to Selznick. "I'm not about to leave at this time." Howard owned and managed a 700-acre cattle farm in Tyringham, Massachusetts, in the Berkshires. Two years had passed since he had accepted the Selznick assignment, and six months since they had last worked together in Hollywood. He felt he had completed the job as efficiently and conclusively as he had been allowed to do and Selznick had had his money's worth. Next, Selznick invited Margaret Mitchell, still hoping to be able to boast that every word spoken in the picture had been written by her, but she would have none of it. In the end, Selznick settled for Jo Swerling, a noted Hollywood script "fixer" and dialogue writer. Two weeks later, they were back in New York, with more reams of notes but with the script in no better shape than when they left. Selznick began casting around for yet another writer— "someone that will be easy to work with and that will be pliable" —with whom to finish the job. His choice was playwright Oliver H. P. Garrett, who demonstrated his pliability by agreeing to accompany Selznick to the West Coast and begin work on the train. Soon there was a Howard-Garrett script as well as a Howard script, but Selznick was still not satisfied. So another writer was added to the *Gone With the Wind* chain gang to rewrite Garrett's rewrite of Sidney Howard—F. Scott Fitzgerald.

Fitzgerald had been hired by M-G-M without much enthusiasm, remembered only dimly by some studio executives as the dashing literary figure of a decade before, and by others, including L. B. Mayer, not at all. He was put to work successively on *A Yank at Oxford, The Women, Infidelity*—which was retitled *Fidelity* in a vain attempt to secure the censor's approval—and *The Three Comrades.* Yet only for *Three Comrades* did he re-

ceive a screen credit, and even then the producer, Joe Mankiewicz, had secretly rewritten sections of the script. When Fitzgerald
read the final version, he erupted in a tormented letter of complaint—"Oh, Joe, can't producers ever be wrong? I'm a good
writer, honest. I thought you were going to play fair." (Years
later, Mankiewicz was to say in his own defense, "Scott's dialogue
was unspeakable. . . . I was considered a damn good writer for
dialogue . . . when I rewrote Scott's dialogue people thought I
was spitting on the flag.")

Then, in the fall of 1938, Fitzgerald confided to his daughter,
Scottie: "I am intensely busy. On the next two weeks, during
which I finish the first part of *Madame Curie*, depends whether
or not my contract will be renewed." In due course, Fitzgerald
handed in a screen version of the story in which the relationship
between Marie Skaldowska and Pierre Curie blossomed as their
work progressed; their love scenes were gentle moments of understanding in the laboratory. But this was not what Bernie Hyman,
the Metro executive in charge of the production, had been expecting. He had envisaged a romantic story with a high Hollywood
gloss and passionate encounters under the stars, so Fitzgerald was
taken off the project. His immediate reaction was to fire off a
telegram to Hyman: RESPECTFULLY SUGGEST THAT THE BEST WAY
TO GET $5,000 WORTH OF USE OUT OF MY CONTRACT IS TO ORDER A
1,200 WORD ORIGINAL FOR SOME SPECIAL ACTORS STOP I HAVE AN
IDEA FOR BEERY AND GARLAND AND COULD CERTAINLY PRODUCE A
COMEDY OF MANNERS FOR SOME YOUNG ACTRESS STOP AM AT YOUR
SERVICE OF COURSE BUT ORIGINAL IDEAS ARE PART OF MY STOCK IN
TRADE THAT YOU HAVEN'T YET TAPPED STOP. Metro's answer was an
envelope from the treasurer containing a standard studio notice
informing him that his soon-to-expire contract was not being
renewed.

Fitzgerald was a tragic misfit in the studio system. His alcoholic
bouts, his dated Brooks Brothers appearance, his inability to command the hypocritical deference that could have bought him
immunity, his deeply sensitive nature that, on the contrary,
prompted his aggrieved letters and telegrams of complaint, made
producers uncomfortable—which they were only supposed to

Scarlett uses chain-gang labor at the lumber mill.
Behind her are the man she loves (Ashley)
and the man she married (Frank). (FLAMINI)

make others—so that when his fate hung in the balance there was no reserve of goodwill working in his favor.

It was no consolation to him that *Madame Curie* proved to be the Lorelei for several other careers before it was finally completed. The picture dragged on for five years, plagued by production difficulties of all kinds; by the time it was released in December 1943, having taken longer to complete than the Curies' experiments leading to the discovery of radium—and at $1,400,000, having cost considerably more—Fitzgerald was already dead.

In the remaining weeks of Fitzgerald's contract Metro loaned him out to David Selznick to rewrite dialogue on a week-to-week basis at $1250 a week. As a teenager, Selznick had persuaded his brother, Myron, to commission the fashionable author of *The Great Gatsby* to write an original script for Elaine Hammerstein, the leading lady of their father's film company. The result was disappointing and the script was never produced, but the experience had kindled Fitzgerald's interest in the movies, first as an actor and later, more logically, as a writer. He had also kept in occasional contact with Selznick, making it a practice to send him an autographed copy of each new work as it appeared.

At Selznick-International, Fitzgerald was doubly removed from doing original work, for not only was he rewriting someone else, but he was expected to use Margaret Mitchell's prose to do it—as he later told Maxwell Perkins, his editor at Scribner's, "One had to thumb through it as if it were scripture and check out phrases of hers that would cover the situation"; yet he found the source material surprisingly good and usually more moving than the other screenwriters' rendition of it. "It is a good novel —not very original, in fact leaning heavily on *The Old Wive's Tale* and *Vanity Fair* and all that has been written on the Civil War," he wrote Scottie. "There are no new characters, new techniques, new observations—none of the elements that make literature—especially no new examination into human emotions. But on the other hand it is interesting, surprisingly honest, consistent and workmanlike throughout, and I felt no contempt for it but only a certain pity for those who consider it the supreme achievement of the human mind."

Fitzgerald's contribution to the script is more fairly judged by

what he took out of it than by what he put in; the most significant
of his changes to survive in the final version were his attempts
to make the drama quieter by chopping long passages of florid
dialogue. Selznick expected Fitzgerald to justify every deletion or
alteration in the margin of the script, and his most frequent
justification for making a change was "Trite and stagy." In place
of a long speech by Ashley to Scarlett describing the wretched
condition of the Confederate army, he substituted an eloquent
line from the novel: "When our shoes wear out—well, some of
the men are barefooted now and the snow is deep in Virginia,"
noting—"Is it news that the South fought without arms?" He
crossed out a long speech in which Ashley praises Scarlett's moral
fiber and commented: "It's dull and false for one character to
describe another." Yet another scene he revised was the moment
when the newly married Ashley and Melanie go upstairs to bed,
watched by Scarlett. The script called for a final round of "Good-
nights" from the couple as they pause at the top of the stairs.
Fitzgerald deleted their lines letting Scarlett watch them in
silent jealously as they disappeared from the scene: "It seems to
me stronger in silence," he wrote.

In three weeks he blue-penciled his way through much of the
first half of the script. Then his working relationship with Selznick came unstuck, virtually on the eve of the start of filming,
over the character of Aunt Pittypat. His version of how he was
dismissed—together with writer Donald Ogden Stewart, who was
also working on the picture—is enshrined in a lecture that he
wrote for Sheilah Graham:

George Cukor comes suddenly into Selznick's office. He looks
worried.

He says to Selznick, "Do I understand we start shooting tomorrow?" "Yes," says David. "But we're not ready," says Cukor, adding that he wants new scenes for Scarlett's arrival at Aunt Pitty's
in Atlanta. "Then we'll just have to work all night," Selznick
replies. One of his current authors on the picture (Fitzgerald)
groans and telephones his fiancée (Sheilah Graham) not to expect
him for dinner. The conference begins.

"What worries me," says George, "is the character of Aunt
Pitty."

"What's the matter with her?" says Selznick.

"She's supposed to be quaint," says Cukor, who is the brain behind the camera. "That's what it says in the book."

"That's what it says in the script too," says Selznick. He opens the script and reads: "Aunt Pitty bustles quaintly across the room."

"That's just what I mean," interrupts Cukor. "How can I photograph that? How do you bustle quaintly across the room? It may be funny when you read it, but it won't look like anything at all."

They argue about this for three long hours, and the two writers try desperately to *make* Aunt Pitty funny and not just *say* she's funny. Which are two different things.

By midnight, Cukor and Selznick fire one of the writers (Stuart). The other writer (Fitzgerald) is sent home and immediately a telegram is dispatched saying that he will not be needed any more.

Being fired from Selznick-International accelerated Fitzgerald's downward slide. His contract at Metro ended; jobs became scarcer and drinking bouts more frequent until, two years later, he was to die of a heart attack at the age of forty-four in the act of leafing through an alumni magazine from Princeton, his old college.

Selznick had another pressing problem besides the script; it was referred to within the organization as "the Cukor situation." In December, *The New York Times* reported that "a closely guarded battle" was in progress between Selznick and M-G-M over some important aspects of the production, including the choice of director. A few days later, the name of Victor Fleming, Clark Gable's motorcycling crony, floated to the surface in the Parsons column as the man expected to replace George Cukor when the main filming started. Despite Selznick's denials, and expressions of confidence in Cukor, the rumors of an impending change of directors persisted.

A combination of factors was at work here. Clark Gable had made no secret of his uneasiness about how his role would fare in the hands of George Cukor, the noted "woman's director," and Metro, with an eye on protecting its investment, was anxious to placate him. So Mayer's men had raised with Selznick the question of replacing Cukor with one of their own directors who had experience in handling Gable, such as Fleming, or Jack Conway. These overtures coincided with Selznick's own growing disenchantment with Cukor. The director's $4,000-a-week-plus contract with Selznick-International was to direct a number of pictures including, naturally, *Gone With the Wind*. He had worked intermittently on the preparation of *Gone With the Wind* but, to Selznick's irritation, had shown little inclination to undertake any of the other film projects offered him.

He turned down *A Star is Born*, saying he wasn't interested in making a picture about Hollywood (ironically, he was to direct the remake several years later), and refused to take over *Tom Sawyer* when Selznick fired director H. C. Potter, preferring, understandably, to direct Garbo in the Metro production of *Camille*. By the time he rejected *Intermezzo* the bloom was off their relationship and Selznick was saying "we can no longer be sentimental about it." But members of his staff sensed that Selznick was probably less concerned about the pictures Cukor had not wanted to direct than about the one he did, *Gone With the Wind*. Selznick had initially perceived it as a romantic drama, dominated by a strong woman's role, eminently suited to Cukor's particular bent as a filmmaker. But as the popularity of the novel grew to epic proportions, a grander vision took hold and he began to get cold feet about Cukor's ability to invest the picture with the scope he now wanted. Only his friendship with his protégé, plus the knowledge that he would be accommodating his father-in-law, prevented another head from rolling—for the time being at any rate.

He did take some precautions, cautioning his writers to bolster Rhett's part as a counter to Cukor's reputation of favoring actresses. "Look, don't let Scarlett romp all over Rhett Butler," he had told Scott Fitzgerald, "George will try to throw everything to her. You and I have got to watch out for Clark." He also instructed Hal Kern, his film editor, to stick close to Cukor at all times to prevent him from getting bogged down in detail and forgetting the larger dimensions of the picture. "Make him force the pace," he instructed Kern. "Don't let him slow down." Shooting began on January 26, marked by the raising of the Confed-

Between Takes

Evelyn Keyes studies the script and Ann Rutherford reads *Redbook* in their mobile dressing room. (FLAMINI)

While filming the delivery of Melanie's baby, Vivien Leigh and Olivia de Havilland posed for this photograph and sent it to Margaret Mitchell. Her husband, John Marsh, wrote back saying Olivia de Havilland looked exactly like Margaret Mitchell when she was writing the novel. (FLAMINI)

Clark Gable goes over the latest rewrite of Rhett's lines. (BA)

Susan Myrick with Clark Gable on the Atlanta set. "Ah cain't affoad a foah doah Fohd." (FLAMINI)

erate flag on the front lawn of Selznick-International by Mary Anderson, and Kern was dutifully stationed behind Cukor. As Cukor called "Action," Kern leaned forward and whispered "Tempo, George." "TEMPO," shouted the nervous director, "TEMPO, TEMPO."

The first scene shot was the opening sequence of the picture— Scarlett on the porch at Tara with the Tarleton twins, played by two young Hollywood newcomers, Fred Crane and George Reeves, who was later to make a name for himself as the screen's Superman. As for Milton Vaughn, the New York elevator boy, Selznick had had second thoughts about him and he was back at his old job at the Savoy Plaza.

Margaret Mitchell once wrote that she had imagined Tara as "an ugly, sprawling habitation built with no architectural plan and growing as the need for growth arose." The handsome facade of white-washed brick erected on the Selznick lot hardly conformed to that notion, but neither was it the overblown palace the producer originally had in mind. At Margaret Mitchell's urging, Susan Myrick had succeeded in persuading Selznick to tone it down; he refused to part with the columns on the front porch, but agreed to make them square, in the authentic Southern style, instead of Hollywood Corinthian. Later, Selznick sent the author his designs for Twelve Oaks and she roared with laughter at its unrestrained splendor. Again Susan Myrick went to work on her behalf, arguing that Southerners would find it ridiculous. "No they won't, Susan," he replied. "They'll say it's just like the mansion my grandpappy had that Sherman burned."

The grounds in front of Selznick's Tara were studded with massive oaks and cedars built from bark and plaster; fresh leaves had to be wired onto the branches every day during filming. Dozens of magnolia trees and apple trees were bought and transplanted, and wax-cloth blossoms attached to the apple trees, which don't blossom in California. Tons of red earth were imported in boxcars from Arizona and shoveled liberally onto the back lot, and for weeks the ears, eyes and nostrils of everyone at the studio were caked with it.

The script of the Tara sequence called for Negro slaves picking cotton and singing in the background (Selznick had hired the

Hall Johnson Choir as singing cotton pickers), little black children chasing turkeys down the drive, baying hounds, and a veritable traffic jam of horses, carriages and farm wagons. The propman's list for the scene read as follows:

> 1 superb hunter
> 1 hunter
> 1 horse for O'Hara
> Flock of turkeys
> 4 dogs
> 4 farm wagons with teams
> Carriage and horses for Ellen O'Hara
> Family carriage and horses

But Susan Myrick pointed out to Selznick that the imminence of the outbreak of war established the time as mid-April, which was planting time not picking time on the plantation; moreover, the drive of Tara was not likely to be overrun with turkeys. When George Cukor filmed the opening shot for which the script direction read: "FADE IN: FRONT OF TARA: LONG SHOT" the turkeys had been replaced by peacocks.

It was a crisp, cool, sunny morning, but the set was drenched in the heat of powerful arc lamps—6400 candles left, front: 7000 candles (behind the camera), and 2400 right. The opening shot was followed by three takes of Scarlett running down the driveway to meet Gerald O'Hara; Cukor ordered the third take printed. Next, the camera was set up closer to the house to film Scarlett complaining about the talk of war and flirting with the twins. Scarlett's opening speech—"Fiddle-dee-dee! War, war, war. This war talk's spoiling the fun at every party"—had an ominous echo. On the same day that it was shot, movie industry stocks registered drops on the New York stock exchange due to eroding foreign markets; Universal was down eight points, Paramount preferred four-and-a half, and Loews one. Hollywood could no longer remain oblivious to Europe's gathering storm. In Italy the Fascist regime had forced the studios out of business by revoking their distributors' licenses. Metro was the only studio still releasing films in Germany and German-occupied eastern Europe, but it was now considered a matter of time before it, too, would have

Overleaf Making whiskey in Shantytown. (FLAMINI)

to stop operating. Though the Communist-infiltrated Anti-Nazi League had fallen into disrepute, anti-Nazi sentiments now had the studios' endorsement. Warner employees found in their pay envelopes an English translation of a German pamphlet *Defilement of Race* with an explanatory foreword by Harry Warner (Jack's brother) calling it "almost a text book for those who follow the appalling philosophy of Nazism."

A sea mist drifted inland and drove the company indoors onto Stage Sixteen to shoot the corset-lacing scene bitterly familiar to hundreds of unsuccessful Scarletts. But the set of Scarlett's bedroom was not finished, and while carpenters raced to complete it Menzies ran all over the place giving directions and occasionally squinting through the camera, and cinematographer Lee Garmes conjured up a window frame to cast a decorative shadow over Scarlett's four-poster bed, shouting instructions to "kill that broad" (a broad is studio slang for a heavy arc light) ; Walter Plunkett danced around the edgy Cukor, desperately trying to consult him about a new costume design—while Kern followed watchfully behind. Vivien Leigh swept into this maelstrom of activity wearing a green quilted bathrobe which she took off to reveal frilled pantaloons. "Action," shouted Cukor . . . "Tempo," whispered Kern. But as Hattie McDaniel began to heave at the strings of Scarlett's corset, Cukor shouted "Cut." Then he said; "Will the visitors please leave the set? We can't work in this confusion." Two men slunk sheepishly out—a reporter from *The New York Times* and an accompanying member of Russell Birdwell's publicity staff.

Cukor's outburst did not come as a surprise, for he was given to displays of waspish temperament on the set. Filming was eventually resumed and Cukor stationed himself beside the cameras, silently making forceful gestures with his fist as if trying to draw a good performance out of the actors by his own physical effort.

Eric Stacey and Ridgeway Callow, the first and second assistants respectively, were a legend of efficiency in Hollywood. Stacey was a tall, unflappable Cornishman who always wore a hat: his main worry was not the filming of *Gone With the Wind* but the fact that he was slowly going bald. Any other missing member of the production could usually be traced to Stage Thirteen, the Washington Boulevard saloon that was considered almost an extension of Selznick-International by studio employees. But when Stacey had to be run to earth he was just as likely to be at the scalp specialist who, for reasons that were lost in the studio's history, had an office on the lot. Stacey was superstitious about tying up his shoelaces until the first shot of the day had been filmed, which meant that he sometimes had to flop around with untied shoes until five in the afternoon. Callow was a small, harassed-looking man with a large red face, a spreading midriff and the gravelly voice of a buck-sergeant, which he used to good effect to marshal Confederate soldiers, slaves, guests at the Atlanta Bazaar, and renegades in Shantytown. Their manifold responsibilities ranged from hiring extras by the hundreds to keeping a record of the menstrual cycles of the leading actresses on the picture so as to know when to leave them out of the shooting schedule; a veteran assistant director used to rattle off the menstrual dates of every female star at M-G-M as a party act. The normal time off allowed was one or two days, depending on the status of the star. A few stars actually got three days. When Stacey quietly arranged for Vivien Leigh to have two days off, even though she was a newcomer, Joan Fontaine, who was about to start filming *Rebecca*—her first important role—heard about it and said, "If Vivien gets two days, so do I."

Cukor continued to work his way through more of the "seemingly small amount of final revised script" Selznick had described in his letter to Whitney, including the scene in which Scarlett delivers Melanie's baby during the seige of Atlanta (which contains one of the picture's few comic concessions in Prissy's singing of "Jes' a Few Mo' Days, ter Tote de Wee-ry Load"), and the shooting of the Union deserter, bent on looting and probably rape, at Tara. On the director's instructions, Olivia de Havilland prepared for the birth scene by spending several hours in the delivery room of Los Angeles County Hospital, dressed as a nurse to avoid recognition, and duly reported to him that labor pains were "not continuous but came in waves." When the scene was filmed, Cukor gripped her right ankle under the bedclothes, out of camera range, and gave it a sharp twist each time he wanted to cue in a cluster of labor pains. All went smoothly up to the point when Scarlett slaps Prissy, who has confessed to knowing nothing about "birthin' babies." Vivien Leigh's slaps left nothing to the imagination—especially the recipient's—and Butterfly McQueen broke into tears of pain and indignation. "I can't do it, she's hurting me, she's hurting me. I'm no stunt man, I'm an actress." Cukor exploded at the interruption; an actress would have continued, no matter what, he shouted. The scene stopped only when he, the director, said so. But the diminutive black actress walked off the set and refused to return until Vivien Leigh had apologized.

Butterfly McQueen differed from the other black members of the cast in more respects than her occasional flashes of temperament. Years of living in New York had eradicated her Southern Negro accent and she had to be coached in her lines by Hattie McDaniel. Between takes she would sit in a corner of the set reading *Esquire* magazine. "Why do you read that, Butterfly?" she was once asked, for this was the *Esquire* of pin-up centerfolds and bachelor living. "I like to look at the filthy pictures," she squeaked.

Early in the filming, a delegation of minor black actors and extras protested to Eric Stacey that some of the lavatories on the back lot bore freshly painted notices saying WHITES, while others said COLOREDS. They threatened to walk off the production unless the signs were removed. Stacey said the notices were the work of a studio carpenter acting on his own initiative and immediately had them taken down. "If you want to get white crabs, go ahead," he told them. The movie industry was a caste-conscious industry in which bit players refused to fraternize with extras, and "dress" extras, who wore their own evening clothes and were paid at a higher rate, would not sit down to eat with ordinary extras. It was not an atmosphere to foster good race relations.

When the killing of the deserter was filmed, a large crowd lurked in the shadows behind the arc lamps on Stage Sixteen. The attraction was neither Vivien Leigh nor the deserter, Paul Hurst, a gorilla of a character actor with a long list of villainous screen credits as gangsters, outlaws, jailbirds, and the like, stretching back to the early days of movies. The crowd was there because word had spread on the studio grapevine that Olivia de

Havilland wore very little underneath the nightgown she was about to slip off in the scene to cover the dead soldier. When the moment came, however, there was an audible sigh of disappointment; Olivia, in a blouse and slacks rolled up to the knee, couldn't have been more covered.

11

The Cukor Situation
Resolved

David Selznick agreed to shoot *Gone With the Wind* in Technicolor for two reasons. Firstly, there was the obligation, assumed from Jock Whitney's Pioneer Pictures, to produce a number of his movies in the new process in return for Technicolor stock options at a specially discounted rate. He had persuaded the Technicolor Corporation to consider *Gone With the Wind* as two movies if it ran over 150 minutes in length (or about one and a half times as long as the average Hollywood production), entitling him to double the number of shares—an added incentive for making a long picture, but one which he tended to keep quiet about. When *Gone With the Wind* was completed, Selznick was to collect 15,000 Technicolor stock options at $3 a share when the going market rate was $11.

Secondly, because of that obligation Selznick had already made and released three feature films in Technicolor and had been converted to a belief in its general effectiveness. Most other producers still regarded it as a costly gimmick that was never likely to challenge the primacy of black-and-white movies; but then, ten years earlier the same producers had written off sound film as a fad.

The process in question was "three strip" Technicolor ("one strip" or Monopack Technicolor was not introduced until several years later), whereby the picture was shot on three negatives running side by side behind green, blue, and red filters respectively; the negatives were converted into a single matrix or master print, from which copies could be made for release to movie theaters. The "three strip" system was shrouded in secrecy because it had still to be patented, and Technicolor took the precaution of never showing outsiders around their entire laboratory in Rochester, New York.

Besides processing the film, Technicolor also owned the cumbersome four-hundred-pound cameras that were rented out to production companies, together with the lenses and the film magazines, for a flat fee of $200 a week each. But the standard Technicolor contract in those early days also required the production company to engage a Technicolor cameraman and an assistant to act as "technical advisers" to the black-and-white cinematographer. Lee Garmes and his camera operator had Technicolor's Paul Hill (later replaced by Ray Rennahan) and *his* assistant to advise them on camera angles, filters, lighting—Technicolor film required almost twice as much lighting as black-and-white to illuminate a scene—and the other mysteries of the new technique of color cinematography. Garmes didn't think the new technique was all that different from the old technique he had been practicing with considerable distinction for twenty years, and the atmosphere around the camera was decidely frosty, particularly when the Technicolor cinematographer, who had no authority to impose his will on the black-and-white cinematographer, would produce his notebook and record that Garmes had rejected his advice on a specific shot, thereby exculpating Technicolor from responsibility for the outcome. Equally irritating to Garmes was the sight of the Technicolor technicians carrying off the cameras for servicing at the end of each day's filming, and bringing them back the following morning.

For an additional $1000 a week, Selznick obtained the compulsory services of Natalie Kalmus, wife of Technicolor's inventor, as color consultant and gratuitous extra headache. Natalie Kalmus had power of veto over any color scheme she felt would not be compatible with color cinematography; she was able to throw out costumes, pieces of furniture, and even whole sets which, in her judgment, would reproduce poorly on the screen. It was true that some colors and fabrics did reproduce poorly— for example, yellow and turquoise tended to look smudged, and so, in a strong light, did purple and violet; reflected light darkened woolens and velvets and lightened the color of silks. But Natalie Kalmus was frequently suspected of confusing personal taste with the exigencies of the Technicolor system; what she didn't like she claimed the camera wouldn't like either. For many Hollywood producers, she was a strong argument in favor of sticking to black-and-white film.

Anticipating the worst, Selznick appointed Bill Menzies "arbiter of all differences of opinion" between his team of designers and Natalie Kalmus. But this did not prevent endless clashes with Platt, Plunkett, Lyle Wheeler, and even Menzies himself, who was occasionally driven to the point of forgetting his role as referee. These engagements usually ended in a compromise, as in the battle of the mulberry walls. Platt had designed mulberry wallpaper which was to be seen briefly through an open door at Twelve Oaks, during the barbecue scene. But Natalie Kalmus decreed: no mulberry, it was too close to the men's beige coats, and they would merge with the background. By filming color tests, Platt proved conclusively that she was wrong, but Natalie Kalmus could dig herself in deeper than a groundhog, and she refused to capitulate. Menzies intervened and finally they accepted his compromise—the walls were painted a pink-hued khaki.

On the first day of production, a hitch developed in the lighting and shooting was held up; Vivien Leigh went over to Stacey and asked him, "What are they fucking around for?" By the end of the first week, the young English newcomer had emerged as a formidable presence on the set of *Gone With the Wind*. She was cool, poised, and meticulously professional. The men admired her but recoiled from her directness and her profanity. (Hollywood believed sufficiently in its own myth to find the combination of exquisite beauty and colorful language shocking.) The women envied her. Olivia de Havilland, who needed ten minutes' contemplation before a mirror in her costume and demure hairstyle—the one Howard Hughes so disliked—in order to enter her role, wondered at Vivien's ability to snap on and off as if by flicking a switch; when "action" was called, she would continue her conversation in whispers on the set for a few seconds longer and then turn into the scene, completely in character.

The younger girls, such as Evelyn Keyes, watched her from a distance, playing the scenes with a firm touch that never faltered and winning arguments with the director and producer, not by means of feminine guile or her status as the star, but through sheer confidence in, and knowledge of, her craft; they saw her and Olivier being lionized at parties and being described as "Hollywood's most romantic couple" by adoring gossip columnists, even though the couple were living under the same roof in open defiance of the movie town's facade of propriety. And they realized that, unlike the gods and goddesses born out

Overleaf Ashley returns home wounded after the punitive raid on Shantytown, to find Union soldiers waiting. (FLAMINI)

of the fantasies, typewriters, and cameras of the studio publicity men, Vivien Leigh—in the words of Evelyn Keyes to her mother in Atlanta—"knew who she was."

But Vivien Leigh was not completely immune from studio pressure. One morning she arrived on the set cursing Hollywood's moral hypocrisy. Selznick was insisting that Olivier move out of the house they were renting in Beverly Hills because they were causing a scandal. When Vivien replied that surely her private life was her own business, Selznick set her right. The "moral turpitude" clause in the contract she had signed extended his authority to her off-screen activities as well. So Olivier moved out of their house and in with Leslie Howard, who happened to be in the same situation, but was able to be more circumspect because the woman with whom he was living was not a celebrity. Behind his soulful screen image, Howard was a tireless ladies' man; his current companion was Violette Cunningham, an attractive English redhead he introduced as his "secretary." Though the description fooled nobody it did keep up appearances, and she was able to accompany him to the set every day without complaint from Selznick—who had barred Olivier, arguing that his presence would be too distracting for Vivien Leigh. Eventually, Violette Cunningham was to accompany Howard to England at the outbreak of the war and would be killed in the London blitz.

At the end of the first week, a large mobile dressing room was towed onto the Selznick lot, heralding the arrival of Clark Gable to start work on *Gone With the Wind*. It was uncompromisingly masculine—the captain's cabin or the big game hunter's lodge. It had knotted-pine walls, and a knotted-pine dressing table; the only other articles of furniture were a deep club sofa and arm chair in red leather. Two heavy brass ashtrays and two English hunting prints of men in pink coats with baying hounds were fastened to the wall. There was a built-in clothes closet and a bookshelf containing five or six books, including *Chicago*—autographed by its author, Maurice Watkins—*The Parnell Movement, with a sketch of Irish Parties from 1843* (*Parnell* was one of Gable's few box-office failures), and a well-thumbed copy of *Gone With the Wind*. Gable always did his homework.

Very early on the morning he was due to report for work,

Gable was awakened by a motorcycle messenger delivering a voluminous memo from Selznick containing the producer's thoughts on the character of Rhett Butler. Gable barely had time to digest its contents before it was time to drive to the studio, where he was joined by his regular retinue: Stanley Campbell, his make-up man; Lew Smith, his stand-in, who a few years later was to die in a shooting incident in a bar close to Metro called the Retake Room; and Ward Bond, for whom Gable frequently found parts in his movies. In *Gone With the Wind,* Bond played the Yankee captain who pursues Rhett and Ashley to Aunt Pittypat's house after the raid on Shantytown.

Anticipating his belligerent mood, Carole Lombard had festooned his dressing-room mirror with stuffed cloth doves of peace. On the dressing table was a gift-wrapped package from her which he found to contain a knitted genitalia warmer and a note which said: "Don't let it get cold. Bring it home hot for me." Gable was, of course, delighted, and spent the rest of the day showing off Lombard's gift.

They filmed Rhett's visit to Scarlett at Aunt Pittypat's Peachtree Street house with the gift of a Paris hat, and then began work on the elaborate staging of the Atlanta Bazaar sequence. The recently widowed Scarlett, all in black, is surrounded by color—the Old Armory festooned with red and blue Confederate flags, the men in their uniforms, and the girls in their finery. Scarlett's appearance in the Bazaar scene wearing a street bonnet is probably the only eccentric costume touch in the whole picture. Susan Myrick and Plunkett tried hard to make Selznick see the absurdity of it, but he would not be persuaded. He felt it helped to underline the contrast between Scarlett's widowed state and her frivolous behavior. Selznick could be as obsessive about costumes as he could about anything else. He wanted to open the siesta scene at the Twelve Oaks barbecue with a pan shot of the girls' dresses standing stiffly against the wall "like headless dummies," as he wrote in the script, somehow believing that the whalebones in the bodice and the wire hoops in the skirts would hold the dresses up. When Susan Myrick tried to tell him that the dresses simply sank flat, he argued with her through a score of memos before finally giving up.

Overleaf To account for their whereabouts, Rhett tells the Yankee captain (Ward Bond) that he and Ashley had spent the evening at Belle Watling's. (PRATT)

The Bazaar scene is more than a festive interlude before the explosion of war in Atlanta, for it establishes Scarlett and Rhett's growing, if reluctant, mutual attraction. Scarlett's dramatic offer of her wedding ring as a contribution to "The Cause," imitating Melanie's example, prompts Rhett's sardonic remark: "I know how much that meant to *you*." Yet when the women take part in a $10-a-dance auction, again for "The Cause," Rhett reveals the ambivalence of his feelings—a combination of contempt and desire—by bidding $150 for Scarlett. A scandalized silence greets his bid, but Scarlett swirls defiantly away in Rhett's arms. Any prospect of a deepening relationship is soon snuffed out; when Rhett airily professes to be gun-running for profit, Scarlett is furious—ostensibly at his lack of patriotic fervor, but actually at his refusal to assume the role of the hero she is seeking to replace the married Ashley.

Cukor had embellished the scene with a defiant speech he had written for Melanie on the justness of the Southern cause. It had echoes of La Pasionaria—Dolores Ibarruri, one of the Communist leaders in the Spanish Civil War and a heroine of the intellectual left—and was evidently intended as Cukor's tribute to her and her cause. Suddenly confronted with this unauthorized vignette in the day's rushes, Selznick was furious. He had complained to the director on more than one occasion about rewriting the script on the set, to which the director's defense was always that the cast had found the script, as written, unplayable. In the heated confrontation that followed, Selznick announced that henceforth he expected to see a run-through of each major scene on the set before it was filmed, in order, as he put it, "to avoid projection room surprises." Cukor objected fiercely to what he regarded as a breach of trust. But Selznick now began hanging around the set, butting in with ideas about camera angles, suggestions about lighting, and helpful hints to the actors.

The truth was that Cukor's skill in selecting small and telling details to convey a sense of developing relationship was working against him. As he viewed the daily footage, Selznick would complain to his associates that he was reluctantly coming around to L. B. Mayer's view that Cukor was too preoccupied with intimate nuances to handle the broad sweep of the picture, and therefore a change of director ought to be given serious consideration. This was quite possibly a premature judgment, considering the small amount of film completed, but that was precisely one of the objections to George Cukor—after two weeks of filming, he was several days behind schedule.

While Selznick procrastinated, Clark Gable's misgivings about working with Cukor were being rapidly confirmed. He could find little common ground with this fussy, gossipy little man of great sensitivity and sophistication, and he was suspicious and resentful of the director's closeness to Vivien Leigh; the two of them had become firm friends, and Gable, rightly or wrongly, felt that Cukor was favoring Scarlett at Rhett's expense. The director didn't help matters much by addressing him as "darling," nor by insisting on a more pronounced Southern accent. Gable was equally insistent in refusing to attempt one, until in the end Selznick intervened on Gable's side. Accustomed to the vigorous shooting pace of "action" directors like Fleming, the star found Cukor's more leisurely rate of progress unnerving and hard to adjust to.

But it wasn't only the director that bothered Gable. Because he was a slow study, the absence of a finished script made him nervous; when Selznick sent revised pages for the next day's scenes by messenger in the middle of the night—which was often— Gable arrived on the set in a torment of uncertainty over his lines. (His morale was not helped by Vivien Leigh's deserved reputation as a quick study.) Interrupted by the director in the middle of a speech, he was unable to pick up where he left off, and had to start again from the beginning. Metro directors knew these things and afforded him the protection he felt he was not getting from George Cukor.

There was also the trouble with his costumes. The clothes made by Plunkett's wardrobe department were a poor fit. Gable complained to Selznick, who agreed to have a new Rhett Butler wardrobe made by Eddie Schmidt, the star's own Beverly Hills tailor. Schmidt quickly produced new versions of Gable's principal costumes, refurbishing the 1860s style with the contemporary touch of wide, padded shoulders.

Gable never complained about George Cukor; he simply

Overleaf   Melanie thanks Belle Watling for providing
her husband with an alibi. (PRATT)

stopped reporting for work. On his second day away from the set Russell Birdwell spotting him leaving Metro in his Dusenberg roadster and asked him why he did not return. "I feel very uncomfortable with George," Gable replied. "That's it." Five days later, the possibilities for shooting around the absent Gable were exhausted; a rumor circulated in the industry that Metro had pulled him out of the picture and the production itself was on the brink of cancellation, and this seemed to Selznick, helped by a very strong suspicion as to the origin of the rumors, to mark the last possible moment for final and decisive action. He talked to Jock Whitney, whose reply was, "Use your own judgment." Then he held a flurry of consultations with his senior staff to hear their view, with Ben Thau and Eddie Mannix at Metro to determine which directors would be available to step into the breach, and with his brother, Myron, and Irene for moral support.

One afternoon, a Selznick secretary came across George Cukor on the set and told him she was getting married. His reaction was typical—"You need a new hair style for your wedding," he said, and immediately telephoned Greta Garbo, Katharine Hepburn, and Joan Crawford to learn the name of the leading Hollywood hairdresser. The answer came back: Sidney Guilaroff. So Cukor called Guilaroff for an appointment and the secretary went to the hairdresser of the stars. Touched, she was on the verge of blurting out a warning, for Cukor, inexplicably, appeared oblivious to the storm scudding down on him. It seems inconceivable that he was unaware of the negotiations and meetings that were taking place over "the Cukor situation," but he gave no sign of it. It is possible that he felt sufficiently secure in Selznick's friendship to discount the possibility of being fired by him; or perhaps he had come to look upon his removal as inevitable, and was resigned to it.

On Monday morning, February 13, nineteen days after the main filming had begun, and nearly two and a half years after he was first signed to direct the picture, Cukor was formally dismissed. Uncertain how he would react and anxious to avoid a scene with his friend and protégé, Selznick dispatched general manager Henry Ginsberg to the set as his executioner. The efficient Ginsberg made a quick, clean job of it; his meeting with

Cukor, in a small office adjoining the set, lasted less than half an hour.

When word reached Vivien Leigh and Olivia de Havilland that this was to be Cukor's last day on the picture, they immediately sought him out in a panic; could it possibly be true? "Yes, I think so," Cukor replied. Still in widows' weeds from the Atlanta Bazaar scene, the two actresses descended like the Furies on Selznick's office. They had an identical investment in Cukor: he had shaped their conception of the character that each was playing, and without his continued guidance they would be ships without a compass. When they entered, Selznick got up from his desk and instinctively backed into the window seat behind it. For nearly three hours the two actresses begged, cajoled, and bullied him to reverse his decision; without Cukor they would be adrift, they pleaded tearfully; already they could feel the characters slipping from their grasp. The entire movie would be adrift.

Outwardly, the producer was sympathetic, but noncommital; to himself (as he later told one of his executives), he was thinking that if Vivien and Olivia were half as impressive on the screen as they had been in pleading Cukor's case in his office, *Gone With the Wind* was going to be a winner no matter who directed it. Having succeeded in calming them down with assurances that he would act only in their best interests, Selznick finally persuaded them to return to the set . . . where they worked the remainder of the afternoon. Both women probably realized that, aside from quitting the production and risking harsh legal consequences, they were powerless to do more than put up a token resistance. "He was my last hope of ever enjoying the picture," Vivien Leigh wrote her husband gloomily. Lesser lights also felt the loss; "The beginning of the end, I fear," Evelyn Keyes wrote her mother. "Cukor was the only man to direct the picture." These misgivings were understandable, since it was evident that Cukor's replacement, when he was named, would be Clark Gable's choice.

Selznick and Cukor issued a joint statement saying that "as a result of a series of diasgreements between us over many of the individual scenes of *Gone With the Wind* we have mutually de-

Vivien Leigh, Leslie Howard, Laura Hope Crews, and
Olivia de Havilland listen as Victor Fleming describes
how the last bottle from Aunt Pittypat's wine cellar is to
be poured and drunk. (FLAMINI)

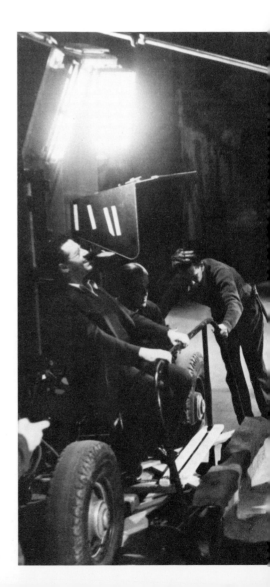

The Directors

An exuberant George Cukor directing Clark Gable and Vivien Leigh in the Atlanta Charity Bazaar scene. (FLAMINI)

cided that the only solution is for a new director to be selected at as early a date as is practicable." Reached by Louella Parsons for comment, Selznick said smoothly: "There's been no formal difficulty with George. It's just that we don't see individual scenes the same way."

Later that day, Susan Myrick dutifully reported Cukor's version of his demise to Margaret Mitchell. "George finally told me all about it," she wrote. "I told him, when I had a chance, that I was terribly upset over what I had heard and he invited me to come in and talk with him. . . . For days, he said, he has looked at the takes and felt he was failing. He knew he was a good director and knew the actors were good ones; yet, the thing did not click as it should. Gradually he has become more and more convinced that the script is the trouble. He has continually taken the scripts from day to day, compared the Garrett-Selznick version with the Sidney Howard version, groaned and tried to change some parts back to the Howard script, but he seldom could make a scene that pleased him."

Referring to the final confontation that had taken place on the weekend between the director and Selznick, she said, "George told Selznick he would not work any longer if the script was not better and he wanted the Howard script back. David told George he was a director not an author and he [David] was the best judge of whether a script was right or not. And George said he was a director and a damned good one and would not let his name go out over a lousy picture." Selznick's reply was, "Then get out."

Cukor was crushed, but he put on a philosophical, even humorous, front. Remembering Marsha Hunt, the girl who was Melanie for a day, he sent her a whimsical telegram saying that now they were both evacuees from *Gone With the Wind*. His favorite retort to questioners was that Selznick had threatened to sue him for spreading alarm and despondency if he talked about the production, and in due course silence over the affair was to become almost an obsession with the director. Invariably, he would insist that he never really knew the reason why Selznick had him replaced; thirty years later, replying to a letter from Joan Bennett reminding him that he directed her Scarlett test, he was to say that he had blanked the whole thing out of his memory.

Keeping his head and his counsel helped Cukor keep Selznick's friendship, and the producer prevailed upon his father-in-law to assign him the direction of a movie tailor-made to his talents, as Hollywood saw them. *The Women,* based on Clare Booth's malevolent Broadway hit, had a cast of 135 women (including Norma Shearer, Joan Crawford, Rosalind Russell, and Paulette Goddard) , and no men; thus Cukor, who was fired from *Gone With the Wind* (largely at M-G-M's instigation) , was hired by M-G-M to direct *The Women,* from which Ernst Lubitsch had been dismissed in the preparatory stages (and F. Scott Fitzgerald before that) , while Lubitsch took over *Ninotchka*—and the wheels of Hollywood went grinding on. Yet though Selznick and Cukor remained close friends, the director never made another Selznick picture.

Jock Hay Whitney called for the accounts; after less than three weeks of filming the picture had cost $800,000, and Ernest Scanlon, the accountant at Selznick-International, estimated that it would exceed its $2.5 million budget by at least a quarter of a million. Rumors still persisted that the production would be abandoned, or at the very least, that M-G-M would insist that Vivien Leigh be replaced by a star with box-office pull. Hollywood's general attitude toward the entire project was conveyed to Selznick in the Academy Award voting that year. He had campaigned hard to win the Irving Thalberg award—a sort of producer's Oscar, established as part of Thalberg's canonization by the industry— but with Cukor fired and the production suspended, the industry was hardly disposed to honor him as a worthy successor to Metro's boy wonder. Selznick's name wasn't even in the top five in the final ballot, and the award went to Hal Wallis. Selznick received another blow to his ego in the shape of Bette Davis's Academy Award for her performance in *Jezebel*; while the fate of the unfinished original hung in the balance, Jack Warner's imitation was making a killing.

As a first step toward refloating his water-logged production, Selznick handed Clark Gable a list of available Metro directors from which to pick George Cukor's replacement. They included Robert Z. Leonard, Jack Conway, and Victor Fleming. Without hesitation, Gable chose Fleming. Then he dashed out to Malibu and roused the director from his bed—it was well after midnight—to deliver the good news. Nothing doing, Fleming replied; for one thing, he was still at work on *The Wizard of Oz,* and anyway, who would want to become involved with *that* white elephant? But Gable knew his man, and he knew that he wanted to be persuaded; he sat on the edge of the bed drinking and appealing for help in the name of their great friendship, until at last Fleming agreed to discuss the assignment with Selznick in the morning.

When Fleming saw the completed footage of *Gone With the Wind* he uttered his now famous criticism: "David, your fucking script is no fucking good." Fleming liked to come across as a man who didn't pull his punches. By now, the script was a flourishing jungle in which revisions, and revisions of revisions, proliferated. After Howard, Garrett, Fitzgerald, and Stewart, the mounting list of casualties fired by Selznick—sometimes after only a morning's work—included screenwriters John Balderston (who had also written *Prisoner of Zenda* for Selznick), Michael Foster, and Winston Miller, and playwrights John Van Druten and Edwin Justus Mayer. In the process, the jungle had developed an exotic foliage of different colored pages, for it was Selznick who introduced the practice—still in common use today—of using colors to distinguish one rewrite from another. Fleming didn't think it added up to a filmable scenario, and insisted on a complete overhaul by a capable writer as his condition for taking over.

Fleming was on the *Wizard of Oz* set when a Selznick executive arrived to say Metro had given its blessing to his immediate release to direct *Gone With the Wind.* The executive was confronted with an astonishing sight: Fleming was directing one of the Munchkin sequences; 116 dwarfs, midgets, and manikins, including perhaps the only twenty-six midget vocalists in the country, swarmed all over the set in Munchkin costume, reducing it to chaos. On an earlier occasion, hundreds of feet of film were ruined when instead of "Ding dong, the witch is dead" they had sung "Ding dong, the bitch is dead, which old bitch, the wicked old bitch," and no one had noticed until the sequence was half over. That was mild compared to some of their other exploits. The studio had put them up in a Culver City hotel, which they were rapidly wrecking. The morning of the executive's visit, filming had had to be suspended when one of the leading Munchkins was found dead drunk in a urinal in the men's lavatory, and now Munchkins were milling around Fleming protesting some grievance. And yet as he shook hands with Selznick's man under a mass of full-sized trees suspended on hydraulics, waiting to be dropped into position, Fleming had a sense of going from the frying pan into a very hot fire. "My god, imagine picking up a project like that at this stage," he remarked. "Still, if Clark's going to sulk I guess I'd better do it."

Clark was no longer sulking when he treated Fleming to a celebration lunch in the Metro commissary, together with writer John Lee Mahin, L. B. Mayer's choice to work with Selznick and Fleming on rewriting the script. On the contrary, he was in high spirits as he toasted "their" production with a bottle of Coke. (The Metro Commissary was dry.)

After working with Selznick and Fleming for two or three nights, Mahin received a summons from L. B. Mayer. "What's going on, John?" Mayer wanted to know. "Is he (Selznick) in trouble?" Well, Mahin reported, the script needed reshaping, but the damage was not irreparable. "I don't know," said Mayer doubtfully. "I hear it's going to be awful long." Mahin replied that at the current script length, it would run about four hours. "They'd stone Christ if he came back and spoke for four hours," Mayer protested. The aphorism pleased him and became his standard remark—and of course, was dutifully propagated by his executives—whenever the length of *Gone With the Wind* was mentioned thereafter.

More than two years had elapsed since the late spring afternoon when Kate Corbaly narrated to Mayer the story of *Gone With the Wind,* but it had remained implanted in his memory. As he witnessed the enviable publicity building up around his son-in-law's unmade picture, he would sometimes remark that, if it had not been for Thalberg's opposition, the novel would

Overleaf Rhett consoles Scarlett after the funeral of her husband Frank Kennedy. (PRATT)

by now be on the screen—made by Metro. Mayer told John Lee Mahin how he wanted the story to go, and instructed him to write a happy ending, one in which Scarlett and Rhett were reconciled. The studio head also said he was thinking of giving the role of Scarlett to a Metro screen queen; having survived one attempted removal by Mayer, from *A Yank at Oxford,* Vivien Leigh now faced another from *Gone With the Wind.*

But Mayer's attempt to "annex" the production through his infiltrators, Fleming and Mahin, sustained a total and unmitigated defeat. Selznick was alerted to the danger by a story in *The Hollywood Reporter* which disclosed Mahin's meeting with Mayer to "rescue" his son-in-law's picture. A reporter from the trade paper had spotted Mahin leaving Mayer's office after their meeting and asked him if they had discussed *Gone With the Wind*; they had, Mahin admitted. "Is anything wrong?" pressed the reporter. Just some rewriting on the script, Mahin replied. When Mahin protested that he had been misquoted, Selznick had Russell Birdwell call him posing as a newspaper reporter and try to trap him by asking leading questions ("I guess you're going to have quite a job to patch up David Selznick's script"), while Selznick listened in on an extension. Mahin avoided the traps, but by now any hint of Metro pressure was a red flag to Selznick; he charged over to Fleming and demanded Mahin's withdrawal. His argument was full of *ad hominem* complaints, but the man in question was not Mahin; the man he was getting at was L. B. Mayer.

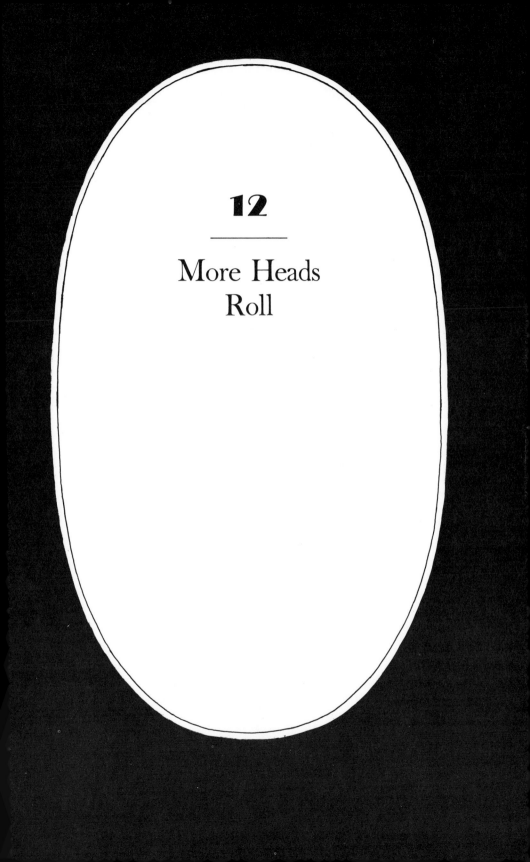

12

More Heads
Roll

At this point Selznick turned to Ben Hecht, whom he ranked with Sidney Howard as one of the two best freelance writers in the business. With his frequent partner Charles MacArthur, Hecht had written such Broadway hits as *The Front Page,* until he discovered that writing movies was more lucrative. His reputation for speed was enshrined in legends of impressive technical feats—rewriting *Hurricane* in two days for Sam Goldwyn; writing *Nothing Sacred* in two weeks for David Selznick. Now he was about to face the toughest endurance test of his career—rewriting the first half of *Gone With the Wind* in a week.

Fleming and Selznick appeared on his doorstep at dawn one Sunday morning and bundled him into Selznick's car. On the way to the studios, they settled on $15,000 as his fee for a week's work on the script. At the studio, Hecht wrote later, "four Selznick secretaries who had not yet been to sleep that night staggered in with typewriters, paper and a gross of pencils." But before any writing could be done, Hecht had to be told what *Gone With the Wind* was about. Discovering that Fleming hadn't read it either, Selznick summarized it for them both in an hour; his narrative left them as mystified as before.

Hecht asked whether any of Selznick's collection of writers had succeeded in producing a passable screen version of this complicated "Ouida-like flight into the Civil War" (as he described it). It was only after considerable rummaging among the piles of colored pages that Selznick was able to unearth Sidney Howard's two-year-old script. Hecht found it "precise and telling," and felt that his main task ought to be to sharpen its focus through further compression.

The three of them then barricaded themselves in Selznick's office and began rewriting Howard's script. While Hecht wrote, Selznick and Fleming acted out the roles for him, with Selznick usually playing Scarlett and Melanie, Fleming having firmly refused to take women's roles. Because Selznick was having one of his dieting fits, lunch consisted of bananas and peanuts. But he

The words of condolence become a proposal of marriage. (PRATT)

was also taking the fashionable new benzedrine wonder pills, which at the time had no reality as a drug to Hollywood people, and he fed them to the other two.

As with Howard, there were endless arguments over where the cuts should come. Hecht found Ashley spineless and unsympathetic and wanted to cut him out altogether, but Selznick insisted on his retention as a typical Southern gentleman. On the fifth day, eating a banana and expostulating on how food digestion obstructed the flow of creative juices, Selznick collapsed and had to be revived by a doctor; on the sixth day Fleming felt blood trickling from his left eye. But Hecht worked round the clock, catnapping to keep his strength, and by the end of the week had completed his assignment.

Selznick was too impatient to catch up with his shooting schedule to wait for the second half, which he privately felt he could tackle himself. The women in the cast were full of foreboding about working with the new director. Olivia de Havilland expressed her concern to Howard Hughes: "Don't worry," he consoled her. "Everything is going to be all right. With George and Victor it's the same talent. Only Victor's is strained through a coarser sieve."

Filming was resumed on March 3, seventeen days after it had been suspended. Fleming started—as Cukor had done—with the opening sequence, Selznick having in the interval decided that Scarlett spent altogether too much of the first portion of the picture in the same sprig muslin dress. So a white flounced dress with a red sash was made to be worn on the front porch of Tara while the muslin was reserved for the Twelve Oaks barbecue. Four copies of each dress had been prepared—the extras were considered necessary for retakes. Such conspicious consumption pushed the total cost of the women's wardrobe to $98,154—or roughly double the men's.

After the richly embroidered chiffon of Cukor's style, Fleming's was sturdy, plain velvet. He forced the pace of the production like a drill sergeant pushing a company of new recruits on the parade ground, one camera set-up following another in breathless succession. In the days that followed, however, it quickly became apparent to his driven crew that Fleming was a

"This is what you were meant for." (PRATT)

capable manager of action and spectacle. It unfortunately became equally apparent that Fleming operated on the principle that he could browbeat results out of cast and crew faster than he could coax them. "So you're the famous Selznick team," he snarled at Stacey and Callow at their first meeting. "By the time we finish this picture you're both going to have a nervous breakdown."

He bullied Thomas Mitchell into sitting on a horse, ostensibly for stationary close-ups. "But my contract says I don't have to ride," Mitchell protested, eyes popping nervously in his jowly red face. "Oh, get on, don't be soft," Fleming replied, waving him impatiently into the saddle, while stagehands out of camera range held the horse by means of invisible wires attached to the bridle. Whether the horse bolted on its own initiative or with some outside encouragement is not known, but Fleming was able to film Mitchell's mad gallop across the fields and the footage did not betray that the terrified actor was holding on for dear life.

All in all, not a good beginning. In a matter of days Fleming succeeded in making himself widely disliked on the *Gone With the Wind* set, the degree of animosity being directly proportionate to the frequency of contact, which put production manager Ray Klune, assistant director Eric Stacey, and Vivien Leigh at the top of the list.

At fifty-six, Fleming was a character of Hemingwayan stamp; he had been a pilot in World War I, a big game hunter, and—in the Twenties—Douglas Fairbanks' cameraman and rousting companion (they had once toured the world's leading golf courses together, playing golf by day and creating mayhem at night). His character was generally believed to have been Howard Strickling's inspiration for Clark Gable's screen image, suggesting narcissistic overtones in their deep attachment for each other.

Along with many contemporary directors—Henry Hathaway and Jack Conway, to mention two others—Fleming cultivated a facade of virile, profane toughness, shunning sensibility because it seemed effeminate, minimizing his creativity as a film maker. Presumably, it was a defense mechanism against the studio system, which invested the producer with the power, and the star with the glory, and often regarded the director merely as a kind of technical overseer of the production. On the set, Fleming was given to gestures of bravado: while making *Treasure Island* off Catalina, he passed the time between takes blasting away at rows of bottles with a .45 automatic on the deck of the *Hispanola;* off it, he was in his element going on hair-raising motorcycle rides through the San Fernando desert or on brothel jaunts in Santa Monica with Clark Gable, who was eighteen years his junior. After appearing in Fleming's picture *The Way of All Flesh* in 1938, German actor Emil Jannings pronounced him *"Zo naif wie ein kind"*—as naive as a child. The facade masked Fleming's complex and brooding personality; it also concealed his poor health, for he had only one kidney.

The positions of the principal stars were now reversed. Gable was in a jovial mood; lunching on the first day of shooting with members of the crew, he told dirty jokes and flashed his new bawdy toy, a trick automatic with a regular butt and a barrel shaped like a penis. He felt reassured by the presence of a director he could trust, who made no attempt to conceal their chumminess, and who deferred to him as the star in the midst of abusing everyone else. In addition, during the holdup in the filming, M-G-M had contributed the promised $100,000 bonus for signing the *Gone With the Wind* loan-out contract toward the final settlement of $286,000—plus income tax charges—Gable had made on his estranged wife, Ria, and she had agreed to sue for divorce; Gable and Carole Lombard were now free to marry.

Ria went to Las Vegas to obtain the divorce, spending the day in bed weeping, with a masseuse, hairdresser, and manicurist in attendance. Protective as ever, Metro dispatched a publicist to her bedside to prevent her from saying anything uncomplimentary about their star, but even so, the wealthy Texas matron managed to get off one parting shot to reporters: "I think a marriage between a star and a society woman has a better chance of succeeding than between two movie stars." The two movie stars in question were only waiting for another break in the filming of Gable's picture to start proving her wrong.

Vivien Leigh had as much reason to be embittered by the turn of events as Gable did to be satisfied. Fleming's blunt declaration, "I'm going to make this picture a melodrama," alarmed her. He further antagonized her by promptly nicknaming her "Fiddle-de-dee"; it was a clumsy attempt at camaraderie that misfired, but so great was her resentment toward Cukor's successor that a more sensitive approach would probably have fared no better.

Fleming didn't help matters when he demanded more cleavage, particularly in the scene when Rhett forces Scarlett to appear at Melanie's birthday party in a *décolleté* burgundy gown after India Wilkes has caught her embracing Ashley. ("For Christ's sake, let's get a good look at the girl's boobs," he instructed the costume department.) Vivien Leigh was well endowed, but her breasts tended to spread sideways, concealing their fullness; to get the Hollywood pin-up voluptuousness Fleming wanted, Walter Plunkett had to tape them tightly together, thrusting them forward and upward, while Vivien cursed, groaned, and complained of being unable to breathe. Laurence Olivier witnessed the procedure. "And all the time I thought they were perfectly lovely," he remarked.

Olivier left for New York a few days later to appear opposite Katherine Cornell in *No Time for Comedy*. Vivien Leigh suspected Selznick of engineering the irresistible Broadway offer in order to remove Olivier's distracting presence from her side, and in a number of ways the separation of "Hollywood's most romantic couple" by 3000 miles worked to Selznick's advantage. The most obvious benefit was that it put to rest Metro's fear of bad publicity arising from Vivien Leigh's relationship with Olivier; Vivien Leigh was plunged into a deep gloom by his departure—"It is really very miserable, and going terribly slowly," she wrote to Leigh Holman shortly afterward. "I was a *fool* to have done it." Henceforth she lived for the moment of reunion, and drove herself without mercy to bring that moment closer. While Gable knocked off promptly at six o'clock, she was willing to work until all hours if it meant getting the picture finished a day sooner; any delay, any slackening of pace annoyed her, and "what are they fucking about for?" became her constant complaint. Selznick took full advantage of her haste; for the rest of the filming she put in a sixteen-hour day, often six days a week. Moreover, the anxiety of separation proved a suitable frame of

Scarlett and Rhett in their honeymoon suite on a riverboat heading for New Orleans. (PRATT)

mind for playing Scarlett O'Hara, and she was to say later that it greatly affected her performance.

Being a girl in a hurry also helped her to accept Victor Fleming as director more readily, and they had a polite working relationship; they also developed a healthy respect for each other's professionalism. As for Clark Gable, he viewed her with amused wariness, rather like Rhett views Scarlett on the screen. There was a lot about her that impressed him, not least her profanity, though it didn't match up to Carole Lombard's. Extremely nervous about his own role, he couldn't help but admire her self-assurance, and he appreciated her efforts to reassure *him*. But her strength of character made him uneasy and he kept his distance. For her part, Vivien Leigh was too much in love with Oliver to be dazzled by Gable or by the prestige of having him as her leading man. But Gable taught Vivien Leigh to play backgammon, and then never won a game; she introduced him to Battleship, a new naval war game played on squared paper, and the two of them would play one or the other in a corner of the set between takes.

Selznick now began to have second thoughts about filming the entire picture in the studio, and decided to venture out on some location work; nothing as far-flung as the South; the countryside surrounding Los Angeles would do well enough. So part of the facade of Twelve Oaks and the grounds were constructed at Busch Gardens, the brewery family's vast estate in the San Fernando Valley some twelve miles north of Selznick-International. While filming of the barbecue sequence was in progress there, a second firing occurred. This time, the object of Selznick's dissatisfaction was Lee Garmes, the film's cinematographer. Garmes was a veteran cameraman whose pictures included *Scarface, An American Tragedy,* and *Shanghai Express* (for which he had won an Academy Award) . In 1936 he had settled in England, where besides working in films he ran his own London portrait gallery on Bond Street, and a photo news agency. But when David Selznick offered him *Gone With the Wind*—at the suggestion of Myron Selznick, who was Garmes's agent—the temptation was too great and he returned to Hollywood. Like most cinematographers of his day, he had never before made a

film in color; but he had come under the influence of its use in
English studios and as a result his images had a muted, subtle
texture quite different from the sharply defined color work prevalent in Hollywood at the time.

But Selznick was not impressed. When he saw Garmes's sub-
dued color effects in the rushes of the early barbecue sequences
he protested in a memo to Ray Klune: "We should have seen
beautiful reds, and blues and yellows and greens in costumes so
designed that the audience woud have gasped at their beauty. . . ."
Taunted by Selznick, he tried to reproduce the dramatic *chiaro-
scuro* effect Selznick seemed to want, only to have the producer
complain that the sequences were too black. "When I ask for effect
photography I do not mean that the whole scene should be so
dark that we cannot tell what is going on." One evening, after
the screening of another picture photographed by Garmes, Selznick bore down on the small, round, dapper cinematographer
and demanded: "Why don't you do that kind of work for me?"
To which Garmes replied: "Because you don't leave me alone." A
week after the picture resumed shooting, Selznick finally summoned Garmes to his office and fired him, in what he described
later as "a very nice talk."

Shortly after that came another important departure. Selznick
had for a long time suspected Russell Birdwell of planning
to defect and form his own independent publicity company. In-
censed, Selznick decided to bug Birdwell's office for evidence, but
he reluctantly gave up the idea when Dan O'Shea warned him
of the possible legal consequences. So Selznick confronted the
dimunitive publicist and said: "Look Bird, I know what you're
trying to do. You want to start your own business. I'll help you,
but don't go behind my back."

Officially Birdwell resigned to form Russell Birdwell & Associates; unofficially he didn't have much choice. For one thing, he
was identified in Selznick's mind with a publicity strategy he now
wanted to reverse, and when Selznick jettisoned a major idea
or policy, it was not unusual for those most closely associated
with it to find themselves overboard as well. To avoid the danger
of overpublicizing *Gone With the Wind* too far ahead of its
release, Selznick decided to shut off the flow of information

about the making of the movie. No pictures were to be released at all, and as little news as possible—"The more we keep under cover exactly what the characters and scenes look like, the more avid the public will be to see the picture itself." For another thing, no publicist was likely to satisfy for very long Selznick's sublimely egocentric craving for personal publicity (indeed, none did; there was a brisk turnover of publicity men at Selznick's studios). It was not enough to be producing one of the most ambitious motion pictures of all time; he had to be seen doing it at every possible opportunity.

Independent publicists were a growing new challenge to studio authority over stars. M-G-M refused to let outside publicists in the studio gates and made it clear that to be subverted by them was an act of disloyalty. But then Birdwell landed Norma Shearer as one of his first clients, and what was good enough for the Queen of the Lot—and one of the studio's principal shareholders—obviously became good enough for rank and file talent. After Thalberg died, leaving her an estate worth $4,469,013 (half of which went for taxes), Norma Shearer fought a long battle with Louis B. Mayer for the continuance of her husband's contract, a princely inheritance of thirty-seven and a half percent of Loews Inc. profits for another four years, and four percent of future production revenues thereafter; in addition, Norma demanded $150,000 per picture to continue appearing in M-G-M productions, and it was common knowledge that Sam Goldwyn had offered her $200,000.

But Mayer proved a vicious and unyielding adversary to his young rival's widow and the dispute dragged on between the lawyers of both sides for six months. In the end, Loews chairman Nick Schenck intervened, concerned about the bad publicity and the growing resentment of former Thalberg associates; he instructed Mayer to come to a quick and equitable settlement. Norma Shearer got what she wanted—plus a $900,000 bonus for staying with Metro.

Having won a fortune, she turned to Birdwell to counteract her image of a superannuated rich widow. Birdwell attempted to portray her as just another working actress with two children, eking out a bare existence on $150,000 a picture. When that

Awakened by nightmares, Scarlett is comforted by Rhett. (PRATT)

failed, he had more success projecting her as a merry young widow with a zest for life, and she was photographed at nightclubs and parties flashing her famous smile and an impressive collection of jewelry. If Birdwell didn't engineer her romance with George Raft (and *he* never said he didn't), the unlikely mating of the screen's Number One Lady and its Number One Gangster was a publicist's dream while it lasted and kept them both in the headlines. But after *The Women,* her career, without Thalberg's guidance, went into a nose dive from which it never pulled out. The nadir was *Her Cardboard Lover* with Robert Taylor, in 1942; it was generally judged one of the worst films of her eighteen years in Hollywood movies. So she turned her back on the casts of Ethiopians, married a Sun Valley ski instructor, and retired.

The search for Scarlett was to remain Birdwell's supreme achievement. Only his later campaign for Jane Russell and *The Outlaw,* playing on the nation's moral attitudes, approached its scope. Then, in World War II, he was to try unsuccessfully to drum up public sympathy for ex-king Carol of Rumania, the aging, balding playboy of the Balkan world, by showing him to be a democratic leader victimized by Nazism; Carol was seeking entry into the United States, where the main attraction was some $80 million in frozen Rumanian funds. ("Madame Lupescu is a very great lady . . . it is a beautiful romance," Birdwell told *Time* magazine. "The king is a brilliant man, a man with great poise and fine judgment.") But Birdwell probably succeeded best at publicizing himself; in 1940 he took out full-page ads in *The New York Times* and other leading publications supporting intervention in the war, and thus began his practice of buying space to tell the world what he, Birdwell, had to say about any issue from communism to the state of the movie industry.

Lee Garmes's successor as cinematographer was Ernest Haller; he had never made a Technicolor movie either, but he had the distinct advantage of having been recommended by Ray Rennahan—the new Technicolor associate on *Gone With the Wind*— which resulted in a better working relationship than had previously existed. Haller was not required to re-shoot any of the Garmes footage Selznick objected to so strongly; in fact, most of it was to wind up in the final version of the picture, with no perceptible difference. Considering the shifts in personnel—and there were more to come—the end result could well have been a mad pastiche of individual styles, but Selznick's picture bore an almost miraculous uniformity. The miracle was largely the result of one man's drive and another man's sharply focused vision. The drive, of course, belonged to Selznick; the man with the vision was not Haller or Garmes, or Cukor or Fleming, but Bill Menzies.

Every day, working from Menzies' rough originals, his staff of young artists, including a young architecture graduate named Macmillan Johnson, turned out dozens of detailed shot-by-shot illustrations, not just of the major scenes, but also of continuity sequences. The principal aim of these three- by four-inch color drawings was definition in the visual sense. They were the blueprints on which each set-up was based; every camera angle, close-up shot, or picture composition was drawn, with the relevant lines of dialogue as captions. The artists worked with a copy of *Gone With the Wind* and Francis Trevelyn Miller's ten-volume *Photographic History of the Civil War,* which contains many of Brady's famous photographs, at their elbows to help their inspiration. Because of the vagaries of the shooting schedule, Menzies and his artists often found themselves frantically working on sketches for the following day's scenes; on such occasions Brady was a godsend.

When he wasn't lying in his office sleeping off a hangover or sitting in a Washington Boulevard bar working on another, Menzies seemed to be ubiquitous. He was in the Art Department supervising the sketching one minute and on the set helping the director to line up a shot the next, or on the back lot directing a scene himself—which he was to do increasingly as the filming progressed—or in Selznick's office seeking approval of another batch of scene sketches, which of course necessitated long arguments. He spent as much time on the set as his drinking and his other duties allowed because, he said, being on a set stimulated his ambition to direct his own pictures; besides, there was always an audience willing to listen to his anecdotes and his memories of Scotland—and there was always someone (usually an extra) with a bottle.

The Shooting / The Camera / The Film

Harry Wolf, clapper boy, talks with Vivien Leigh. (FLAMINI)

Hal C. Kern, center, at work editing the 225,000 feet of film which was printed from the 500,000 feet shot; the final version of the film runs approximately 20,300 feet. With Kern are, from left to right, Richard Von Enger, James E. Newcom, Hal Kern, Jr., and Stuart Frye. Kern Sr. and Newcom won the Academy Award for film editing. (CP)

On the first day of formal shooting, January 26, 1939, Mary Anderson raises the Confederate flag over Selznick–International studios. (FLAMINI)

Ernest Haller, right, who won an Academy Award for cinematography, discusses camera angles with David O. Selznick and Victor Fleming. (FLAMINI)

The use of shadows was unknown in Technicolor, but Menzies succeeded in persuading Natalie Kalmus to allow him to shoot Scarlett and her father in silhouette on the hill at Tara ("Land is the only thing in this world that lasts"). Then, when Scarlett delivers Melanie's baby, he again converted Mrs. Kalmus to the idea of having a light filtering through the window slats of Melanie's bedroom, with the two women outlined against the fading yellow twilight. The scene showing Scarlett and Melanie tending the wounded in the hospital opens with their giant shadows on a wall, yet the two stars were actually in the wrong position to cast the shadows themselves, so Menzies stationed two stand-ins in front of a powerful lamp to mime their gestures in close synchronization.

Vivien Leigh is seen in a calico print dress she wears through a third of the picture, in Atlanta and at Tara. Twenty-seven copies of the dress were made in gradual stages of disintegration that seemed to mirror the collapse of the South. Two were in mint condition for the earlier sequences; a couple more were soiled for use during the birth of Melanie's baby; four were scorched and torn for Scarlett's dash through the burning city and her long homeward trek; the others were sandpapered, frayed, and faded for use during the long hard days at Tara. Selznick was obsessed with the importance of careful aging of the costumes to make them look worn and authentic, and the clothes and uniforms were subjected to numerous rinses in a washing machine in a solution of water, sand, and bleach, with a dingy dye added when the clothes were supposed to look particularly dirty. The last of the series of Scarlett's calico print dresses, however, had to be made with the reverse side of the material, because no more color could be squeezed out of the right side even by this strenuous method.

13

More Whitney
Dollars

Olivia de Havilland felt she needed help with the character of Melanie. Instinctively she turned to George Cukor, and over lunch at his home in Beverly Hills the director made several suggestions on how she should tackle the forthcoming scenes. A week later, Olivia was again confronted with a character problem; this time they met at the Victor Hugo restaurant. After that, she consulted him regularly. They thought it best to keep the meetings secret, Olivia justifying them to herself with the argument that Fleming was either unable or unwilling to devote much time to her problems.

Character guidance was not Fleming's *forte,* especially where women were concerned. As an action director, his natural element was *Test Pilot,* with its aerial scenes photographed with eighteen cameras, and as many as a hundred planes in the air at a time. Whenever Vivien Leigh consulted him about how a scene should be played, all he could answer was, "Ham it up." His decision to make *Gone With the Wind* a melodrama and concentrate on the spectacle did not work in favor of subtle characterizations. But with true British grit, the unknown young actress resisted the director's attempts to reduce Scarlett to a one-dimensional, out-and-out bitch, without any redeeming, or at least extenuating, qualities; at the same time she harangued Selznick about the quality of the script, which the producer was rewriting (revised pages were constantly being delivered to the set) and which was going steadily downhill. Before filming a scene she would moan and protest that it was unplayable—and then play it to perfection. She was, as Selznick used to say of her, "No Pollyanna."

As Scarlett's relationship with Rhett deteriorated, the bickering over the character increased; the precious veneer of civility and cooperation between Vivien Leigh and Victor Fleming was wiped out. "On the set quarrels between Fleming and Leigh popped up over trifles, often ended with Leigh in tears, Fleming in rage," reported *Time.* Matters were not helped when a gossip column disclosed that Vivien Leigh had also been having secret weekly consultations with George Cukor about her role. Every Sunday afternoon, tired and beleaguered, the English actress sought sanctuary at Cukor's to lie beside his pool and discuss Scarlett. No one was more astonished to learn about these visits than Olivia de Havilland.

One morning, Vivien Leigh was complaining as usual about Scarlett's lines. On this occasion, the scene was her rejection of husband Rhett's advances; "I can't do it, I simply can't do it," she complained. "This woman is nothing but a terrible bitch." Fleming started to argue; suddenly he looked at her furiously, rolled up his script and shouted, "Miss Leigh, you can stick this script up your royal British ass." Then he marched off the set and went home to Malibu, where he spent the rest of the day drinking with John Lee Mahin.

Fleming didn't show up at the studio the following day, nor the day after that, and he refused to answer the telephone. On the third day, Selznick, Vivien Leigh, and Gable appeared on his doorstep with a cage of love birds. "Let's have a drink," Fleming said, and a truce was established. But the pressures of the past weeks had taken a heavy toll on his nerves and health; returning to work, he was more explosive than ever. Though Vivien Leigh continued to take most of the heat, she was not the principal cause but a compounding factor; the real problem was David Selznick.

The growing certainty that here was a box-office blockbuster of enormous proportions was transmitted to Selznick not only by what he was seeing in the rushes, but also by the excitement the picture had generated among the people on the set. *Gone With the Wind* began to appear to him as the supreme test of his career, his passport to illustrious immortality; that is how bad accelerated to worse. In his desire for control he debauched himself on the picture, by day keeping a close watch on every aspect of production, and at night writing the script as well as assembling, with editor Hal Kern, a rough-cut version of the picture as it was being shot.

Selznick's insistence on personally approving everything inevitably led to long delays. One morning, for example, the first set-up of the day was ready for shooting when Fleming decided he

Overleaf Still remembering the radishes at Tara after the war, Scarlett gorges herself in a New Orleans restaurant. (PRATT)

didn't like the way Vivien Leigh wore her hair and wanted it changed. Impossible, replied the hairdresser, Hazel Rogers. Selznick had approved the style and she dared not alter it without his authorization. At 10 A.M. Fleming phoned Selznick at home; of course, the producer was asleep and could not be disturbed. So filming came to a standstill waiting for Selznick to return the call. Shortly after noon Selznick called Fleming; he listened to Fleming's objections about Scarlett's hairdo in the scene. Then he ruled that it should remain as it was. At 1:30 assistant director Eric Stacey was able to tie his shoelaces: the first shot of the day had been made.

By April Selznick had fallen hopelessly behind in his writing of the script of Part Two and once again appealed to Sidney Howard for help. This time Howard agreed to return to work on the picture for one week. At his usual fast clip he rewrote several of the main sequences in the second half of the picture, including the final scene between Scarlett and Rhett. He and Selznick had their inevitable run-ins: Selznick wanted a big church wedding for Scarlett and Frank Kennedy; Howard pointed out that nobody in Atlanta could afford one during the Reconstruction. As Howard was leaving for home, a Selznick executive asked him if the script was finally finished. Yes, he replied, but no doubt Selznick would rewrite it and then call him back for further repairs. Of course, he was right, but Howard never returned to Hollywood. A few months later on his Massachusetts farm, he went to start a tractor in a shed; but the tractor had been left in gear, and when he cranked the handle it leaped forward, crushing him to death against the wall.

With his marriage wobbly Selznick was now spending hours at The Clover Club gambling, when he ought to have been at home asleep. To stay awake he took greater quantities of benzedrine, plus six to eight grams of thyroid extract a day, and then sleeping pills to be able to sleep. As he stretched himself on the rack of physical and mental endurance, all his usual failings were magnified and his redeeming qualities dimmed; he became more argumentative, more inconsiderate of the feelings and problems of those around him, more tyrannical, more frequently tired, cross and irritable, and so myopic that an aide had to precede him on the set removing objects from his path.

There was a constant flow of studio delivery boys to the set with flimsy yellow memo sheets. In his impatience, Selznick would frequently appear in person; then the cry of "clear the set" would be heard, the crew would shuffle out, and the stage would be set for another heated argument with Victor Fleming. In a couple of instances everyone was called back and Selznick personally took over the direction of the picture, with Fleming sulking beside him. This happened in the scene of "husbandly rape," when Rhett, whom Scarlett has discovered drinking in the living room, picks her up and carries her upstairs. On the same day, Selznick directed two versions of Rhett's final exit. First he shot the original line from the novel, "Frankly, my dear, I don't give a damn" (Sidney Howard had added the "frankly"); then, because he was doubtful of obtaining the Motion Picture Code's approval to use "damn" on the screen, the scene was refilmed with Gable saying, "Frankly, my dear, I just don't care."

And now, as Selznick screened the daily rushes over and over, his perfectionist nature jumped the rails. Nothing seemed to satisfy him. Tara looked on the screen "like the backyard of a suburban home," and he regretted not building it on location; the color photography ran into belittling contrast with *Robin Hood* and *Garden of Allah,* and they should try to avoid signing a contract with the new cinematographer Ernest Haller, "in case by any unfortunate chance we should have to make still another change." The camera work was nowhere near as good as in *The Great Waltz* (which Fleming had directed in part); all the sets looked unrealistic, and the costumes unconvincingly new; Gable's were a bad fit.

Another object of constant concern to Selznick was the Southern accent—or its absence. One of Susan Myrick's responsibilities was to see that the actors laced the dialogue with enough inflections and cadences of Southern speech to capture the flavor of the South. After each take, Fleming would turn to her and ask: "Okay for Dixie?" If she said it was not, the take was usually reshot. The worst offenders were Gable and Leslie Howard.

Selznick and Ray Klune, production
manager, listen to Victor Fleming, who is
about to be wafted aloft by a crane to film
the pull-back shot. (FLAMINI)

Note the light reflectors on the depot's roof. (FLAMINI)

The Crane Shot

The camera at the highest point. The buildings and automobiles at the far end of the railroad yard were masked by a matte painting. (FLAMINI)

Gable had no ear for accents; Susan Myrick tried without success to get rid of his Midwestern "r" by getting him to repeat such phonetic tongue-twisters as "Ah cain't affoahd a foah doah Foahd." She would also go over each scene with him before shooting, but then in the effort of concentrating on the scene, the accent was usually forgotten. Leslie Howard ruined several takes through sheer indifference. When the director called "Action" the lines would come flowing out in his smooth English diction and the scene would have to be repeated. "Mr. Howard, please don't say "bean," remember it's 'bin,' " Susan Myrick reminded him after one ruined take. "Oh, my word, of course, I forgot," Howard replied. Vivien Leigh picked up the accent quickly and rarely fluffed a line; in her scene with Ashley in the Twelve Oaks library she mispronounced "love." When Susan Myrick explained that the South said "leuve," Vivien replied, "Oh, I see, French." She never got it wrong again.

Margaret Mitchell warned Selznick that the accents had better be right or not be there at all, because Southerners were tired of "the bogus Southern talk they have heard on the stage and screen so often." In a letter to the producer she wrote: "Good quality stage voices are not distinctively Northern or Southern or Eastern or Western, and natural voices of that kind will be far more acceptable to the South than any artificial, imitation 'Southern' talk. Of course, a voice with distinctively un-Southern qualities, a New England twang or a Mid-Western 'r' would be out of place in a Southern film, but I don't believe even that would be as offensive as pseudo-Southern talk in the mouth of a person who did not come by it naturally. . . . So many Southern people have expressed the wish that your actors will talk in good quality natural stage voices, instead of imitation 'Southern,' leaving the atmosphere to be built up by the Negroes and the other actual Southerners who may be in the cast. I believe this is the dominant public sentiment and it conforms so directly with my own ideas."

There's no saying when Selznick first began to think of *Gone With the Wind* as his apotheosis. Perhaps the seed was sown as he stood on the platform watching Atlanta in flames below him, and the realization grew as he watched the daily footage; then again, it could have come in the more acceptable Hollywood form of a sudden flash, solemnized by the hosannahs of invisible choirs and a theophanic glow in the sky. What was certain was that when Selznick approached his backers for more money in mid-April, the production had grown from epic to cosmic proportions. He did not, as we shall see, ask merely for sufficient additional funds to finish the picture—he had none left—but for substantial help in enlarging its scope. He was still planning, for example, to film the battle of Gettysburg and some skirmishes between Confederate and Yankee troops were filmed by Menzies in preparation for it. To broaden the picture's historical perspective he also wrote a series of transitional dissolves that were supposed to introduce the Reconstruction sequence. The first one showed the surrender at the Appomattox; then followed the assassination of Lincoln, with Booth shouting *"Sic semper tyrannis,"* and Lincoln on his death bed. As Lincoln breathed his last, Secretary of War Stanton said, "Now he belongs to the ages," and Dr. Girling added, "And now God help the South." Then came the carpetbagger scene. Fortunately, this pastiche was abandoned in favor of a simple title.

But in the end *Gone With the Wind* remained a picture with a war setting and no battle scenes. War is seen in its destructive effect on people and places, never in its panoply and excitement. The "spectacle" in *Gone With the Wind* consists of scenes of death without glory, like the railway depot sequence, culminating in the famous traveling crane shot of Confederate wounded and dying. It occurs when Scarlett goes in search of Dr. Meade to ask him to deliver Melanie's baby. As she arrives at the depot, it is thronged with wounded men; a train steams in loaded to the buffers with more troops retreating before Sherman's army. The war has reached Atlanta. When Scarlett finds Meade, tending an injured soldier, he bursts out: "Are you crazy? I can't leave these men for a baby! They're dying—hundreds of them!" His words are dramatized by the camera pulling back slowly to reveal a sea of bandaged, bedraggled men covering the ground.

As Macmillan Johnson worked on the design for the big pull-back shot, Menzies kept urging him: "Put more men in, Mac, this is supposed to be a big production." So Johnson piled the scene with Confederate wounded right up to the top of the frame.

But when Selznick enthusiastically handed the design to the camera crew they shook their heads. They estimated that by the end of it the camera would have to be ninety feet off the ground; the tallest camera boom (or crane) in Hollywood could only reach a height of twenty-five, and helicopter rigs were decades away. Then Ray Klune found a construction company that had a crane with a 125-foot arm, and he rented it for ten days. When it was tested, the movement of the heavy vehicle turned out to be too jerky for the camera. So Klune had a concrete ramp built, down which it could free-wheel smoothly, while the camera was simultaneously being lifted off the ground.

Typically, Selznick decided late one afternoon that he wanted the shot made the following day, and demanded 2,500 extras in it—not a difficult number to muster, except at such short notice. All night long, the casting agency was on the telephone, calling men to arms. In the morning, the Selznick lot was flooded with Confederate soldiers of all ages, creeds, and many races. The Filipinos, Japanese, Mexicans, Indians and others, many of whom could hardly pronounce Mason-Dixon Line, let alone pass for beleaguered sons of the South under close scrutiny, were tucked away in shadowy corners of the station depot set. Then, with Vivien Leigh picking her way among the groaning, writhing prostrate figures, the 200-ton vehicle rolled slowly down the incline, and the crane hauled the camera—on a specially constructed platform—slowly into the sky.

By 11:30, the shot was completed and the director called "lunch." It was as if an invisible healing hand had passed over the scene, curing only half the men, who leaped to their feet and ran for the lunch wagons, while the other half remained on the ground. Only 949 were live extras, while over 1000 were dummies. A live extra had lain next to each dummy, rocking it for animation. Selznick was opposed to the use of dummies, but the agency had been unable to meet the full order of 2500 men. Later, the Screen Actors' Guild (which at the time also represented film extras) tried to claim union dues for the dummies as well; Selznick's reply was to challenge it to come up with 2500 extras in the same period of time. The Guild failed to do so and the claim was dropped.

A couple of days later Fleming threw another fit on the set and drove off to Malibu, pausing only to contemplate running his car off a cliff on the way. It was left to the first and second assistant directors, whom Fleming had threatened with nervous breakdowns, to pass the word around that the director had been felled by one himself. Fleming did not go to a hospital, and, in claiming that he had a breakdown, was probably overstating his condition, but he was clearly in no fit state to continue directing the picture. (As Selznick confided to O'Shea, "He is so near the breaking point both physically and mentally from sheer exhaustion that it would be a miracle, in my opinion, if he is able to shoot for another six or eight weeks.") Thus, less than two months after filming was resumed, it had again ground to a halt for lack of a director. Second unit work under Menzies continued while Selznick searched for a substitute. His first choice was Robert Z. Leonard, but Metro said he would not be available. Then Klune suggested Sam Wood.

Wood had over sixty movies to his credit, ranging from several Wallace Reid pictures in the early Twenties to two recent Marx Brothers successes, *A Night at the Opera* and *A Day at the Races*. He was no George Cukor or Victor Fleming, but a proficient technician of limited creative range; he had also been Cecil B. De Mille's assistant, which suggested that he was experienced in handling spectacle. And that may have been just what Selznick was now looking for—a conduit for his own creative ideas. Wood was Fleming's age, and even less popular with the crew; he was grumpy and complaining, and his idea of geniality was to boast that he had three testicles.

A studio executive once met him at the Santa Anita racetrack in the company of a man who (Wood said) had invented a machine that picked winners. The director confided with satisfaction that the man was a masseur and he had paid a hefty sum to cover his engagements for that day in order to persuade him to come to the races. The machine looked suspiciously like an adding machine, but the masseur would crank it vigorously before each race and come up with the number of the horse he said would be the winner. Though the machine turned out to be invariably wrong, Wood continued to place bets on the horses

Overleaf Rhett pours Mammy a glass of sherry to celebrate the birth of Eugenia Victoria, whom he quickly renamed Bonnie Blue. (PRATT)

it allegedly picked to win and by the end of the day he had lost a packet. Some days later he learned that the "masseur" was a known confidence trickster.

Wood started work one April afternoon, and his first scene was to be Melanie and Scarlett's meeting with Belle Watling on the church steps. But Vivien Leigh had invited both David Selznick and Olivia de Havilland to lunch in her dressing room and, as the afternoon wore on, she continued to entertain them both with stories, so beguiling Selznick with her performance that he ignored repeated warnings from Eric Stacey that Wood had arrived and was ready to shoot. The new director was left to cool his heels for nearly three hours. But with Selznick present, Vivien Leigh was safe from Wood's complaints. Perhaps remembering her unfortunate experiences with Victor Fleming, she was making sure that this time it was she who scored the first point.

Selznick went over to M-G-M and showed Al Lichtman, who had negotiated the distribution deal, five reels of *Gone With the Wind*. It was an impressive montage of the principal sequences of Part One, representing most of the spectacle in the picture, plus a couple of scenes of the personal drama from Part Two; included were the opening sequence, the Atlanta ballroom scene, the just-finished traveling crane shot, and a rough assemblage of the fire. Lichtman knew very well why Selznick had come, and was prepared to be circumspect. But by the end of the screening, he was unable to conceal his excitement. The film was rough-cut footage, without music, dubbed-in sound effects, or corrected voice levels, but his distributor's sixth sense told him that here was a money-maker of gigantic proportions. Lichtman said: "Dave, we're home. This picture is going to gross nineteen million dollars." Selznick replied: "I'm glad you think so, Al, because I guess you know why I'm here. I haven't got enough to finish it."

Both of them knew that to be an understatement; Selznick's company was down to its last dollar. It was rumored that he had been forced to appeal to his brother, Myron, for help to meet his last two weekly payrolls. Enlarging the scope of the production, which entailed such additional expenditures as building a part of Twelve Oaks at Busch Gardens instead of on the studio back lot and renting the construction crane for ten days, naturally pushed the costs up. But it had been the production delays that had hemorrhaged Selznick's resources. Time is the most expensive commodity in motion-picture making; while the production was idle without a director, overheads continued to accumulate and payrolls had to be met, with no finished film coming in against which to write off the expenditure.

Selznick approached M-G-M with considerable misgivings, but his request to Jock Whitney had met with a flat rejection, leaving him no choice. He had prepared a new production budget of one million dollars for the completion of the picture. Lichtman was so confident in his own assessment of it that the size of the requested sum, which would have pushed Metro's investment in the picture up to $2,250,000, did not disturb him. He passed it on to M-G-M President Nick Schenck with his enthusiastic forecast that the half-finished picture already had the aura of a major box-office success. Schenck refused to underwrite *Gone With the Wind* any further, and no wonder; with the whole pie almost within his grasp, why would he settle for a slice of it? For if Selznick failed to raise the money, M-G-M would have a legitimate claim to take over the production on its own terms and complete it in order to recover its investment.

Next, Selznick tried Joseph Rosenberg, "Doc" Giannini's successor as Supervisor of the Bank of America's Motion Picture Loans Department. Besides the completed footage of *Gone With the Wind,* Selznick produced another powerful argument in the shape of a Gallup Poll he had commissioned, showing that on a proportional basis, 56.5 million people felt there was "a better than even chance" that they would see the picture. This, Selznick told Rosenberg, translated into a gross of twelve million dollars at the box office.

Rosenberg was impressed with the footage, and the Gallup figures, but not with Selznick's erratic record as a money earner. The bank wanted Metro to guarantee the loan, but again Schenck refused. Being turned down by Rosenberg put Selznick in a tight corner. Today, bank financing of motion picture production is an accepted form of venture capital investment. But at the time, the East Coast banks stayed well clear of Hollywood, and the

San Francisco-based Bank of America was virtually the only bank-source of loans for independent production.

Selznick's backers now found themselves impaled on the horns of a Hollywood dilemma, one which remains familiar to investors in movie production. They were unwilling to deliver another million dollars to Selznick, but unless the picture was completed there was precious little hope of ever seeing any return on the capital they had already lavished on him. So Whitney dispatched his lawyer, John Wharton, to California to negotiate with Rosenberg. On the strength of the producer's Whitney connections, the Bank of America agreed to loan Selznick sixty percent of the total amount, if the corporation was able to raise the remaining forty; the bank's other conditions were that Selznick would set a deadline for finishing the picture (which Selznick did set, but never kept), and provide Rosenberg with a complete script of *Gone With the Wind* (which he never sent).

In New York, the Whitneys and their partners in the Selznick venture very grudgingly put up the extra $400,000. Most grudging of all was Sonny Whitney; when Jock went to see him at his magnificent Seventy-ninth Street town house, he at first refused to accept the Bank of America agreement worked out by Jock's lawyer Wharton, and was all for writing off Selznick-International as a bad investment and throwing Selznick to the Metro wolves. "He's spent his last Whitney dollar," he told Jock. Jock had a difficult and disagreeable time persuading him to go along with the rest of the family. But the Whitneys also knew how to extract their pound of flesh; their price for coming to David Selznick's rescue, probably saving the picture in the form that we know it, was to divest him of control of his company by taking over seven percent of his interest in Selznick-International. This meant that he and Myron no longer had a joint majority holding, and Whitney left Selznick in no doubt that his backers wanted to see the picture completed in the shortest possible time.

A burst of feverish activity signaled the securing of new financing, as if Selznick wanted to demonstrate that he had taken Whitney's admonitions to heart. After three weeks away from work, Fleming reappeared on the set as abruptly as he had left it. But Selznick decided to retain Sam Wood, both to accel-

"You ain't never gonna be eighteen and a half inches again, Miss Scarlett."
(PRATT)

erate the pace of the shooting and to ease the pressure on Fleming. While Fleming concentrated on Clark Gable's scenes, Wood
directed other sequences, and Vivien Leigh now found herself
taking direction from Fleming one day and Wood the next. On
one day, there were five units shooting at once. Besides Fleming
and Wood, there were Reeves (Breezy) Eason filming his special
effects (on which more later), Menzies directing another camera
unit, and Eric Stacey supervising pick-up shots of crowds in an
Atlanta street scene.

The new sense of urgency brought to a conclusion the most
protracted take in the production. This was Scarlett's vow
of survival at the end of Part One. Hungry and exhausted, Scarlett angrily picks a radish from the earth, tries to eat it, and
retches. "As God is my witness," she promises herself (and the
camera), "they're not going to lick me. . . . I'm going to live
through this and when it's over I'm never going to be hungry
again. No, nor any of my folks! If I have to lie—steal—cheat—
kill—as God is my witness I'll never go hungry again." Selznick
wanted to end the scene with a silhouette of Scarlett in a very
early, very clear dawn shot, and the crew began trekking out to
Lasky Mesa in the San Fernando Valley, where the exterior Tara
sequences were being shot early in April to get it.

For full effect, the shot required a perfect, mistless morning,
and perfect, mistless mornings are rare in the San Fernando Valley. A track was laid for the camera to pull back down the hill for
a long shot of Scarlett standing in the red earth with the gray
dawn breaking behind her, and a lookout was posted. If the
sky looked promising around 2:30 A.M., the lookout would give
the word from the nearest telephone. Vivien Leigh would be
roused; everyone would dash out to Lasky Mesa, set the camera
on the track, and wait for the shot, all eyes on the horizon. If the
shot materialized at all, it did so at about 4 A.M. Sometimes, the
crew would spot a mist rolling rapidly in across the hills from
the sea and know that it had been a wasted journey. When conditions were good enough to shoot the scene, Selznick was not
satisfied with the result, and insisted on one more retake.

Thanks to Selznick's demanding nature and the peculiarities
of Valley weather, Vivien Leigh and the production crew (but

not, of course, the producer himself) watched the dawn rising in the hills at least a dozen times in two months, until Selznick was forced to give up waiting for the perfect dawn and pasted one together from the footage taken of several imperfect ones.

The last few expeditions went on to film the opening sequence of Part Two; Thomas Mitchell, Ann Rutherford, Evelyn Keyes, and Hattie McDaniel were also called. Valley weather took its toll on that scene too; "We had to do our early morning trek, only this time I had to be at the studio at 3 A.M.," Evelyn Keyes wrote her mother on May 27. "It was my big scene, very emotional, out on the cotton fields picking cotton just after our illness. We are dirty and sweaty. I am wailing about our plight. Scarlett comes in and slaps me, and she really slapped. I can still feel it! The wind was howling terribly, we were on a high knoll with no windbreak. Every time I'd start to cry we'd all have to sit down and wait for the wind to die down. What a way to do a scene."

One of Vivien Leigh's quirks was her strong objection to retching in the dawn scene, because she considered it "unladylike." She tried several times to persuade Selznick to cut it out of the scene altogether. In the end Selznick suggested a compromise: she need not retch when the scene was filmed, as long as she would "loop" or dub it into the sound track later. Olivia de Havilland happened to be present when Vivien Leigh—with evident distaste—looped the offensive sound for editor Hal Kern at the studio. "I can do better ones than that," Olivia confided to Kern when Vivien had left. Kern (who wasn't too happy with Vivien's efforts) agreed to a demonstration, and had to acknowledge the superiority of her performance. Feeling that his first loyalty was to the picture, he used Olivia de Havilland's retching in the sound track of the picture.

14

Upward and
Onward

In many of the plantation shots Tara is seen brooding in the background, yet the house was on the Selznick back lot, twenty miles from the site where they were filmed. Distance was no obstacle to a process called matte painting, which blended painted backgrounds with already filmed scenes of live actors. It was so named because the area to be painted in later was masked with black matte paint on a glass screen placed in front of the camera when the scene was shot. Widely used in black-and-white cinematography, generally for the purpose of showing cities, mountains, or large crowds in the distance, it was brought into Technicolor movie-making by Selznick—tentatively in *Garden of Allah,* and more forcefully in *Gone With the Wind.*

The three exposed negatives were re-wound in the can and a full-color scale illustration of the missing portion of the scene was then shot onto the re-wound negatives to cover the blackened area with calibrated precision. In all, matte painting was used in over a hundred shots in *Gone With the Wind,* ranging from skies and distant landscapes to more ingenious applications, to complete a number of sets that were in reality only partly finished. Tara itself consisted of the colonaded facade; some of the side views and outhouses, as well as the background vegetation existed only in the form of a matte painting. The same process was used to fill in portions of the house and grounds at Twelve Oaks, to add flags and decorations in the Old Armory, and to create an entire street of burning buildings in one shot of the Atlanta fire. In the railroad depot set, the roof of the station building was unfinished, and the locomotive in the right foreground of the shot of more Confederate troops arriving from the front was a crude mock-up made out of scrap iron: both were finished later as matte paintings. Even some of the wounded lying on the ground in the long shots (though not the famous crane shot) were painted.

To match the colors in the scene, a small piece of negative had to be developed; typically, Technicolor had reservations about the use of matte painting and dragged its feet about keeping Selznick's Special Effects (or Trick) Photography Department supplied with the color samples they requested. But while Technicolor procrastinated, Clarence Slifer, Selznick's special effects cinematographer, accidentally stumbled onto their developing secret—which was to heat the developing agent to a very high temperature—and thereafter was able to make his own color tests. Slifer's discovery opened the way to an unhampered use of matte painting.

In private, Selznick readily acknowledged that the matte painting and other optical effects not only saved him a fortune in set building costs but also produced some visual touches that would otherwise have been impossible. Publicly, it was another story. Like a magician jealously guarding the tricks of his trade, he barely acknowledged the existence of his Special Effects Department, and certainly not the size and scope of its contribution to *Gone With the Wind*. It was quartered in a remote corner of the studio lot, and its staff was supposed to work behind locked doors to keep out any inquisitive visitors who might stray off the beaten track. Hollywood's romantic commitment to glamor— both the bane and the glory of the industry—had him in thrall.

The filming thrummed steadily along at a cavalry trot and Metro began to see its completion as a distinct possibility, and started to make preparations for its eventual release. Frank Whitbeck, who was responsible for producing the Metro trailers, journeyed to Atlanta, hoping to persuade Margaret Mitchell to appear in a short promotional film about *Gone With the Wind*. Whitbeck owned two elephants, which eventually became three elephants, and made a tidy side income from renting them out to studios for jungle pictures. The fact that the Director of Advertising and Promotion at Metro kept elephants in the San Fernando Valley was, of course, well known in Hollywood, and was accepted without question, but visitors from the East would go away shaking their heads. Whitbeck's resonant voice was familiar to millions because he narrated the trailers himself. But the voice that launched a thousand movies failed to shake Margaret Mitchell's resolve to keep out of the limelight of Selznick's production; he met with a polite refusal.

Considerably less mild was her reaction to the Peterson business. Georgia Congressman Hugh Peterson had jumped on the Scarlett bandwagon with a statement regretting that David Selznick had lacked the good sense to choose a Southern actress, such as Tallulah Bankhead, to play the role. It was obvious Peterson was trying to gain some gratuitous political mileage out of *Gone With the Wind;* the fact that Tallulah Bankhead's father was fellow Southern Democrat William Bankhead, Speaker of the House, made it doubly obvious. But Selznick saw only a good stunt and played along. He invited Peterson to Hollywood for a personal inspection of Vivien Leigh, assuring him that the English actress had already won Margaret Mitchell's approval. When Selznick's letter of invitation was published, Margaret Mitchell wrote a stern four-page, single-space protest to Selznick reasserting her neutrality; denying that she had ever approved or disapproved the selection of Vivien Leigh, she demanded "that your publicity leave me in my position as author and not attempt to drag me into the position of co-producer. I do not intend to have my name used to back up your decisions. . . . Ever since the summer of 1936 your film has been the subject of public controversy, and, for no good reason at all, I have been caught in the storm center of the controversy. A large number of the public apparently believes that I have complete control over you and everything you do in making the film. . . . If my friendly attitude is taken advantage of and my polite comments are twisted into something very different from what I said, I will be forced to abandon both friendliness and politeness. If I am rewarded for my courtesy by being placed in a false position and having my name misused, I will be forced to take steps of my own to make my position perfectly clear to the public." Through Kay Brown, Selznick made suitable contrite noises.

But her mortal dread of being dragged into the limelight surrounding the making of *Gone With the Wind* did not mean she wasn't interested in its progress. On the contrary, she continued to devour news of the production from Susan Myrick, Katherine Brown and Wilbur Kurtz. Susan Myrick continued to write to her regularly from Hollywood. At sporadic intervals she could be quite generous with her advice in reply to Selznick's never-

ending flow of questions: could Ashley be wounded—perhaps with his arm in a sling—when he visited Melanie, since this would provide him with an honorable explanation for not being at the front? Yes, he could be on "wound furlough," she replied. But he *had* to be home at Christmastime 1863 if Melanie's baby was to be born without scandal during the fall of Atlanta, on September 1, 1864. (Selznick thanked her for the caution, adding that pregnancy took nine months in California too.) When Selznick told her he was thinking of showing Rhett driving up to Aunt Pittypat's house with Belle Watling in her carriage, she was horrified. It would be ungentlemanly for Rhett to be seen driving publicly with Belle, she warned him. No one could or would receive him after that. Besides, to alight from Belles's carriage outside Aunt Pittypat's would be very disrespectful to Aunt Pittypat.

Everyone saw Clark Gable as Rhett Butler except Clark Gable himself. The role was the longest and most complex he had ever attempted. As a movie star, he was accustomed to tailor-made, man-of-action parts; Rhett required him—probably for the first time—to be someone other than his screen self. His ideas on acting technique were reflected in such remarks as: "When I played my first love scene I was scared to death. The director said, use a longing expression. So I tried thinking of a big, tender rare steak; it worked so well I've been using it ever since." That blazing fusion of actor and part, that oneness, that overriding identification that signals an outstanding characterization was beyond his reach, but, with Fleming's help, he achieved the next best thing; as the critics were to say later, Gable never played Gable better. Having Fleming as his director was his salvation; when he was unable to cope with a scene, Fleming would order the set cleared and rehearse with him alone, sometimes for as long as half a day, until the star felt confident enough to go before the camera. One scene terrified him—when Rhett breaks down and cries at the news of Scarlett's miscarriage. Gable's fears underline a fundamental difference in attitude between the star and the actor; he was unable to see past the fact that the sight of him in tears would be contrary to his hard-boiled image and feared the audience would laugh at him. When Fleming tried to per-

Locked out of Scarlett's bedroom, Rhett turns to Belle Watling for consolation. (PRATT)

suade him that in its context the scene could only increase the audience's sympathy for Rhett, Gable remained unconvinced.

The night before it was due to be filmed, Gable was unable to sleep and complained of stomach cramps. Lombard sat up with him, trying to reassure him, but when he arrived on the set in the morning he was tired and edgy. He became very emotional and threatened to quit movies altogether—"starting with this one"—if Fleming insisted on going through with it. The director succeeded in calming him down and suggested a compromise: the scene would be shot two ways, first with Gable's back to the camera in an eloquent gesture of grief, and then with Gable in a front view, weeping. The set was closed to visitors, and the crew was pared down to the minimum; only two takes were shot, with Gable still grumbling nervously. Of course Selznick used the weeping in the picture. When Gable saw the rushes he was astonished by his own performance. "I can't believe it; what the hell happened?" he asked Fleming.

The occasion called for a celebration and surprisingly Gable rose to it, buying drinks for Fleming and a few members of the production crew. Though friendly on the set, he was not noted for his gestures of largesse. Hollywood was full of stories of his tight-fistedness; while shooting Rhett and Mammy toasting the birth of Bonnie Blue, Gable slipped Susan Myrick the key to his dressing room and asked her to fetch him a bottle of Scotch whiskey. Then he surreptitiously substituted the Scotch for the make-believe sherry—which was actually tea—that Rhett and Mammy had been drinking in the scene. When the scene was reshot, Hattie McDaniel took a deep swig and her huge bulk rattled and shook like a volcanic eruption. In the general explosion of mirth Callow suggested to Gable, "How about leaving the rest of that bottle for the boys, Clark?" "Are you kidding?" Gable snapped, and he marched back to his dressing room with the bottle under his arm.

The King of Hollywood could have had a royal wedding at M-G-M, but shortly after his divorce Gable and Lombard decided to elope to avoid the ballyhoo of a studio extravaganza. Metro handled the arrangements in its most secretive manner. Otto

Winkler, a studio publicity man who often worked with Gable, was sent to scout out an out-of-the-way spot where they could be married. It had to be within a day's drive, yet remote enough to escape detection by reporters. The choice fell on Kingman, Arizona, a town of less than two thousand people, about three hundred miles southeast of Los Angeles. Then Gable was given two days off from filming *Gone With the Wind* and the couple, accompanied only by Winkler, set off for the unsuspecting township in Winkler's blue De Soto coupe. Whenever they needed to stop for gasoline, Gable would first hide in the rumble seat to avoid recognition; Lombard, who wore no make-up and had her hair in pigtails, was unrecognizable in shabby dungarees.

The precautions paid off; they were married quietly and without fuss at the home of a minister of the First Methodist-Episcopal Church, with only Winkler and the minister's wife present, having first changed into their wedding clothes—Carole Lombard in a gray flannel suit designed for her by Irene, Gable in blue serge. Gable gave his age as thirty-eight, and his occupation as "actor"; Lombard, who was thirty, said she was a year younger. Afterward, Winkler dutifully telephoned the details to Strickling at the Metro publicity department; equally dutifully, Carole Lombard sent off identical wires to William Randolph Hearst and his star columnist, Louella Parsons—MARRIED THIS AFTERNOON. CAROLE AND CLARK.

Carole Lombard was well aware that Gable's sexual performance fell short of his reputation. "My God, you know I love Pa, but I can't say he's a helluva lay," she once remarked to a friend. Little did his ardent fans realize, when they wrote him passionate letters asking for one of his pubic hairs, that they were probably better off with the surrogates than they would be with the original. Lombard reportedly blamed his lack of sexual expertise on his past association with older women, who she felt were more easily gratified, and was confident she could put matters right. Their thirty-nine-month affair had been an open secret in Hollywood, but Gable had a Metro star's fear of bad publicity, so they met secretly in hotel rooms, arriving separately, preferably through separate entrances. Gable's first act on entering the

Matte Painting

Street scene during the great fire, in which all the buildings are a matte painting. When the scene was shot, the actors moved in front of a black backdrop. Footage from the fire, filmed weeks earlier, was then added by an optical effects process. (FLAMINI)

In the first photograph, the top of the depot is screened out. In the second photograph, the top of the depot has been sketched in. In the third photograph, the top of the depot and the sky have been matte-painted in; the railroad car is blurred because it is moving into the station. (FLAMINI)

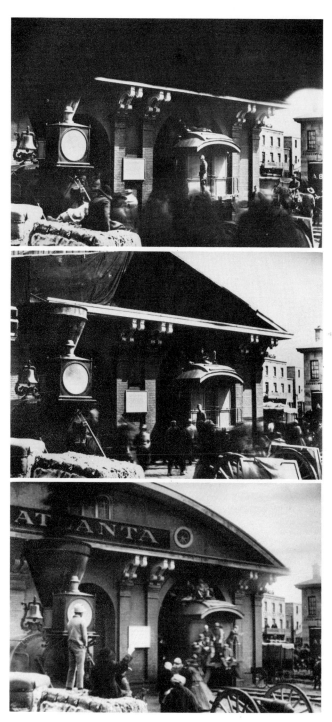

room was always to draw the window drapes. And for a long
time after their marriage, he was unable to make love to his new
wife without first pulling the drapes shut.

When *Intermezzo* went into production, Leslie Howard's attitude on *Gone With the Wind* declined from indifferent to resentful; with two roles to play, he had little time for the job as executive producer of *Intermezzo*, although this was the bait with
which Selznick had hooked him to play Ashley Wilkes in the
first place. He would arrive on the set in the morning, invariably
late, and without knowing his lines; Ginsberg was forever being
dispatched by Selznick to lecture him about not being on time,
and Vivien Leigh scolded him for ruining takes with his line
fluffing. He felt the same way about being carried by Rhett after
Ashley is injured in the Shantytown raid as Gable felt about
crying, and tried in vain to persuade Selznick that it would make
Ashley less susceptible to ridicule if he were to stagger out under
his own steam. "I hate the damn part," he huffed in a letter to his
daughter. "I'm not nearly beautiful or young enough for Ashley,
and it makes me sick being fixed up to look attractive." As for the
picture itself, "terrible lot of nonsense, heaven help me if I ever
read the book." And despite Selznick's entreaties, he never did.

For Vivien Leigh, the book was a talisman against the chaos
of filming out of sequence; she carried it with her on the set—
"to remind myself where I was supposed to be, and how I should
be feeling, until Selznick shouted to me to throw the damned
thing away." Returning to the production after an absence of
several weeks, Olivia de Havilland was shocked at the change in
her—the proclamation in the body of the assault of fatigue, and
in the mind of the pressure on her emotions. To disguise the lines
on her face, the cinematographer changed the diffusion disc on
the camera lens from the lowest (an eighth) to the next lowest
(a fourth). Her mood veered erratically between tantrums and
weeping fits, and the crew gave her a wide berth. Once, as she
stood on the set in the green velvet dress made from the curtains
at Tara, Lydia Schiller, the continuity girl, adjusted the fringe
of her hat to its position in the earlier take. At the touch of yet
another pair of hands Vivien Leigh jumped back, shouting, "For
God's sake, leave me alone."

In her battle with Fleming over the character of Scarlett there was no let-up. One long argument over Scarlett's second declaration of love to Ashley ended with her sending the director to see the screen test she had made of it under Cukor's direction. She had also picked out a line from the script as Scarlett's moment of self-revelation and fought to preserve it. The line occurs when Rhett proposes marriage and Scarlett remembers her mother: "She brought me up so kind and thoughtful, just like her, and I've turned out to be such a disappointment." As Vivien Leigh was to explain later, "To me, it was one of the finer points of the character that she did indeed want to be like her mother more. The Civil War had made that impossible if they were all to survive. It seemed a most important detail indicating something of Scarlett's true nature." Selznick didn't share her view of the line's deeper meaning and would invariably leave it out when he rewrote the scene—which was often. Vivien Leigh would insist on putting it back, and finally won her point.

The slight warp in her sense of mischief became more pronounced. At a dinner party she gave, she introduced her guests to a macabre form of charades called "Ways to Kill Babies." Each player was supposed to mime a way of killing a child. Vivien, for example, pretended to be driving a car and at the same time talking to a child sitting beside her. Then she lifted it onto her lap, murmuring affectionately in its ear, until with a sudden movement, she jerked the phantom child out of the window and drove rapidly off, smiling and humming as she went.

Persuaded that she needed a rest, Selznick gave her a long weekend in which to see Olivier. The actor telephoned her every night after the performance and showered her with expensive gifts. "Is Van Cleef & Arpels a good place to buy jewelry?" she asked a friend one day, holding up a diamond brooch that had just arrived from Olivier. But they had had one brief reunion since his departure for Broadway: five weeks after the play opened, he left directly after the Saturday night performance, made the sixteen-hour flight to Los Angeles, spent a few hours of Sunday with Vivien, and then made the sixteen-hour trip back, arriving too late for the Monday curtain. This time, they were to meet halfway, at the Meulbach Hotel in Kansas City, Missouri. Selznick drove her to Los Angeles Airport and escorted her through the large glass terminal shed to the waiting TWA DC3; movie stars were not covered by studio insurance policies while in flight, but—as Selznick candidly told her—since her role was nearly completed he was prepared to take the risk. On Monday, Selznick went to her dressing room; Vivien was radiant. "Well, how did it go?" he asked. "Oh David, I'm so grateful to you," she replied breathlessly. "Larry met me in the hotel lobby, and we went upstairs, and we fucked, and we fucked, and we fucked the whole weekend."

We will never know how close we came to seeing Scarlett rush out into the night after Rhett Butler shouting "Rhett! Rhett!", and then a final fade-out of the two of them embracing, but Selznick refused to give in to pressure from L. B. Mayer for a happy ending. Instead, he wanted a closing scene which would leave audiences with the hope of a reconciliation; the feeling that perhaps, one day, Scarlett could get Rhett back again.

The scene was rewritten several times before it was shot. For a while Selznick favored a version that went like this:

[SCARLETT *gazes helplessly after* RHETT. *Now* MAMMY *appears behind* SCARLETT.]

MAMMY: Honey chile—

[SCARLETT *turns and flings herself into* MAMMY's *arms.* SCARLETT *sobs like a little girl.*]

SCARLETT: Oh Mammy, he's gone again. How'll I ever get him back?

MAMMY: He'll come back. Didn't I say de las' time? He'll do it again. Ah knows. Ah always does.

FADE OUT—THE END

On the night before the scene was due to be filmed, Selznick, still unhappy with it—and rightly so—changed it to the version that appears on the screen. After Rhett's exit, Scarlett sinks to the ground, sobbing, "I can't let him go. I can't. There must be some way to bring him back. Oh, I can't think about this now. I'll go crazy if I do . . . I'll . . . I'll think about it tomorrow. But I must think about it, I must think about it. What is there to do?

Rhett forces Scarlett to go to Ashley's birthday party, despite the scandal of their being discovered embracing earlier in the day at the lumber mill. (PRATT)

What is there that matters?" Then she hears the disembodied voices of her father, Ashley, and Rhett himself, urging her to go back to Tara—"It's this from which you get your strength; the red earth of Tara," Rhett intones. As she listens to the voices, Scarlett slowly surfaces from her misery; Tara. Tara will have the answers. The camera moves into close-up and she says: "Home to Tara! After all, tomorrow is another day." The film ends with the same extreme long shot that closed Part One; Scarlett in silhouette, standing on the red earth at Tara. Selznick was pleased with his ending for *Gone With the Wind;* he felt it gave the picture "a tremendous lift."

Filmed on June 27, 1939, the scene was the last in the official shooting schedule; that morning the cast and crew received the following invitation to the "wrap party," the traditional bash to celebrate the end of the filming:

> In gratitude for your unfailing efforts and courtesy during the siege of Atlanta and in celebration of the conclusion of the damn thing, we request the pleasure of your company at a little party to be given on Stage 5 immediately after Tuesday's shooting, June 27th.

Vivien Leigh	Clark Gable
Scarlett	*Rhett Butler*
Olivia de Havilland	Leslie Howard
Melanie	*Ashley Wilkes*
Victor Fleming	David O. Selznick
Big Sam	*Jonas Wilkerson*

But with several scenes to be re-shot, other units still shooting, and many trick sequences still to be made, the party lacked a sense of completion. After some desultory drinking, many people drifted back to work; the siege of Atlanta may have been over, but the war had still to be won. What was more, Selznick had opened offensives on two new fronts—*Intermezzo* and *Rebecca.*

As Selznick continued his nightly task of piecing the picture together, he ordered more scenes to be re-shot. The opening sequence continued to bother him, and he ordered a third version of it to be filmed. But Vivien Leigh was now so exhausted physically that she could never have passed muster as an innocent girl of sixteen, so he dispatched her to New York and Olivier, intending to shoot it later (he never did).

Others were more accessible. "When I went around saying goodbye, they said, 'you'll be back,'" Evelyn Keyes reported to her mother. "And sure enough three days later they called me to do an added scene. They are moving so slowly and doing scenes over right and left." She had gone to Omaha as part of a three-day royal Hollywood visit—the opening of Cecil B. De Mille's *Union Pacific,* in which she had a featured role. An enormous crowd lined the streets as De Mille, Barbara Stanwyck, Evelyn Keyes and the other stars of the picture drove into town in an old stagecoach. A dinner in the Auditorium for several thousand guests followed, with hundreds of others watching from the boxes. At the Mayor's luncheon next day, a telegram was delivered instructing her to report back to the studio immediately. It was, of course, signed David O. Selznick. As she arrived at the *Union Pacific* premiere, there were more crowds in the streets. After the performance, a police motorcycle escort took her to the airport where she boarded the plane, still in her evening gown, arriving in Los Angeles the following afternoon. She was nineteen that week.

Selznick didn't know much about music, but he did know what he liked in a film score: he liked busy, heavily orchestrated melody, and a lot of it; he liked themes to introduce the leading characters and more themes to underline the main moods and developments in the movie. In his biography *Selznick,* Bob Thomas relates how, when the producer made *Duel in the Sun* some years later, he requested from Dimitri Tiomkin, the Russian composer, eleven separate themes, including a love theme, a desire theme, and an orgasm theme. "Love themes I can write," Tiomkin told him. "Desire, too. But orgasm? How do you score an orgasm?" "Try," Selznick encouraged him. "I want a really good *shtump.*"

Tiomkin labored over the orgasm theme for several weeks and then assembled the orchestra to play it for Selznick's approval.

Overleaf Chagrined, embarrassed, Ashley endures the formalities of the party celebrating his birthday. (CP)

With Jennifer Jones and Gregory Peck making passionate love on the screen, Tiomkin conducted his composition; the orchestration relied heavily on flageolets, cellos, trombones, and the rhythm of a handsaw cutting through wood. When it was over, Selznick was pleased, but asked to hear it played again. Once more the lovers come on the screen, and once more the orchestra played the theme. At the end, Selznick sighed. "Dimmy, you're going to hate me for this, but it won't do. It's too beautiful." "Meestair Selznick, vot don't you like about it?" Tiomkin demanded in his thickly accented English, trying hard to conceal his exasperation. "I like it, but it isn't orgasm music," said Selznick. "It's not *shtump*. It's not the way I fuck." Tiomkin was livid. "Meestair Selznick, you fuck your way, I fuck my way. To me that's fucking music."

In fact, Selznick did not have a very high regard for Hollywood composers; he was a strong advocate of the use of more classical music and less original composition in film scores. When he chose Max Steiner for the monumental task of composing the score of *Gone With the Wind,* Selznick told him he would prefer "Instead of two or three hours original music, little original music and a score based on the great music of the world, and of the South in particular." But Steiner wasn't the type to hide his musical light under a bushel of old compositions. A volatile Viennese whose musical credits included *Jezebel, A Star is Born, Garden of Allah,* and *King Kong,* he shared Selznick's taste for grand orchestral scores; he divided the picture into 282 separate sections and proceeded to write themes for Scarlett and all the leading characters, for Tara, and for the three separate love relationships in Margaret Mitchell's Southern triangle: Melanie and Ashley, Scarlett and Rhett, and Scarlett and Ashley.

As usual, Selznick had left the choice to the last minute and was now in a hurry for the score. Steiner protested rather dramatically that the producer was asking him to compose the equivalent of four symphonies in as many months, which was impossible. Also as usual, Selznick was unhappy with the first pieces turned in by Steiner. So he secretly commissioned an "insurance score" from Franz Waxman—who was actually at work for Selznick scoring *Rebecca*—in case Steiner should fail to meet the deadline. When *that* seemed to him to lack fire, he sounded out Herbert Stothart about taking over, or perhaps sharing, the assignment. Stothart was Metro's musical director and composer of the scores of *David Copperfield*, *Wizard of Oz* and many other Metro pictures. In reporting the possibility of yet another firing to Whitney, Selznick said Stothart was "simply frantic with eagerness and enthusiasm to do it."

But before the assignment was confirmed, Stothart, who was not exactly the soul of discretion, began proclaiming himself the new composer of the *Gone With the Wind* score. It did not take long for this piece of news to reach Steiner, who immediately doubled his rate of delivery. His butler would wake him up at 5 A.M. each morning and he would compose until midnight; a doctor gave him vitamin injections to keep up his energy level. As Selznick listened to sections of the score performed for him by a small orchestra, his initial reservations disappeared, but he kept up the inevitable barrage of instructions: he urged Steiner to "go mad with schmaltz" for the last half-hour of the picture. Steiner produced 192 minutes of music for *Gone With the Wind;* it was not the treasury of classical favorites Selznick had in mind, but a lush blend of original composition and the musical heritage of the South.

In his anxiety to please all the people all the time, Selznick kept making concessions to pressure groups. When the NAACP protested against the use of the word "nigger," Scarlett's reference to "free niggers" was changed to "freedmen," and lines such as Pork's complaint about having to do farm work, "Ah nare milked no cow, Miz Scarlett, ah's a house nigguh," were cut. As a concession to the Unionist veteran organization, Scarlett shoots a "deserter"; in the novel he was one of Sherman's Raiders. There were a few times, however, when the producer refused to buckle. The Daughters of the Confederacy made anxious noises about the way the South was being portrayed in the picture, based on what they were reading in the papers, and Selznick invited them to view the completed footage. A delegation of two officers from the Los Angeles chapter was dispatched to the studio wearing the ribbons and insignia of office for a special screening. After seeing the film their only major complaint was Scarlett slapping Prissy while delivering Melanie's baby. Southern girls never man-handled their servants, no matter how trying the circumstances, they told Selznick. He promised to re-shoot the sequence leaving out the slap, but after much agonizing decided to risk leaving it unchanged.

15

"The Biggest Picture
of the Year"

Gone With the Wind was one of the last pictures to be completed before the newly formed Hollywood unions succeeded in winning studio acceptance of the five-day week and strict adherence to an eight-hour working day. Had filming started six months later than it did, the picture would have taken considerably longer to make, with disastrous financial consequences. But even so, Selznick was not immune from the prevalent surge of union militancy. As soon as the principal shooting ended, his studio was shut down by a strike of make-up artists and other locals. Their grievance was against Paramount, but Selznick was a more vulnerable target because he was in a hurry to finish *Gone With the Wind* in time for its Atlanta premiere on December 15, and the studio heads bargained collectively. Selznick was also under indictment to appear before the National Labor Relations Board to answer charges of threats and intimidation brought against him by the newly constituted Screen Writers' Guild, which was battling for official studio recognition. He was charged with "interfering with internal affairs of the Guild, making known to employees [of the studio] his hostility and opposition to membership of the Guild." The charges against L. B. Mayer offer a glimpse of the studios' violent opposition to Hollywood's unionization and the unbridled venom with which it was often expressed—"Making speeches to employees in which officers and leaders of the Guild were referred to in opprobrious, vile and defamatory language. Soliciting employees to resign from the Guild and threatening those who refused with discharge. Threatening to close down the studio if certain organizational changes in the Guild occurred."

The producers rejected the allegations but met privately with the Labor Relations Board negotiator to ratify an agreement with the Screen Writers' Guild giving the writers the right—among others—to self-determination in resolving uncertain or disputed writing credits on the screen. This left only the Directors' Guild still unrecognized, but its moment came shortly afterward. In capitulating to the filmmakers' financial and professional demands, the studio heads accepted the principle of the director's "right to first cut," that is, his right to assemble the picture himself. Since the right to final cut remained firmly vested in the producer, the concession was a limited one; even so, many producers—among them David Selznick—honored it more in the breach.

Following his usual practice, Selznick edited *Gone With the Wind* himself, without consulting any of the directors involved. If the warp was predominantly Selznick, the woof promised to be even more so. With editor Hal Kern, Kern's assistant James Newcom, and production assistants Lydia Schiller and Bobby Keon to take notes, he plunged like Laocoön into the 225,000 feet of film printed out of the half a million shot. Although some piecing-together of sequences had been done during the filming, the real work still lay ahead. In endless, nightly sessions—even under deadline pressure Selznick found it impossible to start work until noon—he pored over the disconnected fragments of filmed action in search of his picture; it was a task consisting of an infinite number of micro-decisions—choosing a close-up from one take, a long shot from another, two lines of dialogue from a third, to shape his dramatic tapestry of Margaret Mitchell's novel. Selznick still envisioned a four-hour movie, which meant a final length of about 20,300 feet and an approximate ratio of film printed to film used of ten to one. This suggests that a lot of the picture was left on the cutting room floor, but it wasn't. The enormous quantity of footage was not a true reflection of the number of scenes filmed; proportionately fewer scenes were omitted from the final version than is usual in a movie of average length. The mass of film was the result of Selznick's insistence on "protection," for he expected his directors to provide a stream of takes and a mass of angles in order to give himself as many options as possible in assembling a scene.

The out-takes, or unused footage, have long since disappeared, and there is no record of what sequences were left out of the final edited version of the picture. From all accounts they were minor ones, including, for example, the skirmishes Menzies directed for the battle of Gettysburg that never materialized; a short scene

showing Rhett's affection for Bonnie Blue in which he gives her a toy tea set he had brought her from London; Scarlett finding some of her friends from the Twelve Oaks barbecue, such as one of the Tarleton twins, among the wounded at the railroad station.

Like every other phase of the making of the picture, the cutting of *Gone With the Wind* took on the gruelling pace of a forced march. One session in the cutting room lasted fifty hours; secretaries wilted; Bobby Keon collapsed after forty-seven hours. Only Hal Kern remained standing at the end of it. Kern was a young cutter who had followed Selznick from Metro; his energy never flagged, nor did his devotion. When Selznick would begin to drift off into sleep, Kern would take the hulking producer outside and half-carry him around the building at a brisk pace. If this failed to revive him, Kern would pack him off home to bed.

In this way, a five-hour rough cut was assembled and screened for the principal members of the cast and crew while the strike was still on. But by now the script had become so heavily annotated and revised, so bulging with additional pages, that Selznick found it too confusing to work from, so he stopped and instructed Lydia Schiller to put together a fresh working script based on the edited material. After a back-breaking week bent over the movieola, Lydia Schiler had compiled a scenario which became the official "shooting script" of the production; bound in leather, it was presented to members of the cast who had never received a complete script during the filming of the picture!

Selznick went back to the editing, and by the end of August had completed a second cut with a running time of about four hours and twenty-seven minutes, which he showed to L. B. Mayer, Al Lichtman, and other Metro executives. The film had to be interrupted several times for Mayer to go to the lavatory, but he was quite moved by it; his old reservations forgotten, he left Selznick's studio bubbling with self-congratulation over the prospect of big box-office returns for his relatively small investment. Selznick became very nervous about the danger of fire. "No insurance company will cover you against loss of profit," he told an aide. During the hot months of October and November, he kept

Vivien Leigh in the burgundy velvet dress. To produce the cleavage demanded by Victor Fleming, Walter Plunkett had to tape her breasts together. (PRATT)

the Technicolor matrices in a vault and had garden sprinklers spraying the roof all day to keep the temperature down.

As he continued to fit together the pieces, he ordered more new scenes—for example, Scarlett hiding under the bridge in a rainstorm while a troop of Union cavalry passes overhead. He also asked Ben Hecht to write seven narrative titles, but the words on the screen bear the stamp of Selznick's own florid prose style: "THERE WAS A LAND OF CAVALIERS AND COTTON FIELDS CALLED THE SOUTH . . . LOOK FOR IT ONLY IN BOOKS, FOR IT IS NO MORE THAN A DREAM REMEMBERED, A CIVILIZATION GONE WITH THE WIND." As for the main title, nothing less than the largest lettering ever designed for the movie screen would do. Each word of *Gone With the Wind* was to be framed separately as the title drifted majestically across from right to left; when it was filmed, on Labor Day, it was the camera that moved, pulled along on its dolly by Fred Williams, the head grip. Williams turned on his radio and heard that Britain had declared war on Germany. Work stopped, and the crew discussed the likelihood of American intervention; would they, too, soon be donning uniforms? Williams photographed the Normandy landings on Omaha Beach as a U.S. Army cameraman.

Leslie Howard also heard the news, and left for England as soon as he had finished *Intermezzo;* he died shortly afterward in an air crash in Portugal, reportedly while on a special mission for the British Government. Vivien Leigh and Laurence Olivier heard of the war on Ronald Colman's yacht off Catalina Island; Olivier returned to England after starring in Selznick's production of *Rebecca.*

Before giving credit on the screen, Selznick faced the problem of establishing where it was due. Perhaps inevitably, what eventually appeared was both inadequate and misleading. Selznick told Fleming that though he felt that he, Fleming, ought to receive principal credit for the direction, he wanted to include a combined mention of Sam Wood and Bill Menzies as "associate directors." Fleming flew into one of his rages at the thought of having to share the glory; backed by Mayer, he demanded sole directorial credit as stipulated in the agreement loaning him to

Selznick, arguing that he deserved it for "saving" the production. The producer gave in, but still felt that Menzies's work on the picture merited some form of special recognition. In the end, he fell back on the credit he had thought of when he hired Menzies two years earlier, but which failed to do justice to Menzies's contribution to the picture: "Production designed by William Cameron Menzies." At least he fared better than Woods, who wasn't mentioned at all. Yet Fleming was responsible for fifty-five percent of the direction, at most. With the exception of Rhett's visit to Scarlett at Aunt Pittypat's with the Paris hat, Fleming filmed the main story of Rhett and Scarlett from the moment Rhett pops up from the couch to his final exit—which was actually directed by Selznick in Fleming's presence; those scenes total about 10,000 feet, or slightly less than half the movie. In addition, he shot the few Rhett Butler scenes *without* Scarlett, the opening sequence of the picture, Ashley's furlough, some of Scarlett's return to Tara, some of the scenes in the cotton fields, Scarlett and Ashley's love scene in the woodshed, and Melanie's death.

A further thirty-three minutes (about fifteen percent) were directed by Sam Wood: Scarlett and Melanie's meeting with Belle Watling on the church steps; Scarlett's jealousy as she watches Ashley and Melanie going upstairs to bed, followed by the Reconstruction sequences, including Scarlett's marriage to Frank Kennedy, her scenes at the saw mill, and India Wilkes walking in on her and Ashley embracing; also Melanie's birthday party, and the women in Aunt Pittypat's parlor waiting for their menfolk to return from the raid on Shantytown (up to Rhett's arrival, when Fleming took over); plus Melanie's conversation with Mammy about life at the Butlers' after the death of Bonnie Blue. Still, Wood was indifferent about not receiving any credit, perhaps because he had stumbled onto a valuable consolation prize. His work on *Gone With the Wind* began a close association with William Cameron Menzies which considerably enriched the visual quality of his later movies, such as *King's Row* and *For Whom the Bell Tolls*. Thereafter, the director never shot an important scene without Menzies's approval. Menzies had a tendency to slip away quietly

The Musical Score

Steiner during the recording of the musical score with the MGM orchestra. (FLAMINI)

Max Steiner, who composed the musical score for the film. (FLAMINI)

when no one was looking, but most assistant directors knew where to look for him, and, after a short delay, he would be produced to give a sometimes rather groggy *imprimatur*.

George Cukor had said he was not interested in a shared credit for *Gone With the Wind*. He directed about five percent of the finished movie—Mammy lacing up Scarlett's corset before the barbecue; Rhett calling on Scarlett with the hat; Scarlett delivering Melanie's baby; and Scarlett's disposal of the Union deserter.

In addition to his work as a designer, Menzies also directed about fifteen percent of the footage in the picture. Apart from the Atlanta fire sequence, he filmed Scarlett and her father in silhouette at Tara; Scarlett and Melanie at the hospital; the casualty list scene; Scarlett in the streets of Atlanta during Sherman's bombardment; and her return to Tara, after being left to her own devices by Rhett on the outskirts of Atlanta.

Then there was Reeves Eason, director of the second unit; he was responsible for about one percent, notably the attack on Scarlett in Shantytown. The remaining nine percent was a gallimaufry of process shots, establishing shots, titles (the main titles of *Gone With the Wind* ran on for 600 feet, roughly six times the normal length), and other optical effects. The dawn pull-back shot bringing Part One to a close was filmed so many times, by so many different people, that final authorship would be impossible to establish. Though about five or six reels of Lee Garmes's footage (approximately the first hour) remain in the picture, Ernest Haller received sole photographic credit on *Gone With the Wind*.

If apportioning directorial credit was difficult, determining who wrote what was virtually impossible. But here Selznick simplified matters by claiming that most of the work was done by himself. He said eighty percent of the construction of the scenario was his; he had also written "the last half or two-thirds of the script without anybody's help," *and* most of the lines of dialogue not directly taken or adapted from Margaret Mitchell, with a few more from Howard, Hecht, and John Van Druten. Hecht had apparently received $15,000, plus all the salted peanuts and bananas he could eat, for contributing "materially to the construction of one sequence." And Oliver Garrett? His suggestion that the credit ought to read adaptation by Sidney Howard and screenplay by himself was curtly dismissed as ridiculous. In the end, the sole credit went to Sidney Howard; it was Selznick's posthumous tribute to the playwright's work for the screen.

Selznick insisted on previewing *Gone With the Wind* in absolute secrecy. He was anxious to prevent the press from getting a look at the picture before it was completely finished. He was particularly afraid of the vindictive lash of envy if some reporters managed to track down the preview and the rest did not. Feeling the biggest security risk was the gregarious, long-winded David Selznick himself, Hal Kern refused to reveal where the preview was to be held until they were on their way with twenty-four cans of film, five of the studio's security guards, and Irene Selznick. Their destination was the newly opened Fox Theater in Santa Barbara, which had all the latest sound and projection equipment. But the program was a poor one and the house was practically empty, so they drove to the Warner Theater nearby, where a full house was settling down to watch *Alexander's Ragtime Band.* When the astonished manager agreed to allow them to preview *Gone With the Wind,* the security guards immediately took up positions at every exit and beside the pay phones.

The manager was given an announcement to read to the audience. It said they were about to see "the biggest picture of the year" which had a running time of about four hours, and no one would be allowed to leave the theater once the film began; anyone leaving before it started would not be allowed back in; no telephone calls were permitted (all of which contravened every city ordinance governing public buildings, but no one seemed to mind). When the manager protested that if he did not call his wife his domestic life would be gone with the wind, he was allowed a monitored phone call in which he cryptically summoned her to the theater.

As the four giant letters of the first word of the title began to drift across the screen a gasp of recognition swept through the audience, which then jumped to its feet in an uproar of excitement. Irene buried her face in her hands, and Selznick started to weep.

At the end of the picture there was silence for perhaps five seconds, followed by prolonged applause. Selznick helped pass out the preview cards but he was too dazed to interrogate the audience the way he usually did after a preview. During the drive home, he savored the comments on the cards—"The greatest picture ever made," "The greatest picture since *Birth of a Nation,*" "The screen's greatest achievement of all times. . . ." Still attracted by the idea of a big battle sequence, he had included a question asking whether a battle would be preferable to the existing narrative titles telling that one had taken place. Perhaps because they felt there was too much war in the air already, people overwhelmingly preferred the titles.

A second preview was held some days later with Jock Whitney present, at Riverside, a favorite testing ground with Hollywood producers because of its demographic town-and-gown mix of students and faculty from Pomona College and local white-collar inhabitants. Again, the studio security men sealed off the movie theater; again there was wild enthusiasm for the picture. At the close of Part One, Selznick stationed himself outside the lavatories and began counting the traffic. He had been trying unsuccessfully to convince Metro to run the picture with a fifteen-minute interval, and the numbers convinced him that he had been right.

No battle then; but with less than four weeks to go before the Atlanta premiere of the picture, Selznick decided to open Part Two with a montage of Sherman's march through Georgia. Using existing footage, his Special Effects Department created a collage of ominous warlike effects: marching soldiers, cavalry and gun caissons pouring out of a swirling cone of red Georgia dust, followed by flames, finally dissolving into the Tara cotton patch, all with a single superimposed title—SHERMAN. The montage was completed and rushed to Technicolor, where the film was being processed; it was the studio's last undertaking. The making of *Gone With the Wind* was over.

The final cost, excluding the added overhead for prints, advertising, publicity, and distribution, was $3,957,000. The stars' and supporting casts' payroll totaled $466,688; the extras' payroll, $108,469; and the technicians' payroll, $1,408,997. Sets cost

A fall and a miscarriage. (FLAMINI)

$197,877 to build and another $35,000 in lumber and materials; wardrobe costs came to $153,818. The company purchased $109,974 worth of film stock and $5,511 of sound track stock and spent $10,363 on developing and printing sound track. Lighting came to $134,497; transportation, $59,917; rent and purchase of props, $96,758; location fees and expenses, $54,341.

Included in the stars' payroll was the loan-out payment to Warner Brothers for Olivia de Havilland (Selznick paid no money for Gable). The supporting characters, starting with Hattie McDaniel, received a total of $10,000. The technicians' payroll included Cukor's, Fleming's, and Sam Wood's weekly salaries while working on the picture, and the salaries of William Cameron Menzies and his production staff. The rent and purchase of props included the cost of renting over 1000 horses, plus 375 other animals—pigs, mules, peacocks, oxen, cows, and more than 400 wagons, coaches, ambulances, gun caissons, and freight cars. The cost of the sets and lumber included the construction of 90 sets, among which were 7000 feet of Atlanta street containing 53 buildings, with nearly one million board feet of Oregon pine, Ponderosa pine, and Douglas fir.

Twenty years later, Lyle Wheeler was the art director at Twentieth Century-Fox when the studio was in the throes of making *Cleopatra*. One day, Darryl Zanuck asked him to break down the cost of remaking *Gone With the Wind* on the same scale of the original under prevailing Hollywood conditions. He was curious to see how it would measure up to his increasingly costly and problem-ridden production. Wheeler's answer came out at about $40,000,000, and Zanuck was considerably consoled.

M-G-M planned to release the picture in six major cities for the Christmas and New Year holidays, and then to road-show it in three hundred more cities—that is, show it in one leading movie theater in each area in a specified period of time. Yet another poll commissioned by Selznick showed that $1.65 was considered a reasonable top price to charge for *Gone With the Wind*. But Metro decided on a slightly lower price range—75¢ for the morning and afternoon performances, and $1 and $1.50 (for reserved seats) for evening showings. Considering that Metro had demanded, and got, seventy percent of the gross takings from exhibitors instead of the usual thirty percent, the studio could afford to be generous.

Meanwhile, Metro's publicity department had begun stockpiling articles and photographs to meet the mounting press demand for material. Writers were assigned to prepare major pieces about the stars, the production, and the producer. When Strickling's man interviewed Selznick he was surprised to be treated to a full-scale performance, as if he were a reporter who had to be impressed, rather than someone with no choice but to write favorably about him. But there were no half measures with Selznick; loosening his tie, he launched into a lengthy discourse on the joys and problems of siring a masterpiece, gesticulating, pacing the floor and draping himself against the marble mantelpiece. He followed up the interview with a flow of memos full of suggestions and addenda. Selznick's storm-tossed voyage to safe harbor with *Gone With the Wind* was hardly recognizable in the calm crossing of the studio's official account of the making of the movie. It made no mention of Cukor, Garmes, or the other hands washed overboard, or of Selznick's financial troubles, or, needless to say, of Metro's pressures and machinations. But enough glamorous copy was produced to fill three newspapers, and in fact did. To commemorate the premiere of *Gone With the Wind*, three Atlanta newspapers published special editions consisting largely of editorial fodder provided by M-G-M. Metro also prepared a publicity campaign book for use by its distributors; it was headlined, "MAGNITUDE AND DIGNITY: THE KEYNOTE OF EXPLOITATION." Listed inside were the types and sizes of posters available with an illustration of each, and a catalog of other promotional material including satin bannerettes with portraits of Gable as Rhett, Vivien Leigh as Scarlett, Olivia de Havilland and Leslie Howard, canvas tire covers with pictures of the stars on them, *Gone With the Wind* "fender labels" (that is, bumper stickers), and a collection of oil paintings which were actually doctored stills for display in theater lobbies.

Among the unpublicized incidents was Selznick's battle with the Hays Office over the use of a four-letter word in the picture. The four-letter word was "damn." The same Production Code that barred from the screen detailed acts of killing, miscegena-

Overleaf Rhett proposes a second honeymoon. (PRATT)

tion, venereal disease and sex hygiene, complete nudity (even in silhouette), children's sex organs, bedrooms (except in tasteful domestic situations), and adultery as fun or romantic, specifically barred—under Section V., (1) PROFANITY—the use of the word "damn." As a result, Joseph Breen, the censor, refused to allow Gable's punch line, "Frankly, my dear, I don't give a damn." But Selznick attached great importance to retention of the line as a symbol of the production's fidelity to the novel, so he went over Breen's head to Will H. Hays, the tall, solemn Presbyterian elder (H. L. Mencken always referred to him contemptuously as "Elder Hays") and former Postmaster in President Harding's cabinet, who as head of the Motion Picture Producers and Distributors of America provided the industry with a respectable Gentile front man.

Selznick launched a two-pronged offensive. One prong was a letter to Hays pointing out that the *Oxford English Dictionary* (Selznick was probably the only producer in Hollywood who had a complete, unabridged twelve-volume edition in his library) did not describe "damn" as an oath, but as a vulgarism. To support the argument that the word had gained general acceptance among the public, he also quoted a number of popular magazines such as *Woman's Home Companion* and *Collier's* in which "damn" was used freely. And he pointed out that preview audiences had been disappointed by the omission of Rhett's line—"on our very fade out it gives an impression of unfaithfulness after three hours and forty-five minutes of extreme fidelity to Miss Mitchell's work." The second prong was a call to Hays from Jock Whitney requesting a meeting of the Board of Directors (the New York-based heads of the major film companies) to rule on Selznick's request if Hays refused to reverse Breen's decision. Selznick was banking on the directors' considering the topic too trivial for a meeting and instructing Hays to allow his appeal. But in the end, no meeting was necessary; the first prong was enough to push Hays to compliance, and the immortal line was enshrined in the picture. However, since Selznick was technically violating an article of the Production Code, he was fined $5000.

16

"David—Xmas 1939.
Praise de Lawd. Jock."

Ernst Lubitsch used to describe Howard Dietz as "a man who writes shows on M-G-M stationery." The shows, written with composer Arthur Schwartz, were studded with such memorable gems as *Dancing in the Dark, By Myself,* and *That's Entertainment.* The M-G-M stationery proclaimed him Director of Publicity. It was Dietz who borrowed the symbol of his alma mater, Columbia, to invest M-G-M with its Leo the Lion trademark—throwing in a Latin motto *Ars Gratia Artis,* for classy good measure. He had a ready wit ("A day away from Tallulah is like a month in the country") and good social connections—he was married to a Guiness. He could hold his own in the cut and thrust of the Algonquin Round Table, and the rough and tumble of the M-G-M front office.

L. B. Mayer was suspicious of his successful double life, and didn't much care for him; nor was there much love lost between Dietz and David Selznick. Dietz frequently found Selznick overbearing and wasn't afraid to say so. During one of their arguments when Selznick was a Metro producer, Dietz snapped, "Don't mess with me, David, I'm literate." On another occasion, Selznick wrote a long complaining letter about the publicity campaign on one of his Metro productions and sent copies to all the members of Loews' Board of Directors. Dietz replied: "Dear David; I have just found out what the O in your name stands for; it stands for nothing. Sincerely, Howard." Dietz had the benefit of Nicholas Schenck's protection.

As *Gone With the Wind* was released by M-G-M, promoting it became Dietz's responsibility. It was going to be either the toughest or the easiest movie promotion ever undertaken: tough if the long publicity hammering had numbed the public into such complete indifference that people would stay away from the movie theaters, easy if the picture had caught them just in the moment of peak expectation. It was too early to say which it would be. The more immediate problem was Selznick, for though he had been forced to take a back seat, he refused to leave the driving to M-G-M. His cables arrived nightly at Howard Dietz's New York house. One of them read: I WANT YOU TO BE VERY CARE-FUL OF THE PAPER YOU SELECT FOR THE PROGRAM STOP SOMETIMES THEIR CRACKLING MAKES IT DIFFICULT TO HEAR THE DIALOGUE STOP PROMISE YOU WILL ATTEND TO THIS. Dietz telegraphed back: RE-CEIVED YOUR EPIGRAM STOP YOU CAN REST ASSURED ABOUT PROGRAM NOISE STOP HOWEVER HAVE MADE TIE UP WITH GONE WITH THE WIND PEANUT BRITTLE COMPANY ASSURING EACH PATRON OF THE PICTURE A BOX OF PEANUT BRITTLE AS HE ENTERS THE THEATER.

Arriving in Atlanta, Dietz was soon swamped with requests for tickets to the opening. One old lady haunted the office he had set up in the Georgian Terrace Hotel; "But you don't under-stand," she pleaded. "I'm the president of the local chapter of the D.A.R." Dietz replied: "But *you* don't understand, madam, this picture is about another war." Unable to unravel the prior-ities of the requests pouring in from local politicians, city offi-cials, churchmen, bankers, and the Confederate Soldiers' Home, Dietz decided that the best course of action was to pass the buck. So he called on Atlanta's Mayor William B. Hartsfield and pledged the combined proceeds from the opening night box office and the Junior League Ball, which was to take place on the previous night, to the Community Chest, if the Mayor would assume responsibility for the disposal of the 1400 unreserved seats. The Mayor, who was up for reelection the following year, readily agreed to act as ticket broker. He was put out when he discovered that the reserved tickets included a block set aside for Georgia governor E. D. Rivers, who had invited the governors of Tennessee, Alabama, Florida, and South Carolina, plus their wives. Although Rivers and Hartsfield were both Democrats, the Governor was a New Dealer and Hartsfield a conservative Demo-crat of the old Southern school, and they were cool toward one another. But Dietz had not run out of gambits. "How would you like Clark Gable to be your daughter's escort at the Junior League Ball?" Hartsfield conceded the Governor his tickets.

With some encouragement from M-G-M, Rivers became the first and probably the only governor ever to proclaim a state-wide holiday to mark the showing of a motion picture. Not to be outdone, Hartsfield planned three days of festivities, substantially underwritten by Metro, beginning with a triumphal motorcade into the city from Atlanta Municipal Airfield. Dietz's suggestion that a few people in antebellum or Civil War dress would add a dash of color to the event, eagerly relayed by the Mayor, sent many citizens delving through old trunks—and many more to costume companies to rent ancestral finery for the occasion. Hartsfield also appealed to citizens not to tear off the clothes of the visiting stars as had happened in Kansas at the premiere of *Dodge City.* The Governor and the Mayor were both at the airfield on the afternoon of December 14 to await the arrival of the stars. So was "Good Nabor" Faber of the Atlanta Convention and Greeters Bureau, who weighed two hundred and fifty pounds and wore an antebellum suit and a gold chain of office inscribed "Goodwill Commissioner of the South." His real name was Faber Bollinger, and he told reporters: "You may call me the Grover Wheelan of the South Land."

In one of the open cars that was to take part in the motorcade, four women wearing bonnets, hooped skirts and Paisley shawls somewhat incongruously searched the sky for Clark Gable's plane. They had all been children when Sherman entered Atlanta. Emma Calhoun Connally, seventy-eight, granddaughter of wartime mayor of Atlanta Col. James M. Calhoun, wore a good black brocaded dress, poke bonnet and black chinstrap—her mother's "second day dress." Beside her was a plump, red-cheeked woman in a poke bonnet with a red feather, wearing a broad scarlet chin bow, who buttonholed a visiting reporter and reminisced about her grandmother. This is how it was reported to *New York Times* readers on the front page the following day: " 'My gran'- maw, Mrs. Edward Harper, told me that she went right to General Sherman, and asked him for protection. She was living out, you see,' with a circular gesture of her arm to show that gran'- maw was living outside the city. 'Well, General Sherman, he said: Madam, if you will just come inside the Northern lines I will give you full protection. Well, Suh, my gran'maw Harper said: General Sherman, I'll never leave Atlanta as long as there is a spot as big as my apron—and she held up her apron, which she had made with her own hands from the cotton of our own fields. The general thought she was a brave woman. Madam, you

Scarlett and Rhett watch horrified as Bonnie Blue
is thrown from her horse. (PRATT)

got spunk, he said to gran'maw. That's every word he said to her.' "

The reception committee was told that Clark Gable would be arriving in a separate plane from Selznick and the rest of the *Gone With the Wind* party; they were not told why. With the picture finished, residual resentments against Selznick were coming into the open. When a newspaper story quoted the producer as saying he had "supervised" the directors on *Gone With the Wind*, Fleming, already embittered by the row over his screen credit, refused to attend the Atlanta opening. Selznick argued that the story had been put out by Fleming's own studio, but the director refused even to discuss it. Out of sympathy for his friend, Gable also decided to boycott the Atlanta opening. The elaborate festivities threatened to be an ordeal for him, and Selznick's apparent slight to Fleming was all the excuse he needed to call off his appearance.

Metro succeeded in getting Gable to change his mind, but his relations with Selznick, never very good, were now only held together by the thin filament of Howard Strickling's powers of persuasion. Metro accepted an offer from the fledgling American Airlines of a DC-3 to fly Gable to Atlanta so that he and Selznick would both be spared the tension of a long flight on the same plane. Eager for the publicity, the airline tipped off the local press that Clark Gable and Carole Lombard were stopping over in Tucson, Arizona. When the plane with GONE WITH THE WIND painted on the side landed at Tucson airfield the following morning, the inevitable crowd was waiting to catch a glimpse of the two stars. Gable, who had been drinking with Fleming before his departure, was nursing a hangover, and wanted to get to the airport café for breakfast as quickly as possible. "Folks, I've had a bit of a rough night," he told the people pressing around him. "They tell me you can get ham and some eggs at that café, so please let me through." The crowd parted good-humoredly and Gable was allowed to have his breakfast. Then he brought some back for Carole Lombard, who had remained on the plane.

Selznick landed in Atlanta two and a half hours ahead of Clark Gable, accompanied by Irene, Myron, Vivien Leigh, Laurence

Olivier, Olivia de Havilland, Evelyn Keyes, and Ona Munson. Jock Whitney had arrived earlier, leading a contingent of East Coast money that included a portfolio of Whitneys and Vanderbilts, Herbert Bayard Swope, Nelson Rockefeller, J. P. Morgan, and John Jacob Astor. Selznick's party stepped into the thin afternoon sunshine and a military school band struck up "Dixie." "Oh, they're playing the song from our picture," cooed Vivien Leigh. A local reporter overheard her and asked Dietz who she was. "Olivia de Havilland," Dietz replied quickly. Had it dawned on the Southern press that it was Scarlett O'Hara they might just as well have all gone home.

As they settled down to wait for Gable's plane, it became clear that "Dixie" was the beginning and the end of the band's repertoire and they played it at regular intervals. The sun had gone and a cold wind was whipping across the field when the American Airlines DC-3 taxied to a halt, but the crowd had not thinned. When Gable stepped out, wearing a trench coat, hundreds of people hurled themselves at the plane and the band had to stop playing "Dixie," put down their instruments and help the Georgia State Police to push a lane for him through the crowd.

The procession of open cars drove slowly through darkening Negro suburbs where the crowds stood on the porches of dilapidated houses and in the red earth. On flag-decked Peachtree Street, people were jammed together six deep; contemporary dress rubbed shoulders with faded antebellum finery and Civil War uniforms. The men sported old beaver hats, light trousers, dazzling waistcoats, and velvet jackets, and the women wore hooped skirts, basques, and old miniatures, and carried parasols. In the store windows behind the crowd, the Confederate colors glowed; there were Scarlett O'Hara dolls for sale, and the panoply of the Southern armies glinted in a thousand family souvenirs; weapons, uniforms, buttons, badges, hats, and maps were on display. Nunnally's, the Atlanta candy firm, was selling boxes of candies that contained Scarlett fantasies, Rhett caramels, Melanie molasses strings, Tara pecans, Ashley brazils, Tarleton strawberries, Prissy peppermints, Gerald O'Hara almonds, and Aunt Pitty Pat desserts. On the steps of the old gray brick Georgian Terrace Hotel, the

stars stood bathed in a white floodlight acknowledging the applause, while confetti drifted down from the surrounding rooftops and windows.

In their commemorative issues, the Atlanta papers helpfully printed three versions of the Rebel yell: "Yee-aay-ee," which was used in *Gone With the Wind,* on the advice of Wilbur Kurtz; "Wah-hoo-ee," favored by Dr. Henry J. Harvey of the Ninth Virgina Cavalry; and "Yaaa-yeee," put forward by Confederate General J. R. Jones, who was ninety-six. When Clark Gable arrived at the Junior League Ball, in the dress suit he wore in the ballroom scene of the movie, he was greeted with a rousing combination of all three. Men in gray uniforms that had belonged to their grandfathers cheered him as if he were a Southern hero come to life. Gable raised a sardonic eyebrow in acknowledgment and waltzed off with Mayor Hartsfield's daughter, Mildred. Behind his facade of detached charm, he was still bothered by Fleming's absence and by the demands that were being made on himself. Seeing Howard Strickling deep in conversation with Russell Birdwell, who was in Atlanta as Selznick's publicity consultant, he walked over to Strickling and said, "If this guy gives you any trouble, I'm going home." Strickling hastily assured him that Birdwell was not giving him trouble.

Margaret Mitchell and David Selznick finally met for the first time the next day, at Governor Rivers' luncheon for the Southern governors, for which Metro picked up the tab. Appropriately, they were introduced by their tactful go-between, Katherine Brown. But with the sole topic of their four years' correspondence exhausted by the picture's completion, they found little to say to each other, and when Selznick raised the subject of a sequel to *Gone With the Wind* the diminutive authoress became distant and drifted away. When she was brought together with Clark Gable, a large, curious crowd collected to witness the encounter between the novelist and the incarnation of her hero. Embarrassed by the attention, she took Gable firmly by the arm, led him into the Ladies' Room and locked the door.

A replica of the Twelve Oaks facade covered the front of Atlanta's Grand Theater for the premiere. Outside, there was another very large crowd. They had little hope of getting seats,

Mammy tells Melanie that Rhett is griefstricken and refuses to let Bonnie be buried. (FLAMINI)

for which scalpers were asking $200 for a $10 ticket; they were there to get another glimpse of the stars. Again, some were in period clothes, the women in their hooped skirts taking up five times more space and adding to the squeeze. It reached its worst when Gable arrived with Carole Lombard, shortly before nine. A tremendous surge of the crowd was barely contained by the cordon of four hundred Georgia National Guardsmen; women screamed, and several fainted and had to be held up by the men around them until they could be moved out.

Earlier that evening, Selznick had summoned Susan Myrick to his room in a panic over the Southern accents in his picture. Now that he was actually in the South for the first time in his life, the accents in *Gone With the Wind* seemed weak compared to what he was hearing all around him. Remembering Margaret Mitchell's warning against phony Southern speech, he had left for the premiere fully expecting the Atlanta audience to walk out, perhaps led by the author herself. But he needn't have worried. Vivien Leigh hadn't pouted and flounced on the screen for three minutes before the audience was completely won over. And if her speech wasn't exactly pure middle-high Georgian, these middle-high Georgians certainly didn't seem to care. Hollywood's romantic evocation of the South struck a chord that vibrated strongly throughout the evening. Great waves of nostalgic Southern fervor engulfed the audience. Every reference to the South, every snatch of Southern music in the score, was applauded. When war with the North was announced, the cheers in the audience drowned those on the screen. By the end, many people wept openly. Margaret Mitchell stood nervously on the stage and paid tribute to David Selznick "on behalf of me and my poor Scarlett" and praised "the grand things these actors have done"— her first publicly expressed opinion on the movie. "I feel it has been a great thing for Georgia and the South to see the Confederates come back," she went on. Mayor Hartsfield, obviously as affected as everyone else, thanked the cast and then, with a fine Southern sense of distinction, asked the all-white audience to applaud the Negro performers. None of them was present. Hattie McDaniel was in Atlanta at the time, but was not included in the official celebrations.

Contemporary press reports estimated that a million people crowded into Atlanta, a city of 300,000 inhabitants, on the day of the opening. Which was as it should be, *The New York Times* commented in an editorial, only half sardonically. "Here are our golden boys and girls, the godlike ones visible this once to their adorers." Promotional openings were, it is true, immensely popular; we have the earlier instances of *Union Pacific* and *Dodge City*. The stars never failed to draw large crowds, and local politicians enjoyed sharing the limelight. But in public response, this one was in a class by itself. One obvious reason was the picture's advance publicity, but another was the South's reverence toward Margaret Mitchell's novel which reflected the feelings, including the unrealized and inarticulated sentiments, of many Southerners.

The following day, the *Gone With the Wind* celebrations closed with a luncheon given by Margaret Mitchell at the Piedmont Driving Club. Then everyone left in Jock Whitney's special train for the New York opening. Everyone, that is, except Clark Gable, who flew back to Hollywood, by now totally alienated from *Gone With the Wind* and its producer. To Gable, the picture was a source of two life-long disappointments. One was that he had no percentage share in its huge profits; the second was that when *Gone With the Wind* swept the board with ten Academy Awards in 1940, he was not among the winners. The film won Oscars for the best picture; best actress, Vivien Leigh; best supporting actress, Hattie McDaniel—the first Academy Award to a black performer; best director, Victor Fleming, who boycotted the presentations; best photography, Ernest Haller and Ray Rennahan; best screenplay, Sidney Howard; a special award for William Cameron Menzies "for outstanding achievement in the use of color"; best art direction, Lyle Wheeler; best special effects, Jack Cosgrove; best editing, Hal Kern; and for Selznick, the Irving Thalberg Memorial Award that had eluded him the previous year, when progress of *Gone With the Wind* was stalled and its future uncertain. But the best actor award went to Robert Donat in *Goodbye Mr. Chips,* a sentimental box-office hit.

Though she won an Oscar, Vivien Leigh's memories of the filming were no more pleasant than Gable's. She never had anything good to say about the role that made her famous. During World

War II, she toured the Middle East entertaining British troops, and the highlight of her performance was a parody of Scarlett O'Hara. Movie stardom didn't interest her; between 1939 and her death in 1962 she returned to Hollywood only occasionally to make a picture. Vivien's relationship had an interesting footnote: after her separation from David Selznick, Irene's creative energies found fulfillment as a Broadway producer, and Vivien Leigh created the role of Blanche DuBois in Irene's first production, *Streetcar Named Desire*.

Gone With the Wind dashed toward box-office success like one of Jock Whitney's racehorses released from the starting gate. By Christmas, it was coming up to the million dollar mark. Critically, it was also a winner. Later generations of critics, sophisticated by Fellini, Bergman, Godard, and Kubrick, would sometimes find it unbearably square; they would say that the sweep, the power of the story was still there, and the burning of Atlanta remained one of the finest battle scenes ever put on film, but a faint smell of mothballs was apparent in the lack of cinematic *vérité* of the long second half. Reviews written at the time, however, were glowing. *The New York Times* called it "The greatest motion picture mural we have seen and the most ambitious film-making adventure in Hollywood's spectacular history." Pare Lorentz, the distinguished documentary film-maker, who was the film critic for *McCall's* magazine, wrote: "Mr. Selznick and Mr. Whitney have made a picture that has given movies enormous prestige. They probably have ruined the movie industry, in that the only way the Napoleons of the West Coast can surpass this one is to do what they did: spend money like generals, take three years, employ the best brains in the industry, and cast the best actors on two continents. . . . It [the picture] is a movie version of a novel, fantastic in scope, extraordinary in detail, played better than any movie I've ever seen, and more colossal, stupendous, gigantic and terrific than any picture ever has been, without at any time seeming pretentious." Down-to-earth as ever, *Variety* predicted that *Gone With the Wind* was "poised for grosses which may be second to none in the history of the business." The *New York Post* said: "Just as *Birth of a Nation* was a milestone in movie history, *Gone With the Wind* represents a supreme effort." D. W. Griffith, to whose *Birth of a Nation* Selznick's picture was being favorably compared, was not so impressed. He dismissed the famous pullback shot with the comment: "Chaplin says I got the same effect with a close-up of a few corpses." Jock Whitney gave Selznick a gold wristwatch. The inscription in Whitney's handwriting read: "David—Xmas 1939. Praise de Lawd. Jock."

Selznick was at the top of the mountain. He told friends that during the long, hard haul he felt his father's guiding hand on his shoulder; he didn't mention his father-in-law's less benign grip on his coat tails, but that, too, had propelled toward ultimate success. Selznick's *tour de force* was more than a personal triumph; it was the apotheosis of the Hollywood producer who harnessed the talents of creative men and women to shape a universe that was, in the end, solely his own; the producer who dominated the movies, and dominated the social life (the two were often hard to separate), who imposed his will in the firm belief that the ultimate creative force in movies was his own power. But another force was coming into focus—the artist-director, such as Orson Welles and John Huston, demanding (and often getting) a hitherto unheard-of degree of autonomy—and, in the end, the power of the producer vanished in the general explosion of the cult of the *auteur*.

Selznick was at the top of the mountain. "Everything in *Gone With the Wind*, without exception, is as I wanted it to be," he said. "I took a gamble on my own conceptions and on my own methods." But the gamble was paying off more handsomely for others than it was for himself. In March, he received the first check from Metro representing his company's share in the box-office proceeds. From it, the preferred stock was paid off, and shortly afterward Norma Shearer became the first stockholder to sell her share of the picture to M-G-M.

By the end of 1940, *Gone With the Wind* had been seen by twenty-five million people in the United States and had grossed over $14 million. But Whitney was losing interest in Hollywood and becoming more involved in wartime industry. His confidence in Selznick was eroding, and the two of them had begun to argue about such questions as Selznick's extravagance directly, instead

Overleaf Melanie dies: India Wilkes (Alicia Rhett), Aunt Pittypat, Ashley and his son Beau (Mickey Kuhn), Scarlett, and Rhett come for a last visit. As she waits, Scarlett realizes that Ashley has loved only Melanie and that she could love only Rhett. Rhett finally comes to the realization that there is no hope for his marriage with Scarlett. (PRATT)

of through intermediaries. Selznick-International had not had a profitable year until *Gone With the Wind,* and there was always the danger that Selznick would wipe out the immense profits that were pouring in. He had become more erratic than ever in his business life and was gambling more and more. Whitney's lawyers worked out an intricate scheme for converting his and Selznick's highly taxable profits from the picture into capital gains by selling out to each other and liquidating their company. Selznick sold his thirty-three percent share to Whitney for $750,000. Selznick assumed the contracts of Vivien Leigh, Ingrid Bergman, and the studio's other stars, and bought Whitney's thirty percent investment for twice the amount that Whitney had paid him. Shortly thereafter, they both sold to Metro the interest in *Gone With the Wind* which they had acquired from each other. Whitney was paid $1.5 million for his share, Selznick slightly less. By 1944 the studio owned ninety-eight percent of the picture with C. V. Whitney, and Myron Selznick's estate—Myron having died in 1940—owned the remainder.

Thus Metro reaped the lion's share of the profits of the picture's enormously successful later releases. Al Lichtman's box-office projections proved to be conservative. In 1941, following its extraordinary road-show year, *Gone With the Wind* was put on general release in 8100 theaters around the country, again at increased admission prices, and found another audience of twenty-four million people; in its third time around the country it attracted ten and a half million more. By July 1943 it had grossed $32 million domestically, and the second biggest box-office record belonged to *Snow White and the Seven Dwarfs,* which had totaled $8 million since its 1938 release.

In blitzed London, *Gone With the Wind*'s theme of wartime suffering and separation took on a special significance, and the picture ran at the Ritz Theater for almost the entire length of the war. In Shanghai, it was still showing when the American presence withdrew and the city fell into Communist hands. The Nazis saw Scarlett as a symbol of resistance, and banned both the novel and the movie from German-occupied Europe. When it opened in 1945, the public response was delirious as newly liberated Europeans responded to its stirring message of survival in defeat.

By 1967, it had earned $75 million in rentals for Metro, but was overtaken as the biggest money-making motion picture of all time by *The Sound of Music;* in October of that year, Metro released it for the seventh time in a wide-screen version, having stretched the original 35mm negative to 70mm and added stereophonic sound; it has been released that way since.

The picture had to be reprocessed frame by frame and the quality of the color suffered. In some scenes, such as the opening sequence at Tara, the softer tones look thin and washed out, sometimes so thin that the white screen shows through like an old canvas from which the paint has flaked away. Moreover, the new frame size—narrower, as well as about one and a half times wider than the old 35mm frame—distorts the visual composition Selznick strove so hard to achieve in his picture; a strip had to be sacrificed at the top and bottom of each frame, cutting off the top of the actors' heads at the hairline, and their legs at the ankles, and causing chandeliers and distant horizons to disappear. In its publicity stories about the conversion Metro claimed that the negative of *Gone With the Wind* had in the intervening years been carefully preserved in velvet-lined canisters and stored in a special vault at controlled temperatures; but in fact not all the negative could be found, and the missing portions had to be duplicated from an existing print, adding to the general unevenness of the stretched picture. But caught up in the timeless drama, audiences failed to notice the damage and the picture quickly regained its box-office supremacy. Then, in 1972, came the challenge of a new blockbuster. Based on Mario Puzo's best-selling novel, *The Godfather* was a pre-sold property of *Gone With the Wind* proportions; at today's higher admission prices, it quickly overtook the Selznick picture. But *Gone With the Wind* retains the distinction of having been seen by more people than any motion picture ever made, and only time will tell whether *The Godfather's* popularity will prove as durable.

After the liquidation of Selznick-International, the Selznicks moved to the East Coast. Finding a house took a long time; "The

The Atlanta Premiere

Clark Gable and Carole Lombard at the Junior League Ball the night before the premiere. To the right of Gable and Lombard is Howard Strickling, head of MGM publicity in Hollywood. Behind Gable and Lombard at the extreme left is Atlanta's mayor, William B. Hartsfield. Between Gable and Lombard is Howard Dietz, head of MGM publicity in New York. (TLPA)

Seated in the Grand Theater on the night of the premiere are (front row, left to right) Herbert Bayard Swope, Claudette Colbert, Irene Selznick, and Georgia governor E. D. Rivers; (second row) Jock Whitney, Peggy Marsh (Margaret Mitchell), John Marsh, Clark Gable, Carole Lombard, and Atlanta mayor William B. Hartsfield. (CP)

trouble is David," Irene complained. "He wants a house that looks like Tara and works like the World's Fair." His career suffered from the same obsessive comparison of every project with *Gone With the Wind*. When Gregory Peck saw his lavish designs for the sets of *The Paradine Case*, in which Peck was to star, he said, "My God, David, aren't you going overboard on the grandeur of this little drama in the Old Bailey?" "The picture must have scope," Selznick said. "But why?" the actor asked. "Because I've got to do better than *Gone With the Wind*. I may never make it. But I've got to try." But the shadow of *Gone With the Wind* throttled his ambition and stunted his further growth as a producer, and eventually he stopped making films altogether. He was resigned to the fact that—as he would often say—"When I go they'll put on my tombstone, 'Here lies the man who made *Gone With the Wind*.' " To keep his independent company turning a profit, he loaned out his formidable collection of stars (which now included Peck, Dorothy McGuire and Rhonda Fleming) to other studios, and bought properties which he could resell to other producers who wanted to make them into movies. But his own production record tells a sad story. From the start of his career in movies to *Gone With the Wind*, Selznick produced fifty-six movies. He was now thirty-seven years old. During the remaining twenty-five years of his life, he produced ten pictures. And that included a wartime short for the Department of Public Health.

But that was all in the future. On December 16, 1939, as the Whitney train headed for New York and another glittering premiere, David Selznick was euphoric. In Washington, D.C., they stopped to wait for a connecting train that was to haul them into Grand Central Station. At Selznick's suggestion, the well-heeled group descended on The Variety Club, where the stars and financiers were immediately surrounded by a crowd of considerably less affluent regular members. Unable to resist a gamble, Selznick went over to a slot machine, played a dime, and lost. To hide his self-consciousness, Jock Whitney followed suit. He put a dime in the slot and pulled the lever. In an instant the room echoed with the rattle of coins as the jackpot poured out onto his highly polished shoes.

ACKNOWLEDGMENTS AND SOURCES

A book of this kind owes a lot to the cooperation, encouragement, and reminiscences of many people. I would especially like to thank several protagonists in the saga of the filming of *Gone With the Wind* for taking the trouble to search their memories or their records for facts, figures, and anecdotes. They are: Maxwell Arnow, Russell Birdwell, Kay Brown, Ridgeway Callow, Arthur Fellows, Lee Garmes, Olivia de Havilland, Macdonald Johnson, Hal Kern, Evelyn Keyes, John Lee Mahin, Susan Myrick, Elsa Neuberger, Daniel O'Shea, Walter Plunkett, Ray Rennahan, Ernest Scanlon, Lydia Schiller, Clarence Slifer, Howard Strickling, Edith Udell, John Wharton, Lyle Wheeler, Harry Wolf, and William H. Wright.

I also want to thank Robert Hardy Andrews, Joan Bennett, Pandro Berman, Barry Brannen, Bette Davis, Howard Dietz, Dean Dorn, Melvyn Douglas, Rhonda Fleming, Marsha Hunt, Lee Israel, Eddie Lawrence, Jeffrey Lynn, Lilly Messenger, Lewis Milestone, Stephens Mitchell, Kay Mulbey, Richard Barksdale Harwell, Emily Torchia, Ben Thau, Sylvia Wallace, Minna Wallis, Ruth Waterbury, the late Larry Weingarten, Roberta Winter, Margaret Wyler, the library staffs at the Academy of Motion Picture Arts and Sciences (Los Angeles), the British Film Institute (London), and the University of Georgia (Athens, Ga.), Henry William Griffin and William Pratt at Macmillan, and I am grateful to Henry Grunwald, Managing Editor of *Time,* and Murray J. Gart, Chief of *Time* Correspondents, for allowing me the time off to write the book.

A full bibliography of the works consulted would be too long to print, but the following books and other printed sources were of particular help in my research; Hanson W. Baldwin and Shepard Stone (editors), *Graustark: We Saw It Happen* (Simon and Schuster, New York, 1938); Felix Barker, *The Oliviers* (Lippincott, New York, 1953); John Baxter, *Hollywood in the Thirties* (Paperback Library, New York, 1970); Rudy Behlmer (editor), *MEMO from David O. Selznick* (Viking, New York, 1972); Frank Capra, *The Name Above the Title* (Macmillan, New York, 1971); Bosley Crowther, *Hollywood Rajah* (Holt, Rinehart and Winston, New York, 1960); Bosley Crowther, *The Lion's Share* (E. P. Dutton, New York, 1957); Howard Dietz, *Dancing in the Dark* (Quadrangle, New York, 1974); Finis Farr, *Margaret Mitchell of Atlanta* (William Morrow, New York, 1957); Philip French, *The Movie Moguls* (Weidenfeld and Nicholson, London, 1971); Ezra Goodman, *The Fifty Year Decline and Fall of Hollywood* (Simon and Schuster, New York, 1961); Sheilah Graham, *College of One* (Bantam Books, New York, 1968); Warren G. Harris, *Gable and Lombard* (Simon and Schuster, New York, 1974); Ben Hecht, *A Child of the Century* (Simon and Schuster, New York, 1954); Lee Israel, *Miss Tallulah Bankhead* (Dell, New York, 1972); Gavin Lambert, *GWTW* (Atlantic–Little, Brown, Boston, 1973); Gavin Lambert, *On Cukor* (Putnam, New York, 1972); Aaron Latham, *Crazy Sundays* (Viking, New York, 1971); Samuel Marx, *Mayer and Thalberg* (Random House, New York, 1975); Margaret Mitchell, *Gone With the Wind* (Macmillan, New York, 1936); Peter Noble, *The Negro in Films* (Arno Press and the New York Times, 1970); Hortense Powdermaker, *Hollywood: The Dream'Factory* (Little, Brown, Boston, 1950); Allen Rivkin and Laura Kerr (editors), *Hello Hollywood* (Doubleday, New York, 1962); Gwen Robyns, *Light of a Star* (Leslie Frewin, London, 1965); Leo Rosten, *Hollywood: The Movie Colony, The Movie Makers* (Harcourt Brace, New York, 1941); Bob Thomas, *Selznick* (Doubleday, New York, 1970); Bob Thomas, *Thalberg: Life and Legend* (Doubleday, 1969); Andrew Turnbull (editor), *The Letters of F. Scott Fitzgerald* (Dell, New York, 1966); Alexander Walker, *Stardom* (Michael Joseph, London, 1970); publications include the *New York Times, Los Angeles Times, Los Angeles Examiner, Saturday Evening Post, New Yorker, Time, Los Angeles Magazine,* the London *Times, Photoplay, Daily Variety,* and *Hollywood Reporter.*

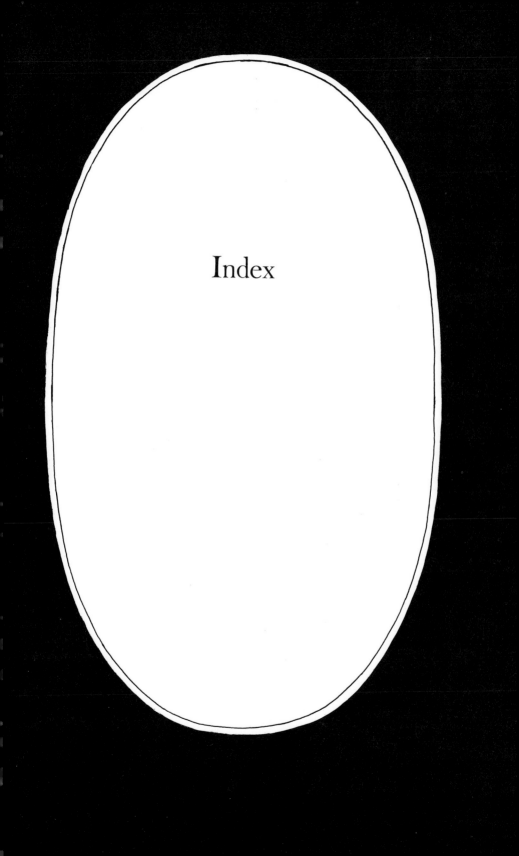

Index